ANARCHISM IN THE DRAMAS OF ERNST TOLLER

Ernst Toller in 1937
(Reprinted by permission of *The San Francisco Chronicle*)

Anarchism in the Dramas of Ernst Toller

The Realm of Necessity and the Realm of Freedom

MICHAEL OSSAR

State University of New York Press

ALBANY

Published by
State University of New York Press, Albany

© 1980 State University of New York

Printed in the United States of America

For information, address State University of New York
Press, State University Plaza, Albany, N.Y., 12246

Library of Congress Cataloging in Publication Data
Ossar, Michael, 1938–
   Anarchism in the dramas of Ernst Toller.

   Bibliography: p.
   Includes index.
   1. Toller, Ernst, 1893-139--Crisicism and interpretation.

   2. Anarchism and anarchists in literature. I. Title.

PT2642.065Z78   832'.9'12   79-20304
ISBN 0-87395-393-2

To the memory of Adolf Klarmann

Contents

Acknowledgements

I should like to express my gratitude to Professors André von Gronicka, Carol Miller, Heinz Moenkemeyer, Martin Reso, John Spalek and George Tunstall for their help and advice, as well as to the staffs of the following libraries and institutions: the Akademie der Künste (West Berlin), the Deutscher Akademischer Austauschdienst, the Faculty Research Committee of Kansas State University, the International Institute for Social History (Amsterdam), the National Endowment for the Humanities, the Deutsches Literaturarchiv of the Schiller National-Museum (Marbach), the Sterling and Beinecke Libraries of Yale University, and the United States International Education Exchange Program.

Finally, I would like to acknowledge permission to quote passages from the following books:

Bertolt Brecht, *Gesammelte Werke in 8 Bänden*, ed. Suhrkamp Verlag in collaboration with Elisabeth Hauptmann (Frankfurt/M: Suhrkamp, 1967), Vols. I and IV

Tankred Dorst, Peter Zadek and Hartmut Gehrke, *Rotmord oder I was a German* (Munich: Deutscher Taschenbuch Verlag, 1969)

T.S. Eliot, *The Complete Poems and Plays 1909-1950* (New York: Harcourt Brace, 1952)

T.S. Eliot, *Selected Essays* (New York: Harcourt Brace & World, 1964)

Peter Hamm, ed. *Aussichten. Junge Lyriker des deutschen Sprachraums* (Munich: Biederstein, 1966)

Jost Hermand, *Unbequeme Literatur: Eine Beispielreihe* (Heidelberg: Lothar Stiehm, 1971)

Donald Keene, ed. *Modern Japanese Literature* (New York: Grove Press, 1956)

Walter Sokel, "Toller," in *Gestalten*, Vol. II of *Deutsche Literatur im 20. Jahrhundert: Strukturen und Gestalten*, eds. Otto Mann and Wolfgang Rothe, 5th ed. (Bern: Francke Verlag, 1967)

Portions of Chapter 6, "*Masse Mensch*: Anarchism and Communism," have appeared in an abbreviated version in the *Germanic Review*, 51, No. 3 (May 1967), 192-208, and are reprinted here with kind permission of Professor William Little.

My special thanks are due to Mr. Sidney Kaufman for permission to quote from Toller's works.

Preface

Until recently German anarchism had been thought a marginal phenomenon. Mention of the term evoked images of emigres like Rudolf Rocker or Johannes Most, or nineteenth century idiosyncratic figures of little moment in the history of German Leftist movements like Max Stirner and John Henry Mackay. But since the publication of Helmut Kreuzer's *Die Boheme* in 1968 and in the aftermath of the discussion provoked by the Rote Armee Fraktion (Baader-Meinhof group) and student publications such as *Radicalinski, Päng, grasswurzelrevolution*, an impressive number of studies has demonstrated the astonishing breadth and depth of anarchist ideas in German political and literary circles—books such as those by Eugene Lunn and Charles Maurer on Landauer, Heinz Hug and Lawrence Baron on Mühsam, Lothar Peter on Pfemfert and *Die Aktion*, Walter Fähnders and Martin Rector on left-wing radicalism and the literature of the Weimar Republic, Ulrich Linse on German anarchist organizations, Michael Baumann on B. Traven, Thomas Riley on J.H. Mackay, Helmut Pfanner on Oskar Maria Graf, Harry Wilde on Theodor Plievier, Arnold Imhof on Franz Jung, and others. Kreuzer notes in *Die Boheme*: "If one surveys the history of Bohemianism in the 19th and 20th centuries, anarchism, more than any other political or sociological idea, proves to be the one the politically inclined bohemians were most disposed to support" (p. 302). And the English writer Herbert Read noted in his *Poetry and Anarchism* (London, 1940): "I believe that the poet is necessarily an anarchist, and that he must oppose all organized conceptions of the state" (p. 15). Erich Mühsam, a German writer and participant in the Munich Revolution who later died in Oranienburg, wrote in words nearly identical to Read's:

> [It] must be said that all art is necessarily anarchist, and that a man must first be an anarchist in order to be an artist. For all artistic creation is based on the longing for liberation from coercion and is in essence free of authority and external compulsion. The inner coherence and order of art, however, is strongly connected to the relationship of the libertarian individual with the whole organism of society. To restore this relationship between man and humanity, which finds its highest expression in art, and which is crushed and destroyed in the bureaucratic mill of the state—this is point of our...activity. [*Kain*, 2, No. 1 (April 1912), 9]

It seems that of all the German literary movements, the Expressionists and the literati of the "Expressionist decade" conform to Mühsam's, Read's and Kreuzer's strictures most closely. Writers such as Leonhard Frank, Ludwig Rubiner, B. Traven, Martin Buber, Gustav Landauer, Erich Mühsam, Benedikt Friedländer, Franz Oppenheimer, Carl Sternheim, Franz Werfel, Carl Einstein, Mynona, Reinhard Goering, Oskar Kanehl, Franz Jung, Oskar Maria Graf, René Schickele, Theodor Plievier, Max Hermann-Neisse, and Ernst Toller were all demonstrably influenced by anarchist ideas.

My purpose in this book is to trace the development of these ideas in one of the most important and successful of the Expressionist dramatists, Ernst Toller. Toller's popularity and later eclipse and the fact that for a brief moment he was confronted with the necessity and the opportunity for political action make him a paradigmatic figure in the history of German libertarian literature. For this reason, his political failure is all the more moving and instructive. Certainly historians of the Weimar Republic, one of the most fecund periods of German intellectual life, have always speculated on what might have been, and "what might be" is in a sense the central question of Toller's drama.

We shall find that the very ambiguities and problems that haunt Toller and bedevil his critics are the ones that occupy scholars of anarchism: are his solutions to the ills of society in any sense realistic, or are they valuable solely in a negative sense as a critique of certain excesses inherent in authoritarian socialism? Do his views on the tactics of revolution necessarily foreclose any possibility of success? Is Toller merely another version of Erich Mühsam's radical street-lantern lighter, who is all for a revolution so long as his lanterns aren't removed to be used as barricades? Were the soldiers' and workers' councils that Toller, Landauer and Buber advocated a realistic alternative to a centralized parliamentary system in a modern, industrialized society or were they merely romantic vestiges of nineteenth century anarchist thought that had unaccountably survived? Is a third way possible, one between the extremes of a parliamentary system that is nothing but the executive committee for capitalism, on the one hand, and the ossified bureaucracy of state socialism, on the other?

Toller's plays, in posing questions like these, acted as a kind of litmus paper in that they provoked his critics and his audiences to political judgments; they represent, in the Brechtian sense, highly effective didactic theater. In fact, one could make a case for the view that this very effectiveness in achieving what is so obviously their primary purpose is in itself an indication of artistic merit, albeit not merit that can be described and analysed in conventional terms. For this reason, a substantial part of our task will be to examine just what effect Toller's plays had on their critics and how they were perceived—how they served as a touchstone that caused each critic to define for himself the limits of his ideology and the means he was willing to approve to promote it.

In the following pages I have of course consulted previous renderings, particularly those in the *Seven Plays*: Ashley Dukes' translation of *Die Maschinenstürmer*, Edward Crankshaw's of *Die Wandlung*, *Die blinde Göttin*, *Feuer aus den Kesseln*, and *Wunder in Amerika*; Vera Mendel's translation of *Masse Mensch* and *Hinkemann*, and Hermon Ould's of *Hoppla, wir leben!* In addition, I have consulted Edward Crankshaw's version of *Eine Jugend in Deutschland* (*I was a German*) and R. Ellis Robert's of the *Briefe aus dem Gefängnis* (*Look through the Bars*). However, I have adapted and modified these where it seemed necessary or appropriate.

In the case of Toller's works, the original edition cited is given in the notes (or in the text), followed by references to the corresponding volume and page number of the new Toller edition by Wolfgang Frühwald and John M. Spalek, *Gesammelte Werke*, 6 vols., Reihe Hanser 250-255 (Munich: Hanser, 1978). Volume 6, *Kommentar und Materialien*, has unfortunately not yet appeared as of this writing.

For the reader's convenience, I have translated the titles of Toller's works in the bibliography; other titles are translated the first time they appear in the text.

1

I was a German

It is the artist's job to create the sun when there is none.—Romain Rolland: *Jean-Christophe: La Foire sur la Place*[1]

From the time he was invited as a young ex-soldier to attend a conference called by the publisher Eugen Diedrichs to seek a non-annexationist peace, until his suicide in 1939, Toller was rarely off the front pages of German or foreign newspapers. His first play, *Die Wandlung*, written before the Munich Revolution of 1918-1919 and performed while its author was in prison for the part he played in that revolution, was such a theatrical sensation that it prompted public agitation for Toller's pardon—an offer he refused. One scholar notes, "During the Weimar Republic a Toller production that was not banned, subjected to a riot, or at least protested against publicly was an exception."[2]

Toller's works were translated into languages ranging from Bulgarian and Esperanto to Gujarati and Japanese, and his plays were performed in Moscow, Sarajevo, Tallinn, Riga, Copenhagen, Tokyo, London, Paris, Buenos Aires, Helsinki, Urbana, Brooklyn, Berkeley, Princeton and Poughkeepsie. He was a friend of Nehru. Through his intercession with President Roosevelt, the Archbishop of Canterbury, and various heads of state, a large scale relief effort was mounted for refugees of the Spanish Civil War. His good friend, sometime collaborator and fellow emigré, Hermann Kesten, notes:

> I walked with him through Tripoli, and an Arab chauffeur pressed his hand and said: "You are Toller!"
> I went with him to a pub in the East End of London and the waiter reached across the bar to shake his hand, and said: "Comrade Toller!"
> I went with him to a cafe in Paris and a *flic* at the bar gave him his hand and said: "Vous êtes Toller!"
> The Russians admired him, Chinese intellectuals lionized him, Spanish Republicans adored him and American journalists were [sometimes] not indifferent. He was as popular with the little man as baseball players are in America. Students in Zagreb carried him on their shoulders. I heard Italian secret agents, sent to spy on him by Mussolini, quote from his

Schwalbenbuch in Taormina. He was equally popular and forgotten, fanatically loved and fanatically hated, treated with ridicule as a has-been and imitated.[3]

Ernst Toller was born in Samotschin, a small town now in Poland, on December 1, 1893. His maternal great-grandfather, the first Jew to settle in the town, was granted certain civil rights under the patronage of Frederick the Great; his paternal great-grandfather, said to be a man of great wealth, came from Spain. Toller's mother Ida, née Kohn, and his father, Max, a pharmacist, ran a general store. His father ultimately achieved a position of some importance as town councillor.

Samotschin was a town run by a German minority, largely Protestant with an admixture of Jews, in a Polish Catholic province, Posen. Toller very early became acquainted with the fact that some men were more equal than others, that Jews were permitted to make common cause with the other Germans against the Poles, but otherwise were scarcely tolerated themselves. When a little girl came to play with Toller, who was at the time still young enough to be in a dress, her nanny called:

Don't go there—that's a Jew. Ilse lets go of my hand and runs away. I don't understand the sense of her words, but I begin to cry, without stopping. Marie runs toward me, takes me into her arms, shows me her coral necklace, I don't like the necklace, I tear it apart.[4]

Through his friendship with Stanislaus, the nightwatchman's son, Toller began to observe the subtle and not-so-subtle process of the inculcation of prejudices between religions, between rich and poor, between nationalities. When Toller was sent to the county seat, Bromberg, to attend the *Realgymnasium* (a scientifically-oriented secondary school) he began to write, first poems and then news articles for the local newspaper, the *Ostdeutsche Rundschau*. His first attack on the establishment came with the anonymous publication of the following notice:

Last week, the worker Julius died. He writhed in agony on the train station floor from 3 until 9:30 without anyone helping him or calling a doctor. Has it come to this, that a dying man can be pelted with stones ...by schoolboys? When the police heard about it, they let it be known that it didn't concern them, since Julius lay on the property of the Royal Prussian Railroad. Did they have to stick to the letter of the law here, where a man's life was at stake? What difference did it make whether he lay on city property or elsewhere? You say that Julius [the village idiot] doesn't deserve such fuss? If this had happened to an animal, help would have been available immediately.[5]

When the enraged mayor demanded the author's name and the affair was eventually smoothed over by his father, the town councillor, Toller learned his first lesson in political influence.

Toller was an indifferent student at Bromberg; he spent his time reading forbidden writers (Gerhart Hauptmann, Ibsen, Strindberg, Wedekind) and his money having term papers written for him by a firm in Leipzig. He sent his first plays to the Bromberg Municipal Theater, but received no reply. After the death of his father and a tragicomic love affair with a local actress, Toller passed his exams and left Germany to study at the University of Grenoble in February of 1913.

In Grenoble, a university popular among foreign students, Toller led a rather relaxed existence, congregating with fellow German students, gambling, and sending home telegrams like "All money lent to a Turk. Turk disappeared."[6]His studies, which concentrated on Dostoyevsky, Tolstoy and Nietzsche, were interrupted by the assassination at Sarajevo and the mobilization. Toller took the last train to Germany before the border was sealed and immediately volunteered in Munich for service, after nearly being attacked by an angry crowd which took him for a spy because of a French label in his hat. After basic training at Bellheim, Toller volunteered in March of 1915 for service at the front, where he was to spend thirteen months, first at the Bois-le-prêtre and then in the vicinity of Verdun. Of the intoxication that had swept over nearly all of Germany in August of 1914, nothing was left. Toller describes the moment of truth in words which recur often in his works:

> One night we hear screams, as if a man were suffering terrible pain, then it is still. Someone must have been mortally wounded, we think. But after an hour the cries return. And now it doesn't stop. Not this night. Not the next night. Naked and wordless, the scream whines—we don't know if it comes from the throat of a German or a Frenchman. The screaming takes on a life of its own; it accuses the earth and the heaven. We press our fists to our ears in order not to hear it, but nothing helps—the screaming revolves like a top in our heads, it stretches the minutes to hours, the hours to years. We wither and grow decrepit between one scream and the next. We learned who is screaming, one of ours, caught in the barbed wire; no one can save him. Two tried and were killed. Some mother's son fights off death desperately, God damn, he makes such a big stink about it, we'll go mad if he hollers much longer. Death stuffs his mouth shut on the third day.[7]

Finally, just after volunteering for the air corps, Toller was taken ill and was

3

transferred to a hospital in Strassburg and released in May of 1916.

After some weeks spent in a sanitarium, Toller went to the University of Munich, where he studied law, art history, and literature with Arthur Kutscher and through him met a number of Germany's leading writers, including Max Halbe, Karl Henckell, Frank Wedekind, and Thomas Mann, who read and praised his poetry.

In 1917 the publisher Eugen Diederichs invited the young student and ex-soldier to a conference at Burg Lauenstein in Thuringia to discuss the direction Germany would take in the future. Among the participants were the sociologists Max Weber and Ferdinand Tönnies, the writers Walter von Molo, Richard Dehmel, the historian Friedrich Meinecke and a number of other leading cultural and academic lights. Toller was bitterly disappointed at the wealth of academic analysis of Germany's plight and the dearth of action designed to do anything about it. However, impressed by Max Weber's courage, he followed him to the University of Heidelberg where he founded a pacifist group of students, the Cultural-Political Association of German Students. The group was soon quashed by the High Command of the army. The men in the group were drafted into the army, the women, several of whom were Austrian, were deported. Toller, who happened to be in the hospital, was warned, and fled to Berlin.

In Berlin, Toller continued his anti-war agitation. He wrote to the Nobel Prize winning author of *Die Weber (The Weavers)*, Gerhart Hauptmann, asking him to oppose the war publicly and received no answer. He corresponded with the anarchist Gustav Landauer and made the acquaintance of Kurt Eisner, a pacifist and leader of a left-wing splinter group of the SPD (Social Democratic Party), the USPD (Independent Social Democratic Party).

When Eisner led a strike of munitions workers in Munich in January of 1918, Toller followed and was soon arrested. In prison, he wrote the final scenes of his first play, *Die Wandlung*, and immersed himself for the first time in a systematic study of Marxist and anarchist literature: Marx, Engels, Lasalle, Bakunin, Mehring, Luxemburg and the Webbs. The depth of these studies can be gauged by the many details of *Das Kapital* that have found their way into his plays, notably *Die Maschinenstürmer*. Toller writes of this period:

> Only now do I become a socialist; my sense of the ...structure of society sharpens, of the lack of necessity for war, of the terrible lie of the law that permits all to starve and allows few to enrich themselves, of the relationships between capital and labor, of the historical significance of the working class.[8]

Eventually Toller's mother was able to arrange for his release from prison and transfer to a psychiatric clinic, an experience he later turned to account in *Hoppla, wir leben!* He was released from the clinic in the summer of 1918.

Shortly thereafter, on November 7, 1918, Kurt Eisner led a demonstration in Munich from the Theresienwiese to the Landtag. The demonstration ended in the proclamation of a republic with Eisner at its head—two days before the similar revolution in Berlin. On November 10, Toller, who had been ill with influenza in Landsberg, left for Munich, where he was elected Vice-President of the Central Council of Workers', Farmers' and Soldiers' Councils. In the days after the initial exuberance following on the effortless seizure of power, the various rightist and centrist forces began to recoup. In Berlin, Karl Liebnecht (a beacon to the workers for his vote against war credits in 1914) and Rosa Luxemburg were murdered. The Chancellor Friedrich Ebert (elected President in February) made his notorious pact with General Gröner and Gustav Noske, accepting their services to "protect law and order" and assure an orderly demobilization. In Bavaria, the reaction also grew: the Majority Socialists Erhard Auer and Trimm called for a counter-revolutionary militia to "safeguard the revolution."

On February 21, 1919 Eisner, on his way to the Landtag to tender his resignation, was murdered. In the confusion that followed, the first so-called Council Republic was set up on April 7, with the Majority Socialist government under Josef Hoffmann fleeing to Bamberg. Toller describes the new government:

> The people's commissars are elected. Here too one sees the ignorance, the nebulousness of the German Revolution. Sylvio Gsell, the physiocrat, proponent of "free money" and free-market economy becomes Minister of Finance. [But] Dr. Neurath, the Marxist, is designated President of the Central Economic Office. How are these two men to work together? I am offered three positions, one after the other; I reject all three. As head of the People's Office for Foreign Affairs, Dr. Lipp is chosen, [a man] whose abilities no one knows. He has no face, only a full beard, wears no suit, only a frock coat—these two properties seem to be the basis of his qualifications. A worker whom I ask about Dr. Lipp tells me he knows the Pope personally.[9]

Dr Lipp, after dispatching a somewhat bizarre telegram to his friend the Pope complaining that the previous government had taken the key to the toilet in its flight, subsequently went mad and was forced to resign.

After a week, the government collapsed and was replaced by a second, Communist Council Republic. The Communists (KPD), who had originally refused to support a government it was clear they could not control (arguing that the "phoney" Council Republic was premature) now found conditions ripe. Toller

5

was replaced and briefly arrested, but then allowed to lead the artillery in defense of the Republic against the Hoffmann forces ensconced at Dachau. Although ordered to bombard Dachau, Toller realized that with the support of the local populace and farmers, the city could be taken without bloodshed. But his agreement with the Whites to withdraw was shattered by an *agent provocateur*, and thus Toller captured the town and became the "Victor of Dachau." Again Toller refused an order, this time to shoot the captured White officers:

> No matter how brutal the laws of civil war may be (I know the counter-revolution has mercilessly murdered Red prisoners in Berlin), we are fighting for a more just world; we demand humaneness and so we must be [ourselves] humane.[10]

It was clear to Toller that with 100,000 troops marching on Munich from Berlin, there was no point in the senseless resistance to the last man that the Communists were demanding. After trying unsuccessfully to prevent the murder of right-wing hostages, Toller went into hiding when the White troops entered Munich on May 1. He evaded capture for several weeks with the aid of a number of friends, among them the poet Rainer Maria Rilke. Eventually, on June 5, he was betrayed for the 10,000 RM reward on his head, tried and sentenced to five years imprisonment at Niederschönenfeld. Probably the few weeks in hiding saved him from the fate of so many other revolutionaries who, like Gustav Landauer, were summarily "shot while trying to escape."

In Niederschönenfeld Toller wrote the plays *Masse Mensch (1921)*, *Die Maschinenstürmer* (1922), *Hinkemann* (1923), and *Der entfesselte Wotan* (1923), and a number of volumes of poetry: *Das Schwalbenbuch* (1924), *Gedichte der Gefangenen* (1921) and *Vormorgen* (1924). In 1923, Toller, the political naif (according to East German writers such as Hans Beyer), wrote of his satire on the rising nationalist tide, *Der entfesselte Wotan*, with astonishing prescience *(Mein Kampf* had yet to be published):

> Whom am I attacking? These types who according to my deepest conviction have dragged us into the most miserable slime, and who will push the people in deeper and deeper if they do not free themselves from their influence. The German[y] of Goethe, Hölderlin, Büchner ...what does it have in common with ...Ruge, with Theodor Fritsch, with Adolf Hitler?[11]

Das Schwalbenbuch is a cycle of poems inspired by the ludicrous spectacle of all the power of the Bavarian prison bureaucracy being brought to bear in order to destroy for utterly no reason the nests that a pair of swallows, emissaries of freedom, continued to try to build in the cells. The swallows, cheered on by the entire population of prisoners, fought on undaunted initially, but finally succumbed after a long and difficult war.

On June 16, 1924, Toller was released, thirty years old, having served his full sentence minus one day (an effort to forestall demonstrations). On his release, he produced an impressive variety of essayistic and political writings, work that could not have passed the censor in Niederschönenfeld. He documented the excesses of Bavarian justice in *Justiz. Erlebnisse* (1927) in order to do what he could for his still imprisoned comrades and show that like other power centers in the Weimar Republic, the judiciary represented the same conservative forces that had dominated Wilhelmine Germany. His views are amply and convincingly confirmed by E.J. Gumbel's book, *Vier Jahre politischer Mord (Four Years of Political Murder)*, which documents the unequal justice meted out to agitators of the Right and Left between 1919 and 1922.[12]

In 1924 Toller began a period of extensive and frequent travel: to Leipzig in August of 1924, to the Middle East and Palestine in March, 1925, to the Soviet Union between March and May of 1926, to the United States from September to December of 1929, to Republican Spain in the spring of 1932 and to Switzerland in 1933.

During this period Toller found time to publish four plays, *Hoppla, wir leben!* (1927), *Bourgeois bleibt Bourgeois* (1929), *Feuer aus den Kesseln* (1930), and *Wunder in Amerika* (1931), as well as the important volume of essays, *Quer Durch* (1930). In 1929 he joined the *Gruppe revolutionärer Pazifisten* (Group of Revolutionary Pacifists), other members of which were Helene Stöcker, Kurt Tucholsky, Alfons Goldschmidt, Walter Mehring and the leader of the "activists," Kurt Hiller.

Fortunately Toller was in Switzerland on the day of the Reichstag fire, and he never again returned to Germany. On May 10, 1933 his books were burned. It was the same day he finished writing his autobiography, *Eine Jugend in Deutschland*. Later that month Toller gave a sensational address to the formerly apolitical P.E.N. Club meeting in Dubrovnik, evidently with the connivance of its President, H.G. Wells (who had succeeded John Galsworthy). The official (Nazi) German delegation walked out. Toller said in that speech:

> I will be reproached in Germany for speaking against Germany. That is
> not so; I am opposing the methods of those who rule Germany today,
> who however have no right to equate themselves with Germany. Millions
> of people in Germany cannot speak and write freely. When I speak here,
> I speak for these millions, who have no voice.[13]

Toller had married a young German actress, Christiane Grautoff, in London in 1934. Hermann Kesten remarks of the marriage:

He married in London a charming actress, who, half as old as he, had gone into exile for his sake, and with whom he was occasionally happy.[14]

In 1935, the second part of Toller's autobiography, *Briefe aus dem Gefängnis*, appeared in Amsterdam. His concern for his fellow prisoners is evident in every page of his prison letters, which contain numerous protests to authorities on their behalf, and which chronicle a never-ending war against brutality and senseless regulations. These letters, which were not collected until 1935, must be read, however, with some caution, since Toller did not have all the relevant documents at his disposal and in some cases altered and combined letters, in others disguised and invented the names of recipients in order to protect people still living in Nazi-ruled Germany. The material that Toller did have had been smuggled out of Germany at great risk by a friend, Dora Fabian, who was imprisoned for her efforts and later committed suicide under suspicious circumstances.

In 1937 his satirical comedy, *Nie wieder Friede*, was published, and in 1939 his last play, *Pastor Hall*. In 1936 Toller had come to the United States, where he lived most of the time in Santa Monica and wrote film scripts for MGM, among them *Der Weg nach Indien* and *The Heavenly Sinner*, a comedy about Lola Montez, in collaboration with Sidney Kaufman. Earlier films include *Menschen hinter Gittern* (1931), which was produced in English as *The Big House* (1930), and *Pastor Hall* (1940).

Toller's suicide on May 22, 1939 remains somewhat of a mystery. We have Christopher Isherwood's description of his generally depressed state of mind, we know that he was discouraged at the obstacles placed in the way of his art in Hollywood and that he was seeing a psychoanalyst. The fact that the relief funds he had so successfully raised for the refugee children on both sides in the Spanish Civil War fell into the hands of Franco, the failure of his marriage and the war situation certainly all played a part. Yet just before his death he had given an impassioned speech to a P.E.N. Club meeting in New York, and he spoke with his friend Ludwig Marcuse about his plans for the future on the eve of his suicide. He died with a ticket to London in his possession.

Perhaps the most moving tribute was written by the novelist Hermann Kesten, who had received Toller's last letter in Paris, written a few days before his death:

In spite of his fame he was modest, without malice toward colleagues, and always ready to help them. He suffered from the mixing of his political and his literary reputations, although he himself helped to create his legend. He had many weaknesses.

But he was fearless, tireless, undaunted, on all occasions ready to help an individual, a worthy cause, the general well-being ...and truly, he loved life. He was my friend.[15]

2

Toller and His Critics

One may cross the world by two paths and only two. *All* or *Nothing*! The one is to fight against everything. To win or else to die. The other is to fight against nothing....But even though I have these opinions they don't cheer me or give me the slightest strength. I am a weakling with a marvelous sword inferior to none.
I can't stand it unless I fight, and yet I'm unable to win. That means that death is the only possible course for me. But I dislike the thought of death. I don't want to die! Then, how am I to live?—Ishikawa Takuboku: *Romanji Diary*[1]

"How am I to live" is a question that each philosopher has had to ask himself as a professional obligation. But it is also a question that each man has to come to terms with willy-nilly as a human obligation, and one which Ernst Toller evidently learned in 1939 that he could not answer. This study will analyze Toller's attempt to deal with this problem in ideological terms, from his early plays where the question is asked in the sense of Takuboku's first paragraph —how is one to arrange one's life—to the later plays and prose works where the problem transforms itself into a poignant and palpable sense of being trapped: how is one to endure this world.

In *Hoppla, wir leben*!, the erstwhile revolutionary, Wilhelm Kilman, draws his conclusions from his estimate of the political constellation of an unspecified country in 1927 and becomes an opportunist and a compromiser. For his efforts two attempts are made on his life —one by Karl Thomas, a leftist who regards Kilman as a cryptofascist fraud, and then another, successful, one by a rightist student who feels that Kilman has sold out to the Jews and Communists. Toller (and I don't wish to imply any further invidious comparisons) must have felt very much like Kilman, as he saw himself attacked by both capitalist and Communist critics for what is in essence the same failing—a lack of system. John Spalek notes:

Toller's works are also rejected [by Marxist critics] because of their "abstract quality," their abstract view of man and morality, and their mystical elements. In other words, Toller is accused of a lack of realism and an awareness of the historical process....He is frequently described by his critics as a "Gefühlsmensch," a basically irrational and impulsive person, guided by his passions, an enthusiast who easily over-estimates his abilities, an utopian idealist, and an orator intoxicated by his own words.[2]

When critics acknowledge Toller's lack of political orthodoxy, whether to attack it from the left as the necessary consequence of a bourgeois humanism that thinks it can make an omelette without cracking an egg, or to greet it from the right as a mitigating circumstance, as the judges in Toller's trial did, they are at the same time acknowledging a supposed deficiency of system in his philosophy. Indeed, many of them would deny, and have denied, that he has a philosophy at all. Even those academic critics such as Karl S. Guthke, who consciously strive for objectivity and have no political ax to grind, seem to feel that this alleged lack of system is a grave flaw which mars Toller's work, perhaps fatally. They regard him as a fuzzy-minded idealist, a hopelessly naive romantic who longs for a fairy-tale ideal realm without giving us any convincing suggestions as to how this happy state is to be achieved. Guthke writes:

> The lack of clarity and realism is, however, only one weakness of the Expressionist credo; another is the platitude....To us today, the well-meaning, arrogant combination of exaggerated, insufficiently thought-out idealism and pathetic sense of mission, of being a savior, in the manifestos and appeals that these young men directed at the conscience of mankind with such childishness seems almost unintentionally comical.[3]

Apart from the question of whether drama is the place for detailed blueprints of programs of social engineering, one wonders why a writer merits criticism for showing precisely that the ideal happy state is *not* to be achieved. Toller wrote from prison to Tessa in 1920:

> Outside: Blood-murder-torture-hunger-the distress of millions. That oppresses one even more. And the presentiment of the fate of Europe in the coming decades. The incomprehensible force that leads me along the one, terrible path. If only I could believe in a more pure development, as I used to. Humanity—always helpless, always crucified. Justice—a bitter taste is on my tongue. I believed in the redemptive power of socialism, perhaps that was my "life-lie"[*Lebenslüge*], perhaps....[4]

Against these words of the twenty-seven year old poet, a poet whose play on the totalitarian mentality, *Der entfesselte Wotan* (Wotan Unbound, 1923), was so accurate that when it was revived in 1959, the producer found it necessary to point out that it had been written in 1923 and not updated, the promises of Jean-Paul Marat in 1780 sound like a grotesque parody:

The lot of the poor, always downtrodden, always subjugated and always oppressed can never be improved by peaceful means....The people have broken the yoke of the nobility; in the same way they will break that of wealth. The great point is to enlighten them and make them aware of their rights, and the revolution will function infallibly without any human power being able to oppose it.[5]

Like Ishikawa Takuboku, Toller had discovered the ineffectuality, the uselessness, the impotence of his poetry and his ideals, his "marvelous sword inferior to none."

Modern philosophy in general has moved from ambitious systematic edifices to a more modest and unashamedly subjective and solipsistic atomization, from Hegel to Nietzsche—perhaps because in the twentieth century one has come to realize the extent to which indulgence in theoretical speculation necessarily falsifies one's apprehensions of reality. In the same way, men have always demurred when they have been asked to attach labels to their political philosophies, even Karl Marx, who was fond of asserting, "ce qu'il y a de certain c'est que moi je ne suis pas Marxiste."[6] An honest man, one who like George Orwell is concerned that his political ideas remain free to interact with his experience, who is concerned about their nexus with the real world, feels instinctively that he betrays his principles by accepting a name for them. For a name is always a label, a *pars pro toto* which reduces an organic totality to a fragment, a fossil. This vague feeling of being called upon to perform a discreditable act in denominating and codifying one's political philosophy has trickled down so far that one can observe great numbers of coy politicians paying obeisance to it every day. Originally, it evidently grew from a certain sensitivity to the degree of complexity of the interaction between moral and political theory and political realities. Toller complains: "Everyone gives me some label"[7] Elsewhere he writes: "I regard myself as independent of political parties.[8] This ideological declaration of independence is to a large extent responsible for the tone of Toller criticism. Spalek notes: "The controversy which surrounded Toller's work in the twenties was almost entirely political in nature. It...had little to do with the literary qualities of his works."[9] Toller's remarks also point to his basically anarchist political orientation. The party and its discipline necessarily prevent and encroach upon the sanctity of the individual.

It is my contention that Toller's political ineffectuality, that the apparent theoretical lack of rigor which so bothers his critics of leftist, rightist and academic persuasion, exemplifies not a fatal flaw in himself, but one in us, his interpreters. It is an expression of the constitution of the world rather than a statement about Toller himself. Toller's ramified and complex political ideas admittedly do not correspond to those of any organized party. But to infer from this a lack of political philosophy is to falsify drastically an intellectual position for which, on the contrary, the sanctity of moral principle was absolute. Jost Hermand, in an extremely interesting and sensitive discussion of *Hoppla, wir leben!* in his recent book, *Unbequeme Literatur: Eine Beispielreihe (Uncomfortable Literature: A Series of Examples)*,[10] about which we shall have more to say later, emphasizes that Toller's dramatic technique was essentially dialectical. Far from being a mere mouthpiece of the author, the hero, Karl Thomas (and the other revolutionaries in the play), embody a whole spectrum of conceivable political attitudes which interact in the manner of a kind of Brechtian *Lehrstück* (didactic play). Hermand writes:

> Seen in this way, Toller proves to be a quite consistent thinker, even with respect to the phenomenon of revolution. After he had in his *Wandlung* attempted the leap into utopia, he revealed [in the works] since *Masse-Mensch* an unusually sharp eye for the inner dialectic of all revolutionary processes, as only Büchner and Hauptmann had before him. In his works he is constantly concerned with the gulf between ethics and politics....On the basic of this tragic knowledge of the terrible brutality of all historical revolutionary processes Toller sharply rejected the "banal optimism" of the "extreme left" his whole life long. The attempt of the KPD [the Communist Party of Germany] to play fast and loose with the future sometimes seemed to him positively absurd.[11]

Hermand says of *Hoppla, wir leben!*:

> This play is neither "bourgeois" nor "proletarian" art. Its greatness lies in the fact that it strives to be more than mere [partisan] propaganda, without, on the other hand, degenerating into "humanitarian" platitudes.[12]

And he concludes with the observation: "It was not his ideal 'to straddle the fence,' as Kurt Hiller once wrote. That he did so nonetheless reflects unfavorably not on him, but on the unwillingness of others to come to terms with the possibility of a 'third way.'"[13] Exactly what this third way consisted of, it will be our task to investigate.

Toller perceived that evolution and even revolution were necessary, but in a sense superficial. He saw that man must change radically and profoundly within himself or unavoidably suffer disaster. Nietzsche said that we possess art lest we perish of the truth,[14] but for Toller the "marvelous sword" of poetry was used to cut through to the truth in all its starkness and unpleasantness. Once achieved, the starkness of this insight never left him, and it gave him the strength to eschew superficial tactical coups and moral compromise in order to make his fellow men feel the necessity and profundity of the choice which he knew faced all men with the same intensity as it faced him. In this sense, he was a saintly man, a German George Orwell, a German Eustache de Saint-Pierre. Eustache, in Georg Kaiser's play *The Burghers of Calais*, in giving up his life to point the way to his fellow men, succeeded and the souls of his compatriots and the harbor of Calais were saved. Toller did not, and the fate of our souls and our "harbor" is still in doubt. Yet, if they should be lost, we shall have to decide whether the fault is a naively and excessively idealistic example, or some deficiency within us.

Fourier is said to have never forgotten seeing a cargo of rice being dumped into the sea to drive the price up. Obviously he did not become a utopian socialist solely on that account, but just as obviously many of the features of his "phalansteries" are traceable to it. Similarly, Toller developed his ideology through a constant process of interaction with political realities; in fact he alludes to Fourier in a description of his feelings on returning to civilian society after the war:

> Again I think of Stefan, my childhood friend, of his hatred of the rich, of my mother's reply that poverty was God's will. The earth has food for all in abundance; man's spirit has found means and ways of mastering nature, of transforming stone into true gold—into bread. And still, here, millions of men die of hunger, while elsewhere grain is dumped into the sea....Unreason and blindness rule the people, and the people suffer their dominance because they distrust reason, which could control the chaotic, order it creatively and give it shape. Because man grows organically, he calls his golems (the economy, the state) organic structures, and so he appeases his bad conscience. For is he not helpless before the incomprehensible and irresistible omnipotence of a world that includes death....he loves freedom and yet he is afraid of it, and he would rather abase himself and forge his own chains of slavery than dare to create and to breathe, freely and responsibly.[15]

He altered many of his most important political judgments in the course of his short life, filled with events of the poignancy of those related in *Eine Jugend in Deutschland*, in *Das Schwalbenbuch*, in *Justiz. Erlebnisse*. Yet at the core of his mind there remained a gyroscope which always guided him, the orientation of which remained fixed. At the beginning of his career, in *Die Wandlung*, Toller expressed an optimistic faith in the possibilities of human regeneration:

> Mother! Don't you feel how the earth ferments? How all the earth becomes one powerful womb, that trembles in childbirth? Think of the

torment when you were about to give birth to me—that is how the earth is convulsed....A torn, bleeding womb to give birth to mankind anew.[16]

And even later, after five years of imprisonment and on the "day of the burning of my books in Germany" in 1933, he was able to write in *Eine Jugend in Deutschland*:

I don't believe in man's "evil" nature; I believe that he does the most terrible things out of lack of imagination, out of inertia of the heart.

Have I not myself, when I read of famines in China, of massacres in Armenia, of tortured prisoners in the Balkans, laid my newspaper aside and without pausing continued my daily tasks? Ten thousand dead of starvation, a thousand shot—what did these numbers mean to me? I read them and had forgotten them an hour later. From lack of imagination....From inertia of my heart.[17]

Even in what is perhaps his most pessimistic and cynical work, *Hinkemann*, Toller maintains this faith in at least the *possibility* of regeneration, for Hinkemann's wife Grete has not ridiculed him for his war injury as he believes she has, and is in fact filled with remorse when she sees the extremes to which his love for her has driven him. This flood of optimism, which later ebbed to a trickle, was never undiscriminating, nor was it based on an idealization of the proletariat. It was not an example of "socialist nonrealism." On the contrary, Toller observes in *Briefe aus dem Gefängnis*:

For years now I have been living close to proletarians. Can anyone live more closely together than we did—crammed together in a cell block? I am getting to know the workers as never before. Outside one sees the surface of a man; almost never does one see him naked. And just because I have seen the naked proletarian, I recognize the dangerous self-deception of those writers who think they are educating the masses by proclaiming, "O holy worker, O God-like worker, you child of justice, love, purity," and amid vigorous kowtowing disport themselves with servility....If we do not through our work develop his [the worker's] spiritual and intellectual powers, do not create those fine, ramified relationships that bind men to an idea, to a cause, then we will breed partisan factions, but never communities [*Gemeinschaften*].[18]

Here, too, one recognizes Toller's inclination toward an anarchistic rejection of the political party in favor of the community, informed by creative spirit (*Geist*). Like the best of realists, like Goethe, Zola, Tolstoy and Dostoevsky, Toller sees the masses as fickle, easily swayed, capable of the most extreme cruelty. But we are all men and therefore all potential "nameless ones," like

15

the demagogue in *Die Maschinenstürmer*. Toller does not condemn us on that account, but neither does he exculpate us. He strives to realize certain of his potentialities and suppress others. From the time he handed scenes from *Die Wandlung* to enthusiastic workers on strike in Munich[19] until the end of his life, Toller was able to see human depravity as a result of "inertia of the heart"; to believe in the possibility of the moral regeneration of a raped, misled, exploited and exhausted people. His journey was a sentimental one, but it was not one which led him to close his eyes to reality on that account. Toller, grew very much aware that this is a world in which the traveler is not met by universal indulgence on his way to his goal. It was a terrible and final irony that the large sum of money he had collected for the relief of refugees in both Fascist and Republican-held parts of Spain during the Spanish Civil War fell into Franco's hands. Voltaire could not have devised a more telling symbol of the failure of Toller's hopes.

I have indicated in general terms the kinds of criticisms that have been made of Toller's works by writers of various ideological persuasions, and noted one rejoinder, that of Jost Hermand, with which I basically agree. Toller's philosophy is, in my view, anything but naive, nor is it vague and ill-defined. On the contrary, it is to be taken as a dialectical working-out of various ideological possibilities. The result is a system which is non-trivial and self-consistent; one which can be described as idealistic, but one whose evident realism (in all of the plays after *Die Wandlung*, which does not pretend to mirror reality, but rather points a new way) cannot be ignored. In fact, the seriously distorted view that has dominated Toller research to date and led to the common view that he was a man ruled by his emotions and out of touch with the realities of Weimar Germany is largely a result of an unjustified generalization of the attitudes of *Die Wandlung* to all his other works. *Die Wandlung* is uniquely optimistic among Toller's works—it is the only one of his plays written before his experiences in the Munich Revolution, and it was intended to be a vision of the ideal, rather than a realistic assessment of the possibilities for a radical restructuring of society. In 1917 no one in Germany knew, least of all Toller, what would follow the war; what was certain was that the people yearned for an end to the slaughter. But neither Toller, nor Friedrich Ebert, the unwilling head of the provisional government, who "hated revolution like sin," nor anyone else quite saw in 1919 that the people knew what they did not want, but did not know what they wanted, as Toller put it. It would be difficult to surpass in its hard-headed realism Toller's analysis of the reasons for the failure of the Munich experiment in *Eine Jugend in Deutschland*.

It will be expedient to postpone a detailed consideration of the various criticisms of individual plays. But the results of the researches of two writers who have attempted to define Toller's ideology, the American, W.A. Willibrand, and the East German, Martin Reso, will serve to indicate the directions in which I feel progress can be made. Willibrand summarizes his results in the following words:

> In the study of his proletarian dramas we saw that Toller opposed (a) revolutionary violence and the sacrifice of individuals to the welfare of the group; (b) the glorification of the proletariat; (c) the Utopian vision of a well-ordered economy as a panacea. And...he posited a spiritual and moral transformation for the achievement of a better social order....Man would be assured of happiness only in so far as organized society were capable of giving it. The best society has tragic limitations beyond which it cannot help suffering humanity. Some alleviation if fleetingly suggested as lying in the domain of religion, the exploration of which was beyond the powers of Ernst Toller....Toller was closer to a true conception of humanity than Marxism could ever be. In spite of his obvious metaphysical limitations, he saw that the need of a meaningful life caused people to turn to the chauvinistic demagogue of both the right and the left. Hence the possibility and also the necessity of a more spiritual aspect. [20]

These words reduce the complex web of a highly articulated philosophy to a few sentences, the truth of which can be admitted, but only in a general sense, as Martin Reso shows.[21] Toller did not set out to be a philosopher, but the limitations of his metaphysics, his intellectual powers and political acumen, are by no means so evident as Willibrand claims. His plays, and even more his essayistic writings, letters and autobiography will speak for themselves. As late as 1930, political realists like Carl von Ossietzsky were writing:

> Hugenberg will never let his Golem become too independent. When Hitler no longer fits into his plans, he will cut off his resources and the National Socialist movement will disappear as mysteriously as it mushroomed during the past two years.[22]

In the same year Toller wrote:

> We stand before a period of reaction. Let no one think that the tenure of fascism, be it ever so moderate and devious, will be a short transition period. The revolutionary, socialist, republican energy that the system will destroy will not be rebuilt for years....It is time to dispel dangerous illusions. Not only democrats, also socialists and communists tend to feel one should let Hitler rule; then one would most easily see him ruin himself. But they forget that the Nazi party is defined by its will toward

power and the use of power. They will be glad to achieve power democratically, but they will never surrender it at the behest of democracy....If nothing happens [to avert it] we are on the verge of a period of European fascism, a period of the temporary extinction of political and spiritual freedom, whose end will only come in the train of ghastly, bloody struggles and wars.

It is New Year's eve, 1931. This time the phrase is [literally] true: it's one minute before midnight.[23]

We also have the testimony of Ernst Niekisch, a fellow-prisoner at Niederschonenfeld, as to Toller's grounding in theoretical matters:

...with devotion he carried on his studies, which ranged from literary history and philosophy to questions of theoretical socialism. When I organized a series of lectures on Kant's epistemology for some friends, he was one of the most zealous members of the audience and returned again and again, in many discussions, to the problems of epistemology. Spengler's work, *The Decline of the West* agitated him spiritually and Freud's psychoanalysis captivated him....[24]

Reso, too, reproaches Toller for ideological innocence in order to show that his humanistic outlook, his "unorthodox Marxism," militated against the advocacy of any effective mass movement based on the strength of an organized proletariat and the class struggle:

Toller's vision of man is magnificent, but not pertinent. It has the error of all utopias. The attempts at solution in his works are too ideal to be realized. His ideas are profound, ethical and humanitarian....[25]

Reso emphasizes that this comfortable profundity is really useless, a kind of curiosity, since it is ineffectual:

Apart from the proclamation of the idea as the fundamental element of the whole movement, one sees very few well-founded economic insights and general demands. What was demanded were wishes that were altogether acceptable at the time of the origin of the program [of the Cultural and Political League of German Youth, 1917] but any hint of tactics was lacking. One cannot conduct politics this way.[26]

It is my contention that Toller's philosophy concerned itself with all of the tactical and theoretical problems which agitated the socialist and revolutionary world from 1848 on. He presented a critique of capitalism, of alienation, of the effect of international economic competition, of colonialization; he considered revolutionary tactics, the role of the revolutionary leader, the extent to which education of the masses is effective, the possibilities and justification of revisionism. He agonized over questions of whether the revolution could be accomplished without employing means which vitiated its goals. He concerned himself with the role of workers' and soldiers' councils. And this list could be extended.

He did not solve all of these problems, but not because of intellectual insufficiency. They were resolved neither by Toller nor by Lenin, Bernstein, Luxemburg, nor by the whole pantheon of socialist thinkers, because very many of these problems were simply insoluble. Toller's proposals, we shall find, lie in all their essentials within the tradition of the communist-anarchism of the Kropotkin wing of European anarchism. In nearly all of the conflicts listed above, Toller sides with the anarchists and arrives at solutions which assert the primacy of the individual over the party.

In order to show this we need to begin by examining in some detail the tradition of European anarchism in order to define its characteristics. We shall then focus on the development that these ideas underwent when they are applied to conditions in Germany. With this necessary work of definition and background accomplished, we shall apply this scheme to Toller's plays. Of Toller's twelve full-length plays, those that deal with the relationship between bourgeois and proletarian figures will, of course, most concern us. It was in these early dramas that Toller tried to define and work out his political philosophy in dialectical fashion and to delimit it from the competing political currents of the day. Each play attacks this problem from a different direction. In *Die Wandlung* Toller emphasizes the importance of the spiritual matrix from which the "new man" must spring. In *Masse Mensch* he again distinguishes between his conception of the "new man" and that of the authoritarian Marxists, this time emphasizing not so much the spiritual as the ethical aspects of this philosophy. In *Die Maschinenstürmer*, on the other hand, Toller deals with the danger from the right, from capitalism, and places revolutionary action within an economic rather than an ethical context, pleading for a kind of syndicalism. In *Hinkemann* Toller shows the insufficiency of *all* political attempts to improve man's lot by rearranging society. In *Hoppla, wir leben!* (in this sense the mirror image of *Masse Mensch*), he concludes that those revisionist ideologies which can be realized will lead to the wrong goal, whereas those which refuse to indulge in compromise cannot be realized. Each of these attempts at definition forms an essential part of Toller's political ideology.

What we shall find will be a system that began on an instinctive level as an intuitive revulsion against war and the society that had produced it, but which very soon took on a consistent and carefully delimited ideological content. The emphases and accents of this philosophy were altered to contend with the various problems that confronted it, but its core remained surprisingly constant. Reso himself is aware of this anarchism in Toller, though he chooses to reject it as ideological confusion, a mass of contradictions. A few quotations will suffice:

> He wanted the dominance of the masses and fought for the rights of the individual; he advocated political action and severed his ties with his party; he sought the revolution and shrank from its consequences.[27]

Reso notes elsewhere:

> It was a difficult path, and he never walked it to the end, for his whole contradictory nature urged him into other ties, forced him to leave behind the mass organization that offered him the only guarantee for the accomplishment of his goals in order to fight his own particular battle....For him, not partisan associations but devotion to the ideal was decisive.[28]

Just what this struggle and this ideal consisted of, we shall investigate in detail. Toller's ideals, morally and theoretically self-consistent, never changed, but the Hitler epoch, with its revelations of the depths of human depravity, caused him to give up hope that his vision of a new society, a humane social structure, could ever be achieved without compromises and means which, although they of course did not approach those of his adversaries in cruelty, were nonetheless odious to him. Who can summon the courage of the Woman (in *Masse Mensch*) and forswear violence in the face of Hitler? This question Toller could not answer. He wrote in a speech against Hitler, "I was a convinced pacifist, but reality set me right."[29]

As the above sketch indicates, it will not be the purpose of this book to inquire into the aesthetic merits of Toller's works. An unbiased critic would have to concede, I believe, that Toller's plays were successful not because of the beauty of his verse, nor because of the formal perfection of his dramatic plots. At times (and frequently) his poetry is an embarrassment to the benevolently disposed critic. Such poems of his that are reprinted in anthologies are present largely as acts of piety and representatives of historical moments rather than as exemplars of sublime political poetry. Toller's prose works, of considerable importance both artistically and as documents of his times, have only recently been seriously studied.[30]

And yet, Toller's plays *were* successful—perhaps more so than those of any Expressionist playwright after Brecht. I believe this is so because they addressed certain ideological and ethical dilemmas that agitated the Germany of the 20's (as indeed they still do today), and addressed them in an extremely effective and affecting way. The dramatic structure of Toller's Expressionist plays is no more traditional than that of, say, Strindberg's *Ghost Sonata*, and one would do him an injustice to judge his worth by applying traditional standards. His popularity and his later eclipse closely parallel those of German anarchism itself, and it is by examining Toller's work as a political statement and the resonant chords he struck within this anarchist context that one can best explain his significance and determine his place as an artist. Toller's ideological concerns were closely bound up with the larger phenomenon of European and German anarchism in the 20's, the importance of which has only recently been investigated in books such as those cited in the bibliography by Hans Manfred Bock, Fähnders and Rector, Eugene Lunn, Ulrich Linse, Charles Maurer and others. It is this phenomenon that we want to examine in order to understand Toller's significance fully.

3
Anarchism: The Historical Tradition

It is the leap of mankind from the realm of necessity into the realm of freedom.—Friedrich
Engels: Anti-Dühring[1]

The difficulty of arriving at a satisfactory definition of anarchism has been
recognized by nearly everyone who has written on the subject. Paul
Eltzbacher,[2] who presents a compendium of the ideas of seven leading anarchist thinkers under a variety of rubrics in order to then determine what they
have in common, is unable to discover any common denominator save their rejection of the state in some form or other. A movement that includes personalities as diverse as Max Stirner, Ravachol, Johann Most, Gandhi, Tolstoy
and Kropotkin presents formidable problems to the systematizer, and
ultimately we shall have to adopt a Wittgensteinian solution and say that we
know mainly in an operational sense whom we are willing to call an anarchist
and to whom we are disposed to deny the designation. One thing we can say is
that anarchists in general regard man himself as infinitely perfectible and consider that crime, poverty, the soulless mechanization of the production of
goods, loneliness, isolation and the other manifest ills of modern society are not
necessary features of all conceivable societies, but instead the consequence of
the distortions caused by government and the state. It follows that the state
should be eliminated and the "government of men" replaced by the
"administration of things." The exact form this administration will take varies
a great deal from thinker to thinker—from the essentially egotistically oriented
Max Stirner, influenced by Nietzsche but also by Hegel, through the
mutualism of Proudhon, to the collectivism of Bakunin and the anarcho-
communism of Kropotkin. But all envisage some sort of assemblage of groups
freely cooperating for mutual benefit—even Stirner, with his oxymoronic
"Society of Egoists." For each realizes that in addition to being an individual
concerned with protecting the integrity of his personality from the incursions of
the state and all other institutions, man is a social animal that requires not only
companionship to fulfill himself emotionally, but also mutual aid (to anticipate Kropotkin's theory) to enable him to cope in a material sense with a

highly complex world.

A second dichotomy characteristic of anarchism is its double aspect as both an economic and political ideology. Oscar Jászi has noted, "The fundamental element of anarchism is an extension of classic liberalism from the economic field into all other fields."[3] Just as the laissez-faire economist wishes to banish the state from economic life insofar as possible in favor of the invisible hand of the market place, the anarchist banishes the state from social and political life in favor of decisions freely arrived at on an *ad hoc* basis by those intimately concerned. In fact, one equation commonly proposed is that between anarchists and classical liberals. Alan Ritter,[4] in a closely-reasoned and convincing argument, has examined the commonplace notion that anarchists are really liberals (in the United States in the 1970's we would say conservatives) at heart. He agrees that in addition to the manifest tendencies within anarchism that link it with various leftist ideologies, there is a large conservative component. In general, one can say that in their sense of powerlessness, of being politically manipulated and disenfranchised, exploited by the wealthy and by a society constructed for the wealthy, in their opposition to private property and private controls of the means of production, the anarchists were ready to make common cause with the socialists and were, in some cases at least, capable of employing the impressive socialist mechanisms for removing the bourgeoisie from the levers of power.

But in their longings for a natural and non-institutionalized society, for free associations of mutual aid, for non-coercive economic arrangements to replace the present system of property and wages, in their rejection of political and government interference in economic activity, and above all, in their libertarian and individualist leanings, the anarchists discovered to their surprise a kinship with conservative thought.

Although its roots have been traced back as far as Zeno and Aristippus, anarchism like socialism is after all basically a child of the industrial revolution, though some writers emphasize its basis in the crafts and among skilled workers. James Joll in *The Anarchists* notes: "The anarchist movement ...is, at least in part, the result of the impact of machines and industry on a peasant or artisan society. It throve on the myth of revolution as it developed after 1789; yet, at the same time, it was the failure of political revolutions and constitutional reforms to satisfy economic and social needs which led the anarchists to challenge the methods and goals of the revolutionaries themselves."[5]

The new non-coercive society will obviously represent a revolutionary change from the present, and consequently its attainment presents the anarchists with a distinct problem. Either man will have to undergo a spiritual revolution prompted by example and persuasion, as Tolstoy suggests and as Gandhi has demonstrated, or there will have to be a social revolution—more than likely a bloody one. Tolstoy's metaphor for the former possibility is particularly endearing and rustic.

> Men in their present situation are like bees that have left their hive and are hanging on a twig in a great mass. The situation of the bees is a temporary one, and absolutely must be changed. They must take flight and seek a new abode. Every bee knows that, and wishes to make an end of its own suffering condition and that of the others; but this cannot be done by one so long as the others do not help. But all cannot rise at once, for one hangs over another and hinders it from letting go, therefore all remain hanging. One might think that there was no way out of this situation for the bees.[6]

At this crucial juncture, Tolstoy continues his parable by emphasizing the moral force of the individual, who, relying on his own reason and conscience, succeeds where the unthinking collective does not: It is only necessary that "...one bee spread its wings, rise and fly, and after it the second, the third, the tenth, the hundredth, for the immobile hanging mass to become a freely flying swarm of bees."[7]

But if history is any sort of reliable guide, it is the latter alternative that is more likely, and this brings us the third dichotomy in anarchist theory. The likelihood is manifestly remote that those in control of the levers of power and those who benefit from the toil of the exploited masses will voluntarily relinquish their privileged position. After all, it took many generations of human history to produce one Tolstoy. And the probability is even more remote that without a powerful, highly organized and centralized anarchist movement the state can be seized and demolished by anarchists. When we read of anarchist congresses failing because of a refusal to vote, every vote being an encroachment on the rights of the minority and the individual (cf. Godwin: "The deciding of truth by casting up of numbers [is an] intolerable insult upon all reason and justice."[8]), or when we read that playing in an orchestra or acting in a play is incompatible with the sanctity of the individual because it is the imposition of one man's ideas or emotions on others, we are inclined to ridicule the anarchist ideal, or at least to despair of attaining it. George Adler, in his (hostile) article on anarchism of 1902,[9] quotes the report of a police spy in London to the effect that in the 1890's there were no more than ten native anarchists in all England and finds the estimate credible. (Certainly one feels that Joseph Conrad never suffered much anxiety that the bizarre group of anarchists he described in *The Secret Agent* would ever seize control of England.) And Ulrich Linse, who describes in several books and articles the soul-searching sectarian controversies over the question of centralization and participation in the labor movement among the German anarchist groups from 1871 through the Weimar period, notes: "The Federation of Communist-Anarchists, however, apparently owing to the decline of the other left-wing radical movements (in 1923), did not achieve their organizational high-water mark until 1923-24 with an approximate membership of 500, and reached about 10,000 to 15,000 workers with their agitation."[10]

The anarchists were faced with the dilemma that they would forever remain ineffectual and certainly fail to achieve their goals unless they formed strong, centralized organizations ready to seize control by force, if need be. But if they did these things, the goals they achieved would not be theirs. The dilemma is well expressed in Bertolt Brecht's play, *Die Massnahme (The Measures Taken)*:

> What baseness would you not commit
> In order to eliminate baseness?[11]

Yet elsewhere, in his poem "An die Nachgeborenen" ("To Those Who Will Follow Us"), Brecht writes of this same baseness:

> And yet we know:
> Even the hatred of baseness
> Distorts the features.
> Even the rage at injustice
> Makes the voice hoarse. Ah, we
> Who wanted to prepare the soil for friendliness
> Could not ourselves be friendly.[12]

James Joll begins his book, *The Anarchists*, by quoting Trotsky's denunciation of the Mensheviks as typical of one approach to interpreting history: "You are miserable isolated individuals. You are bankrupt. You have played out your role. Go where you belong, to the dustheap of history." He goes on to remark for the "historians of success":

> When a revolution succeeds, historians are concerned to trace its roots and unravel its origins, so that very often, the whole chain of events leading to it over many decades is represented as an inevitable process, and each idea or episode is judged by the extent to which it helped or hindered the final result. On the other hand, the revolutions which fail are treated as blind alleys, and the men and ideas that inspired them are rarely studied for their own interest .... Yet, if the aim of the historian, like that of the artist, is to enlarge our picture of the world, to give us a new way of looking at things, then the study of failure can often be as instructive and rewarding as the study of success. A recurrent type of failure

25

and its causes may throw light both on the psychology of individuals and on the structure of societies.[13]

William Godwin (1756-1836)

Of all the anarchists we shall consider, William Godwin was the first to present a theory of anarchism rendered in a form of unparalleled purity, unalloyed by compromise and empiricism. Moreover, his work and ideas provide the foundation on which later thinkers built, even when they modified it. For these reasons, we shall examine these ideas in some detail.

The fundamental principle of Godwin's political philosophy is well stated in his remark: "There is but one power to which I can yield a heart-felt obedience, the decision of my own understanding, the dictate of my own conscience."[14] We shall see that this anti-authoritarian, even anti-political, aspect of anarchism is its most pervasive, indeed well-nigh its defining characteristic. Oscar Wilde, for example, wrote in a similar vein: "There is no necessity to separate the monarch from the mob; all authority is equally bad."[15] And Proudhon issued a categorial rejection meant to include not only authoritarian monarchs, but democracy as well: "Whoever puts his hand on me to govern me is a usurper and a tyrant; I declare him my enemy."[16] It should not therefore surprise us to learn that scholars have detected anarchist ideas in nearly every heresy which has appeared on the stage of history: in the Albigensians, the Anabaptists, in Müntzer, Meslier, Jacques Roux, Morelly, Sylvain Maréchal, Fichte, Multatuli, Thoreau, Whitman, Aristippus, Zeno, Fénelon, Diderot, in Winstanley's Diggers, and in the Spartacus revolt. Even Rousseau has been called a spiritual ancestor of the anarchists, though as James Joll, Ernst Cassirer and Peter Gay point out, it was his theories of education and the famous first sentence of Book I of Le Contrat social that appealed to the anarchists, and not the idea of the social contract itself, which they rejected. But the heretic, who by definition resists what he considers an unjust and coercive use of power by established authority, does not necessarily reject all manifestations of authority, nor does he propose a program of direct action to eliminate it. William Godwin did summarily reject authority, as the above quotation indicates, and it is he who must be considered the first anarchist in the modern sense of the term—at least, the first man to develop his ideas on the subject in a systematic way in his Enquiry Concerning Political Justice (1793), a work which was written in the heat of the French Revolution and perhaps inspired by Burke's Reflections on the French Revolution. Godwin's theories proceed from the principle that justice and happiness are linked, that man will do good if only he can recognize it, and that doing it will make him happy. Godwin shows himself a true representative of the age of reason, and in a sense mirrors Kant's confidence in the efficacy (not to mention the moral necessity) of an individualist ethical system—the individual himself must choose how to behave, and if he is able to choose intelligently and in accord with the categorical imperative, Kant and Godwin are confident that universal human reason will lead him to affirm by and large those values which most societies mistakenly try to enforce by coercive means. To anticipate, we will be able to classify Godwin (and Max Stirner) on the right end of the spectrum of anarchism—as an "individualist anarchism," in contrast to more socially-oriented varieties such as anarcho-syndicalism and communist anarchism. In the case of Stirner (or Nietzsche, for that matter) we are not at all certain that extreme individualism will necessarily engender justice, and justice happiness. Stirner wrote: "Let me withdraw the might that I have conceded to others out of ignorance regarding the strength of my own might! Let me say to myself, what my might reaches to is my property; and let me claim as property everything I feel myself strong enough to attain, and let me extend my actual property as far as *I* entitle, that is, empower myself to take.... "[17] It must be noted, however, that Stirner's life was a good deal tamer than his theoretical posturings. Stirner points out in *The Ego and His Own* that children, for example, while they appear weak, actually wield enormous power by virtue of their lovableness. Thus, power must be defined in a rather broad sense.

Godwin's view of human nature was much more agreeable—in fact, totally optimistic. Man was infinitely perfectible: "Perfectibility is one of the most unequivocal characteristics of the human species, so that the political as well as the intellectual state of man may be presumed to be in a course of progressive improvement."[18] Evil he explains in the following way: "All vice is nothing more than error and mistake reduced into practice and adopted as the principle of our conduct."[19]

If vice is error, then it can be corrected by reason, since the mind is a *tabula rasa*, on which a prudent education can write the truth. All crime has a cause, and if the cause is eliminated, the crime will be, too. Most crimes result from the unequal distribution of wealth, and thus ultimately from property. Like Proudhon, Godwin regarded private property as theft and thought that its abolition would abolish crime as well. The progress of science would lift the burden of disagreeable toil from man's shoulders. Reason would control and check potentially disruptive emotions like ambition and vanity: "Do you want my table? Make one for yourself, or, if I be more skillful in that respect than you, I will make one for you. Do you want it immediately? Let us compare the urgency of your wants and mine, and let justice decide."[20]

Cooperation of the sort envisioned by Godwin, however, was entirely voluntary and non-institutionalized, unlike Proudhon's People's Bank scheme, which we shall have to consider later. The logical consequence of Godwin's individualism and faith in the efficacy of reason in taming the passions becomes most evident when we examine his view of ideal interpersonal relationships: "I shall assiduously cultivate the intercourse of that woman whose accomplishment shall strike me in the most powerful manner. 'But it may happen that other men will feel for her the same preference that I do?' This will create no difficulty. We may all enjoy her conversation and we shall all be wise enough to consider the sensual intercourse a very trivial object."[21] We have perhaps even more difficulty in suppressing a smile at the following chapter entitled "On the Mode of Excluding Visitors": "Let us suppose that we are ourselves destined ...to give this answer that our father or wife is not at home when they are really in the house. Should we not feel our tongue contaminated with the base plebeian lie? ...He must in reality be the weakest of mankind who should conceive umbrage at a plain answer in this case, when he was informed of the moral considerations that induced me to employ it."[22] Godwin goes on then to suppose that we refuse out of simple dislike; "for some moral fault we perceive or think we perceive in him. Why should he be kept in ignorance of our opinion respecting him, and prevented from the opportunity either of amendment or vindication?"

Because Godwin holds such an optimistic view of the possibilities of voluntary cooperation in forging a viable society, he views government as a disagreeable nuisance: "Government can have no more than two legitimate purposes, the suppression of injustice among individuals within the community, and the common defense against external invasion,"[23] though, as we have seen, rationality in league with education will soon eliminate injustice anyhow. Other anarchists, for example, deny even the need for punishment.

Democracy, while it is the best of the known forms of government, is not ideal, involving as it does the delegation of one's power to make decisions. Further, it divides men into two classes—the governors and the governed—on a spurious basis. Godwin advocates the dissolution of powerful, centralized bureaucracies into local units of participating government which he called "parishes." Laws could then be dispensed with and all would participate in all decisions.

Education, too, ought to be decentralized. It is not, in any event, the function of the state, nor even of society. The general aim should be for the individual to internalize moral principles to such an extent that a considerate, benevolent and tolerant social association will result which can safely abjure coercion. Ritter in the article referred to above points out the distasteful aspects of tyranny of public opinion. Similarly, George Orwell comments on the anarchist Houyhnhnms in *Gulliver's Travels*:

This illustrates very well the totalitarian tendency which is implicit in the anarchist or pacifist vision of society. In a society where there is no law, and in theory no compulsion, the only arbiter of behaviour is public opinion. But public opinion, because of the tremendous urge to conformity in gregarious animals, is less tolerant than any system of law.[24]

Orwell, the reluctant socialist, proves to be a reluctant anarchist as well, though he would admit, one supposes, that of the two sorts of compulsion, public opinion is preferable to coercion. Moreover, what Godwin means by an internalized system of ethics is not identical with what Orwell calls "public opinion."

Godwin's analysis and vision were immensely popular when *Political Justice* was first published and enjoyed a vogue not only among such men as Coleridge and Godwin's benefactor, victim and son-in-law, Shelley, but also among working men. By the time he died, his work was forgotten, though Woodcock traces his influence to the nineteenth century English labor movement, to Robert Owen whom he knew personally, to William Morris, Bernard Shaw and Herbert Read.

Proudhon (1809-1865)

Of all the classical anarchists, perhaps the one whose life exhibits the most similarities to Toller is Pierre-Joseph Proudhon. Like Toller's his theoretical writings were in a highly effective prose (cf. *De la Justice dans la Révolution et dans l'Église*) which was however far from scientific in the Marxian sense. Woodcock calls him, "a deliberate, anti-systematic thinker who distrusted static conclusions and final answers."[25] The Comtesse d'Agoult wrote in her *History of 1848*: "His unexpected and striking manner of speaking ...excited the curiosity of the public to the highest degree," just as Toller's friend Hermann Kesten refers to him as "a dazzling speaker ...a born actor.... "[26] The federalist social system that Proudhon advocated reminds one of the councils of 1918-1919 in Bavaria. Woodcock says of the "progressive societies," the workers' associations that Proudhon proposed as the basis of the new society: "...he appears to see them partly as educational, intended to give the proletariat a true consciousness of the economic realities that underlie the social situation, and partly as functional, actual cells of the new order, organized on a 'collective and limited liability' basis, for the purpose of regulating a mutualist exchange of goods and services...."[27] Similarly, in his *Idée générale de la Révolution* (1851), Proudhon speaks of decentralization, federalism instead of nationalism, and of direct workers' control of the means of production.

Proudhon resembled Toller not only in his rhetorical and propagandistic talents and in his vision of the organization of the new society, but also in his attempts at achieving it. The resistance to all forms of coercion, of collectivism, the doctrine of "respect," the rejection of violence all comport with Toller's attempt to achieve his goals by education and by example. During his brief period of command of the Red forces defending the revolution in 1919, Toller released White prisoners, only to have the same men fight against him the next day. Proudhon writes in 1846 in his famous reply to Marx's offer of collaboration in a committee of correspondence:

> ...let us not, because we are at the head of a new movement, make ourselves the leaders of a new intolerance, let us not pose as the apostles of a new religion, even if it be the religion of logic, the religion of reason. Let us gather together and encourage all protests, let us brand all exclusiveness, all mysticism; let us never regard a question as exhausted, and when we have used our last argument, let us begin again, if necessary, with eloquence and irony. On that condition, I will gladly enter into your association. Otherwise—no![28]

Proudhon's words and Marx's reaction to them could scarcely find a closer parallel than Toller's colloquies with the Communists, led by Leviné, and his subsequent defense of his actions against attacks by Paul Frölich on the occasion of his trip to Russia. In a similar vein Toller complained to Paul Z[ech]: "I regard myself as non-partisan.... As a writer I speak to all those who are willing to listen, regardless of which party or group they belong to. The idea means more to me than the slogans of the day; man [means] more than a party identification card."[29]

Perhaps the most remarkable parallel between Proudhon's and Toller's thought is to be found in the notion of the malevolent God. Proudhon's slogan "God is evil" is well known. He writes:

> I affirm that God, if there is a God, bears no resemblance to the effigies which philosophers and the priests have made of him; that he neither thinks nor acts according to the law of analysis, foresight and progress, which is the instinctive characteristic of man; that, on the contrary he seems to follow an inverse and retrograde path; that intelligence, liberty, personality are constituted otherwise in God than in us; and that this originality of nature...makes of God a being who is essentially anticivilized, antiliberal, antihuman.[30]

The concept of a malevolent God is central to Toller as well. I cite the following passage from *Masse Mensch* as an example. The Woman replies on being called a blasphemer:

Did I disgrace
God?
Or did God
Disgrace Man?
O monstrous
Law of guilt
In which men
Have to become ensnarled.
I call God before the bench!
I accuse.[31]

And later on, she says, in a passage that illustrates both Toller's conception of the malevolent God and his anarchistic tendencies:

Whoever calls for blood of men,
Is Moloch.
So God was Moloch.
The State Moloch
And the Masses—
Moloch.[32]

These ideas are a precipitate of Toller's childhood experiences with God the Avenger. After being told that a neighbor, Frau Eichstädt, was burned to death in a fire because "the Lord" apparently willed it so, Toller lay in his bed and meditated had been on his yet unpunished misdeeds. He recounts his murder of God in these words:

That's the reason for the fire? The reason for this terrible punishment: Is God so severe? I think ... of Frau Eichstädt, burned to death.... The room is dark. I lie in bed and listen. To the right of the door is a round, elongated glass tube that I am forbidden to touch; the cleaning girl, Anna, crosses herself before she dusts it. "That's where the Jews' God lives," she growls. My heart beats faster. I'm still afraid to try it. What if he leaps out of the little scroll and screams, "I am the Lord! As your punishment ...!" I no longer let myself be intimidated. In one leap I'm at the door; I climb on the cabinet, tear the "Lord" down; I smash the little glass tube. "He" doesn't move. I throw it on the floor, spit on it, take my shoes and beat it.... Happily I get into bed; let everyone find out that I have been beaten the Lord to death.[33]

We have seen that the similarities between Toller and Proudhon are significant and involve their views of human nature, of the constitution of the ideal just society, and of the methods for achieving such a society. Now we must outline Proudhon's thought itself somewhat more systematically.[34]

Proudhon rejected the schemes of Fourier, Saint-Simon and the utopian socialists as being mere rearrangements of power which leave intact the concept of the state. Proudhon, who was one of the few anarchist theoreticians to come from peasant and petit-bourgeois origins, saw the root of the trouble in the idea of property itself. Thus he rejected, in the early phase of his career at least, the industrial concentration which had so transformed the France he had grown up in, and he rejected such symbiotic schemes predicated on industrialism as Fourier's "phalansteries" and Louis Blanc's rigidly controlled communes. Proudhon, the printer, had a very strong feeling for the dignity of satisfying work: "Work is the first attribute, the essential characteristic of man."[35]

The problem was to arrange society so that the amount of work one did corresponded to one's abilities and needs, so that the working man need not toil to enrich idle proprietors. Property was to be replaced by possession of the tools of one's employment; credit was to be abolished and replaced by the *Banque du Peuple*. The bank (which Proudhon projected in 1849) was designed to eliminate interest on credit and to replace the currency by exchange of scrip based on units of working time. Although it gained many subscribers, it was never put into practice, owing to Proudhon's arrest.

In spite of Proudhon's conviction that the dignity of their labor conferred moral excellence on the proletariat, he also realized, like Toller in *Die Maschinenstürmer*, that the working man was no saint to be unduly idealized. He admitted in words that could have been spoken by Jimmy Cobbett in *Die Maschinenstürmer*: "Man is by nature a sinner, that is to say not essentially a wrongdoer but rather wrongly made, and his destiny is perpetually to recreate his ideal in himself."[36] Unlike the Communists and utopian socialists such as Fourier and Saint-Simon, Proudhon did not believe that social engineering, that transforming society would make it possible for man to be good. More is required: in fact it is exactly the creation of a new man for which Proudhon pleads and which he regards as necessary. In 1846 it was possible to see this necessity as a promise that could be fulfilled. In 1921/22, when Toller wrote *Hinkemann*, it had become a last hope which would evidently never be realized.

Proudhon's passion for justice led him after 1848 to predicate a society based on negation of private property and negation of the state. But revolutionary change would be ineffectual, a mere change in masters, if it were merely economic and not accompanied by a political revolution as well. E. H. Carr quotes Proudhon's explanation of a vote he cast in the National Assembly: "I voted against the Constitution not because it contains things of which I disapprove and does not contain things of which I approve. I voted against the Constitution because it is a Constitution."[37] The kind of society of producers' councils Proudhon envisaged is described in the following passage: "For there to be a relationship between interests, the interests themselves must be present, answering for themselves, making their own demands and commitments, acting.... In the last analysis everyone is the government, so there is no government. Thus the system of government follows from its definition: to say representative government means to say relationship between interests; to say relationship between interests means absence of governments."[38]

Proudhon, like Bakunin, saw social change as an inevitable process, and thought that the faculty of justice, so strong in himself, could be developed through education, though it is the last of the faculties of the soul to mature, as we see from the example of children. This touching faith in the efficacy of example and education as a force for good appears in an interesting light in this remark by Woodcock: "Besançon was a center of theology, and as he proofread the effusive apologetics of the local clergy, Proudhon found himself slowly converted to atheism...."[39]

Although Proudhon had preached abstention from voting, he nevertheless stood for election to the National Assembly. Like Kropotkin, he came to see the necessity for political action toward the end of his life, with the arrival in politics of the "most numerous and poorest class." Proudhon, however, wanted this political action to be based on mutualism, on the kind of councils to which we have already referred. To be governed by any sort of political system would be intolerable. He says in a famous passage:

To be governed is to be watched over, inspected, spied on, directed, legislated at, regulated, docketed, indoctrinated, preached at, controlled, assessed, weighed, censored, ordered about, by men who have neither the right nor the knowledge nor the virtue. To be governed means to be, at each operation, at each transaction, at each movement, noted, registered, controlled, taxed, stamped, measured, valued, assessed, patented, licensed, authorized, endorsed, admonished, hampered, reformed, rebuked, arrested. It is to be, on the pretext of the general interest, taxed, drilled, held for ransom, exploited, monopolized, extorted, squeezed, hoaxed, robbed; then at the least resistance ...to be repressed, fined, abused, annoyed, followed, bullied, beaten, disarmed, garotted, imprisoned, machine-gunned, judged, condemned, deported, flayed, sold, betrayed and finally mocked, ridiculed, insulted, dishonoured. That's government, that's its justice, that's its morality.[40]

Kropotkin (1842-1921)

G. D. H. Cole remarks: "Kropotkin, when he came to write of *Mutual Aid among Men and Animals* and to develop to the more clearly articulated theory of Anarchist-Communism, found in Bakunin much on which to build, and relatively little to discard."[41] Cole divides anarchism into two broad orientations—the individualist and the collectivist. To the former belong such men as Stirner[42] and Benjamin Tucker; to the latter, Bakunin, Kropotkin, Réclus, and Grave.

This distinction is crucial, and we shall need to come to terms with it again in its application to Toller's political behavior. It posits two important elements in socialist theory: first, that one can be a "collectivist" and an "anarchist" simultaneously (in a sense very different, however, from Stirner's monstrosity, the Society of Egoists). Second, it is possible to be an anarchist and a socialist simultaneously, but a distinction is to be drawn between collectivists like Bakunin and Kropotkin and what the anarchists saw as authorization socialists like Marx. In particular, we shall find that anarchism is a theory that proceeds from a libertarian *political* (or, rather, anti-political) starting point, and then presupposes a variety of economic and social models which it presumes will allow the individual that degree of social freedom which it regards as essential. Marxist socialism, on the other hand, is, in the first instance, a theory of *economic* organization of society which attempts to obtain the greatest degree of economic (and thus social) autonomy for the individual by granting his economic equality—a natural orientation for someone who considers that the structure of society is determined by economic relationships. The distinction, to some extent, is predicated on that between Hegelian idealism and Marxist materialism.

Thus, in deciding to what degree Toller is an anarchist or to what degree he is a humanistic socialist, we will need to be guided by the *direction* in which he compromises when compromise becomes necessary. Does he recognize the primacy of political (or anti-political) ends or that of economic ends in his attempts to alter society? This is the central question we shall have to answer. Two dramas, *Masse Mensch* and *Die Maschinenstürmer*, provide in paradigmatic form the essence of the conflict—the position of the Nameless One representing authoritarian socialism and that of the Woman representing the anarcho-communist solution. In this sense, then, the theoretical presuppositions of Kropotkin are relevant to our task.

The difference between Kropotkin's basically anarchist orientation and the reformist tendencies of his friend and fellow exile Stepniak is clearly defined in his early attitude toward the support of political reform in Russia. Kropotkin regarded the ballot as anathema to his conception of political liberty: "...simply an instrument in the hands of the dominating classes to maintain their dominion over the people. These rights are not even real political rights, since they protect nothing for the mass of the people."[43](It was a popularly elected Reichstag in Germany, after all, that had approved Bismarck's anti-socialist law.) These ideas are elaborated on in Kropotkin's first major work, *The Conquest of Bread* (1892). In this book he demanded a rapid revolution, which was to effect a total transformation of society involving the complete abolition of government and the consequent appearance of the new man. As a practical means of gaining the support of the masses, Kropotkin advocated a new means for the distribution of food, the lack of which he took to be instrumental in the failure of the French Revolution. The details of this system were, however, unspecified, Kropotkin having Goodwin-like faith in the ability of people to deal adequately with their problems, once the constraints and distortions of political institutions had been removed.

Based on his studies of the medieval town, Kropotkin visualized a network of communes covering the countryside and cities, each as nearly self-sufficient as possible with its own factories, shops and farms. The parks and land around Paris, for example, could be cultivated and each person from the age of twenty to fifty would learn several occupations and would work with his hands as well as with his brains for five hours a day. "Such a society," he wrote in *The Conquest of Bread*, "could in return guarantee well-being to all its members; that is to say, a more substantial well-being than that enjoyed to-day, by the middle-classes. And, moreover, each worker belonging to this society would have at his disposal at least five hours a day which he could devote to science, art and individual needs which do not come under the category of *necessities*."[44] The scheme reminds one of nothing so much as the kind of settlements advocated by the Billionaire-son in Georg Kaiser's play, *Gas*.

Kropotkin was convinced by his scientific researches and statistics on experiments with Jersey and Guernsey cattle that advances in agriculture and science would make his dream possible. Like Fourier's *phalanstères*, the communists would eat together in communal dining halls (although the possible option of private facilities was conceded by Kropotkin). Volunteers would survey housing needs and quarters available and would redistribute the space at hand so equitably on a rational basis that no serious disputes would arise. He writes: "And to those who are not yet comfortably housed the anarchist communist will be able to say: 'Patience, comrades! Palaces fairer and finer than any the capitalists build for themselves will spring from the ground of our enfranchised city. They will belong to those who have the most need of them; ...they will serve as models to all humanity; they will be yours.'"[45]

In all of this Kropotkin always stops short of providing details of how all the ends are to be achieved, and how disputes are to be settled. The criticisms that

Karl Guthke levels at Expressionists like Toller, Leonhard Frank, and Kaiser could apply as well to Kropotkin:

> But when they go on to formulate directly [their] ideals and goals, we generally discover the superficial philanthropic ideas dredged up from the 18th century, which impress us as solutions much too naive for the problems in question. There is, for example, Georg Kaiser with his *Gas* trilogy, where, among other things, a return to nature is offered as a panacea which is so naive and uncompromising that next to it Rousseau's ideal gives evidence of incomparably wiser profundity and superiority.[46]

Kropotkin's answer to such criticisms was that anarchism was as "scientific" as Marxism in its belief that the complex laws of the social and economic organization would determine the exact nature of the libertarian society to emerge from the ruins of the coercive and maiming system of capitalism. In fact, his famous article on anarchism in the eleventh edition of the *Encyclopedia Britannica* shows that he considers having put anarchism on a scientific basis his chief contribution to its development. But these laws and this social organism are so complex and highly articulated that it would be folly for the anarchist to pretend to give a more than general blueprint of the future, a fact explicitly recognized by the anarchist conference at St. Imier in 1872. Cole quotes the remarks of Malatesta at a conference of Bakuninists in 1876:

> How will society be organized? We do not and we cannot know. No doubt, we too have busied ourselves with projects of social reorganization, but we attach to them only a very relative importance. They are bound to be wrong, perhaps entirely fantastic.... Above all else, our task is to destroy, to destroy every obstacle that now stands in the way of the free development of social law, and also to prevent the construction of these obstacles, no matter in what form, or the creation of new ones. It will be for the free and fertile functioning of the natural laws of society to accomplish the destinies of mankind.[47]

In this respect Toller differs somewhat from Malatesta and Kropotkin, though his remarks in the letter, "To a Socialist Delegate," make it clear that he feels that, in order to act, the revolutionary must simplify and reduce the reality that confronts him to its essentials. He writes:

> I reproach you and your comrades for permitting the struggle in the Ruhr. There are men who are always right [i.e. blameless] because they always let things take their own course—they have the least grounds to be proud of their sense of reality... Naturally, in each historical situation

there is only a limited number of possible decisions. But did anything happen to determine the direction of the course of action? Each political situation permits several actions. Whether someone is in command of the situation can be seen from whether [or not] he chooses among very few, ideally two, courses of action. Someone not in command of the situation sees the possibility for infinitely many courses of action.[48]

In *Fields, Factories and Workshops* (1898), Kropotkin, while not gainsaying the need for technological advance to free man from drudgery (indeed we have seen that in the *Conquest of Bread* he presupposes such technological progress), argues for a system of decentralized industry combined with agriculture, particularly in England, where the trend toward specialization of the economy and of production had gone too far. In this he directly contradicts the predictions of Marx and Engels. He did not deny the observable tendencies toward socialization in such industries as ship-building, but held that other new areas of endeavor were constantly appearing in which individual handicrafts were important and which would constitute a prevailing countertrend. Kropotkin felt that it was necessary for scientists and other intellectuals to be involved in the drudgery of society so that they would see the desirability of devoting their efforts to the mundane but useful task of mitigating such drudgery. He was pleased to learn that a Mrs. Cochrane of Chicago had invented a washing machine, for example. However, he also felt that work itelf had a certain dignity and the author ought also to be a printer, and the painter of scenes of farm workers in the fields ought also to have worked in the fields.

Consistently enough, Kropotkin proposed a system of mixed vocational and academic education, devoted to basic skills and concepts rather than specific techniques aimed at fitting a child into a particular social slot. Cole remarks:

> The reader of Kropotkin's writings is struck again and again by the contrast between the essential reasonableness, and even moderation, of what he says about matters such as these, and the intransigence of his more political writings. Even in these, he has little of the bitterness that is characteristic of much Anarchist literature. Even when he was most indignant or furious, he remained an essentially lovable person, and there was in him not the smallest trace of that streak of insanity that is continually showing itself in Bakunin's work. Bakunin managed to be dictatorial as well as the enemy of dictation: Kropotkin had no wish to dictate to anybody. He did really believe in freedom and regarded coercion as an unncessary result of wrong social institutions.[49]

And George Bernard Shaw noted that Kropotkin was ''amiable to the point of saintliness, and with his full red beard might have been a shepherd from the Delectable Mountains.''[50]

Cole goes on to make the telling point that Kropotkin never convincingly explains the presence and the dominance of so much coercion in present-day societies, in view of his theory that man is basically a reasonable creature, libertarian in disposition, and given to mutual aid and free cooperation. Nor does he explain why coercive institutions, once abolished, would not return. This optimism, however, was characteristic of a good many "scientific" socialists of the day as well. Toller (in agreement with the psychiatrist Otto Gross, as we shall see later) writes: "Believe me, no child is evil to begin with—perhaps it was mutilated, made fun of, its feelings scorned, and so now it surrounds itself with an armor of intractability and maliciousness. Only love that does not attempt to teach, to moralize, can give the child the certainty: 'I have nothing to fear; I am respected just as I am, and although I am the way I am!'''[51]

Kropotkin's optimism is most evident in his work *Mutual Aid: A Factor in Evolution*, in which he undertakes to refute theories of Social Darwinism such as that of Thomas Huxley, and at the same time cast doubt on the Hobbesian view of an anarchical state of the war of all against all. Kropotkin contends that the struggle for limited food resources has historically led to cooperation. Those who survive are not necessarily physically the fittest, most selfish and most brutal, but those exposed to the least natural adversity. The horses of Siberia do not grow more fit owing to the winters they must endure. Instead, it is the horses of more temperate climates that flourish. Kropotkin writes: "The first thing which strikes us as soon as we begin studying the struggle for existence ...is the abundance of facts of mutual aid, not only for rearing progeny ... but also for the safety of the individual, and for providing it with the necessary food.''[52]

Kropotkin's basic thesis is that man is naturally cooperative, and that this urge toward mutual aid is even stronger than his egoism. Thus the collectivist anarchism of Kropotkin is the very opposite of the individualist anarchism of Stirner, and Kropotkin was for example at pains in his works on ethics to combat Nietzsche, whom he regarded as a danger. To support this basic theses, Kropotkin was fond of citing Darwin's example of the blind pelican, fed by its fellows, and the British Life-Boat Association. Cooperation was even possible on an international scale—witness the *Compagnie Internationale des Wagons-Lits*.

The question of the ideal disposition of property was a stumbling block. Proudhon had advocated collective ownership of the major means of production, with the small producer in possession of such tools as he could personally use. But the communist-anarchists, unlike Lassalle's General Association of

German Workingmen, were against producers' cooperatives of any sort, on the theory that only the community ought to own things. This introduced the problem of defining the community as a non-coercive entity. Kropotkin foresaw two stages: a transitional collectivism, with communal ownership, giving way to true communism based on the principles of Sorel and of the *Critique of the Gotha-Program*—from each according to his abilities, to each according to his needs. As in Marxism there is a "withering way," only here, the state must be destroyed at once, and it is the concept of ownership which later on withers away.

With the death of Stepniak, Kropotkin's efforts were turned in several new directions. This change corresponded to various developments: the general decline in anarchist popularity, the loss of faith in the imminence of an anarchist revolution in western European countries, the need to come to terms with assassinations and acts of terror (the so-called "propaganda of the deed") propagated by men calling themselves anarchists and finally the evident success of socialist and reformist movements, especially in Germany. As Bertrand Russell pointed out in *Proposed Roads to Freedom*: "Anarchism attracts to itself much that lies on the borderland of insanity and common crime,"[53] and the editor of the *Encyclopedia Britannica* saw fit to append to Kropotkin's article on anarchism in the eleventh edition (1910-1911) a list of anarchist-perpetrated atrocities, introduced by the remarks:

> It is important to remember that the term 'Anarchist' is inevitably rather loosely used in public, in connexion with the authors of a certain class of murderous outrages, and that the same looseness of definition often applies to the professions of 'Anarchism' made by such persons. As stated above [by Kropotkin], a philosophic Anarchist would repudiate the connexion.... But the following résumé of the chief so-called 'Anarchist' incidents is appended for convenience in stating the facts under the heading where a reader would expect to find them.[54]

Because of such acts of terror, many men whose philosophies were in fact anarchistic in nature refused to admit it, either before the world, or to themslves—among them Tolstoy and William Morris. Unlike Toller, Kropotkin shrank from publicly denouncing acts of terrorism, though he made it clear (as even the editor's note above indicates) that there was no place in his philosophy for political murder, and still less for violence directed at the innocent. Yet he felt (here again like Godwin) that it is not the place of one man to pass judgment on the motives of another, and pointed to the desperation on the one hand caused by repressive regimes and laws restricting political activities (e.g. the anti-socialist law of Germany passed in 1878 in response to attempts on the life of the Kaiser), and to officially sanctioned violence of constituted governments themselves on the other.

Two works of this period demonstrate Kropotkin's aversion to political terror—an aversion which anticipates his reaction to the brutality of the Bolsheviks after he had returned to Russia. They are *The Terror in Russia*,[55] a work which undertook to describe the brutalities of Czarist Russia to the English, and *The Great French Revolution*.[56] The latter serves as a corrective to the interpretations of the day, in that it emphasizes in true Brechtian fashion the role of the peasantry in the Revolution and in the making of history rather than that of the bourgeois politicians of more conventional studies. The so-called leaders were actually followers—an insight akin to that of the playwright Georg Büchner and his character Danton that the individual is only foam on the wave of history. In this interpretation, Kropotkin has adopted the notion of class conflict from the Marxists, but (and here he resembles Bakunin) without the contempt for the peasants and *Lumpenproletariat*.

Kropotkin's position on the terror of the French and Bolshevik revolutions and his pro-Entente position during the World War earned him the mordant criticism of most fellow-anarchists, but they also reveal a consistency of thought and suggest certain affinities to the German revisionist, Bernstein. Indeed, Hulse calls him the Bernstein of the anarchists and summarizes their similarities in a highly instructive paragraph:

> A forthright and prolific writer, he [Kropotkin] was willing to follow his ideas where they led and to incorporate current political observations into his thought. Although ...he remained committed to his anti-capitalist, anti-static doctrine, within the general outline of his philosophy he demonstrated considerable flexibility. Bernstein's assumption that existing institutions could be used to achieve the peaceful transition to Socialism and Kropotkin's belief that in the final analysis physical force would be necessary in the struggle were obviously far apart, but it is significant that each regarded the use of force as an evil. Both held the idea that it would be wrong for a small, revolutionary élite to try to seize power by violence; both saw physical combat as a defensive weapon, to be used by the masses if the regime in power initiated the violence. Both Bernstein and Kropotkin assumed that a reformer or a revolutionary had an ethical obligation to restrain hate and irrational violence, and this was not true of most of those who called themselves anarchists or orthodox marxists.[57]

While the Fabians in England and the Social Democrats in Germany were making visible progress, the anarchists were viewed more and more either as criminals or hopelessly idealistic dreamers. Kropotkin's response, beginning in the 1890's was to become increasingly reformist—to move further from the "individualist" pole of anarchism and closer to the collectivist one. So by the time Shaw wrote his indulgently sympathetic *The Impossibilities of Anarchism*, Kropotkin's anarchism had moved closer to the revisionism of the Fabians and of Bernstein. When Bernstein's *Presuppositions of Socialism* was reviewed by N. (Max Nettlau?) in *Freedom* in 1899,[58] the reviewer praised Bernstein for the anarchist tendency of his arguments against Marx, while at the same time rejecting his willingness to accomodate himself to capitalism. Kropotkin points out that Bernstein's critics had accused him of apostasy but not answered his arguments, which were unanswerable.[59]Similarly Toller notes in a letter of 1921: "I detect conservative elements within myself. One could perhaps say that the revolutionary becomes one only out of love for a utopian conservatism."[60] This resembles the position of Tucholsky and the *Gruppe Revolutionärer Pazifisten* (Group of revolutionary Pacifists) that Toller joined (in 1929), along with Walter Mehring, Tucholsky and Kurt Hiller, eschewing membership in the KPD or SPD. Tolstoy wrote of Kropotkin with great understanding: "His arguments in favor of violence do not seem to me to be expression of his opinions, but only of his fidelity to the banner under which he has served so honestly all his life."[61]

In his humane but at the same time realistic position on violence, Kropotkin anticipates Toller's dilemma in the face of increasingly successful Nazi tyranny, and also his solution. Ultimately, he argues, one cannot make an omelette without breaking an egg, but then, having broken the egg, one had better make the omelette.

James Joll points out that because Kropotkin seems to offer "the best of so many worlds,"[62] he has attracted a great many of the most disparate followers. Benito Mussolini found his works "overflowing with a great love of oppressed humanity and infinite kindness,"[63] while Oscar Wilde writes: "Two of the most perfect lives I have come across in my experience are the lives of Verlaine and of Prince Kropotkin: the first, the one Christian poet since Dante; the other, a man with a soul of that beautiful white Christ which seems coming out of Russia."[64]

4

Heirs to European Anarchism

The laws and statutes of a nation
Are an inherited disease,
From generation unto generation
And place to place they drag on by degrees.
Wisdom becomes nonsense; kindness, oppression:
To be a grandson is a curse.
—J.M. von Goethe: *Faust*[1]

It is a commonplace that anarchism grew and flourished (to the extent that it flourished at all) primarily in the Romance part of Europe—particularly in Spain, Italy and France. According to the Italian sociologist Cesare Lombroso anarchism was the result of epilepsy and pellagra, deficiency diseases that occur among the people of Southern Europe because of their dietary habits.[2] George Woodcock writes, for example:

> Anarchism has thrived best in lands of the sun, where it is easy to dream of golden ages of ease and simplicity, yet where the clear light also heightens the shadows of existing misery. It is the men of the South who have flocked in their thousands to the black banners of anarchic revolt, the Italians and Andalusians and Ukrainians, the men of Lyons and Marseilles, of Naples and Barcelona.[3]

Anarchist sentiment in Germany was outflanked very early by the Marxists and the SPD, generally conceded to have been the strongest socialist party in Europe before World War I. Richard N. Hunt describes the immense influence of the SPD twenty-two years after Bismarck's persecutions:

> The 1912 elections brought the Social Democrats their biggest victory yet, with 4,250,329 votes, or 34.7 per cent of the total, and 110 mandates. With a third of the nation behind it, the SPD was now the largest party in the Reichstag. By the beginning of 1914, membership had passed the million mark. The Social Democratic press, including 90 dailies, reached 1.4 million subscribers. The party boasted a flourishing women's move-

ment and youth section, an elaborate adult education program, even a special school for training future party officials. The various undertakings of the SPD were worth, in capital assets, 21.5 million marks and gave full employment to 3,500 people....Like the German working class in general it now had more to lose than chains.[4]

This is not the place to retrace the reasons for the growth and dominance of the SPD.[5] It is my contention, however, that in spite of the impressive and oppressive institutionalization of a rival leftist party which "had more to lose than chains," as Hunt puts it, anarchist thought did not on that account disappear from the German political spectrum. On the contrary, it continued to grow *within* the SPD and other "established" left-wing institutions; it made itself felt in the debate on war credits in 1914 and within the Independent Socialists (USPD) after the split of 1917 and even among the Spartakists. These men were not always conscious of belonging to an anarchist tradition (indeed the "canonical" German anarchists, men like Stirner, Rocker, Weitling and Most exerted very little influence in Germany during their lifetimes), nor did they always refer to themselves as anarchists. Martin Buber, for example, about whose work *Pfade in Utopia* (*Paths in Utopia*, 1950) we shall have more to say later, referred to himself as a mystical or religious socialist. Even Rosa Luxemburg is writing from an anarchist point of view when she argues for the anarchist weapon of the mass strike and against centralism in "Leninism or Marxism?":

Now the two principles on which Lenin's centralism rests are precisely these: 1. the blind subordination, in the smallest detail, of all party organs, to the party center, which alone thinks, guides and decides for all. 2. the rigorous separation of the organized nucleus of revolutionaries from its social-revolutionary surroundings.

Such centralism is a mechanical transposition of the organizational principles of Blanquism into the mass movement of the socialist working class....The indispensable conditions for the realization of Social Democratic centralism are: 1. the existence of a large contingent of workers educated in the political struggle. 2. the possibility for workers to develop their own political activity through direct influence on public life, in a party press, and public congresses, etc.[6]

While pretending to argue for *true* Social Democratic "centralization" and against a Leninist élite, she is actually arguing for anarchistic decentralization. When she claims: "The ultracentralism asked by Lenin...is not a positive and creative spirit. *Lenin's concern is not so much to make the activity of the party more fruitful as to control the party*,"[7] she is writing quite in the spirit of the anarchist Proudhon, who described centralized Marxism in 1864 in the following words:

> A democracy having the appearance of being founded on the dictatorship of the masses, but in which the masses have no more power than is necessary to ensure a general serfdom in accordance with the following precepts and principles borrowed from the old absolutism: indivisibility of public power, all-consuming centralization, systematic destruction of all individual, corporative and regional thought...inquisitorial police.[8]

There is, then, as these few quotations show, a significant body of anarchist thought *within* the various German leftist parties which are generally considered Marxist in nature, and it is a kind of anarchism which often (indeed in the case of Toller or Buber) thinks of itself as "socialist," utopian or humanitarian. Although many writers have noted the anarchist character of Marxist goals such as the classless society and the withering away of the state, it is important to realize that significant groups within the German Marxist parties (particularly in the Communist Workers Party, the KAPD) advocated anarchist means and tactics as well, as the above quotations demonstrate. We shall have more to say about anarchist currents within the Marxist parties in our discussion of Martin Buber's subtle analysis of the notion of "utopian socialism."

Toller, who until his imprisonment in Niederschönenfeld thought of himself as an Independent Socialist, wrote in *Quer Durch*: "Every real socialist strives for anarchy, freedom from authority, as his goal."[9] Although he does not ignore the formidable difficulties in the way of anarchism in a highly organized society, it is evident in his discussion both of the penal system and of the factories in the USSR that temperamentally and philosophically he favors the kind of anarchist-communism advocated by Kropotkin. Of the former he notes: "Here we shall not discuss the question of whether prisons are among those institutions which socialism has the duty to extirpate. I hold this view."[10] Kropotkin, in his essay, "Law and Authority," an essay which does not assume that man is totally good, as his critics charge, exclaims:

> Burn the guillotines, demolish the prisons; drive away the judges, policemen and informers... treat as a brother the man who had been led by passion to do ill to his fellows...and be sure that but a few crimes will mar society.[11]

In similar terms, Toller defends during his trip to Soviet Russia two sixteen-year-old Russians who "raped" farm girls of twenty-one and twenty-four during a festival while drunk, and were sentenced to three and four years imprisonment. Toller's guide tells him: "…'Our courts must punish the youths so severely out of consideration for the peasants,'" whereupon Toller notes: "Every regime must take into consideration [the opinions of] the classes that support it—their interests, their traditions, their customs."[12] The only way to obviate such injustice would be to destroy the state as such. In the chapter "*ZIT*"[13]of *Quer Durch*, Toller provides a counterpart to the much less sympathetically described chapter, "Ford."[14] He discovers in Russian factories the same inhumane mechanization of the worker he had found under capitalism in the Ford works: "Through this mechanization, the number of working operations possible in a give time was multiplied by thirty. This oppresses me. Is this to be our goal: mechanization of man, the stifling in him of all that is creative?"[15] It is doubts like these that cause "M," writing in *Die rote Fahne* (*The Red Banner*), to condemn the drama of Toller ("the favorite of the bourgeoisie, admirable as a human being but politically ignorant") as counterrevolutionary:

> Toller's enthusiastic hymns to benevolence and the brotherhood of man—not only between workers but between the oppressed and the oppressors…—is this not the typical artistic formulation of the principle of company unions, of cooperation between management and wage slaves?[16]

Toller resolves his doubts in the following way:

> In our highly-articulated society…it would be senseless to want to return to handicrafts and cottage industry. The problem is actually such that the sum of the necessary mechanical work must be reduced to a minimum so that opportunities for creative development during leisure hours are made available to men. It simply depends on whom the worker does his work for.[17]

This is exactly the position of Kropotkin in *The Conquest of Bread*, described above, in which Kropotkin, far from rejecting modern industry, notes for example: "In well-managed coal mines the labour of a hundred miners furnishes enough fuel to warm ten thousand families under an inclement sky…. Truly we are rich—far richer than we think…richest of all in what we might win from our soil, from our manufactures, from our science, from our technical knowledge, were they but applied to bringing about the well-being of all."[18]

Among the many "heretical" figures, unorthodox Marxists who while calling themselves German Socialists exhibit marked anarchist elements in their thought, two figures, Gustav Landauer and Martin Buber, demonstrate particular ideological affinity with Toller himself, and it is to the first of these that we must now turn.

Toller, Gustav Landauer and the Communist Anarchism of Kropotkin

We shall see in our discussion of Toller's play, *Die Maschinenstürmer*, that Kropotkin's *Mutual Aid* appears to have had a demonstrable influence on Toller's formulation of the conflict. In fact, the conflict between Social Darwinism and Kropotkin's reply to it in *Mutual Aid*. In fact, the conflict between Ure and Jimmy in that play is a personification of the conflict between Social Darwinism and Kropotkin's reply to it in *Mutual Aid*. This same concept of mutal aid was also central to Gustav Landauer's variety of anarchism; it was Landauer who had translated Kropotkin's book into German in 1904 under the title *Gegenseitige Hilfe in der Entwicklung* (the 1908 edition appeared as *Gegenseitige Hilfe in der Tier-und Menschenwelt*). The startling congruence between Kropotkin's examples and the language of Toller's imagery indicates that Toller used Landauer's translation in the composition of *Die Maschinenstürmer*. Further evidence is provided by a number of passages from *Quer Durch*.

We know from *Eine Jugend in Deutschland* that Toller was intimately familiar with Landauer's original work. He writes: "The evening before I leave Heidelberg, a letter arrives from Gustav Landauer, whose *Aufruf zum Sozialismus* (*Call to Socialism*) has moved and influenced me profoundly."[19] Kurt Hiller, in his polemical preface to the Rowohlt anthology of Toller's works, explicitly and wrongly denies the East German critic Martin Reso's accusation that Toller was an "unconscious" anarchist influenced by Landauer, that he "subconsciously advocated anarchist ideas."[20] According to Reso, "Toller did not count himself among the anarchists, even though he felt in sympathy with them."[21] He notes with regret: "Since the Woman in the play has the dominant role, Toller is coming out unambiguously for the individual; he values the right of the individual more than that of the class."[22] Reso sums up his criticism of Toller's concept of the new man by again linking him to Landauer's anarchism:

And so...a utopian picture of the "new man" was presented, but in the process it was "overlooked" that this man who was demanded, hoped for, for whom [Toller] propagandized can only be a product of changed economic and social conditions, that he can become a socialistic and therefore truly new man only by proving himself in practical social life. In Toller's particular case, the pernicious influence of Landauer is evident—[Landauer], who had said: "One of the worst errors of the 'Marxist' was the notion that 'one achieves a revolution by creating revolutionaries,' whereas actually, on the contrary, one achieves revolutionaries only by creating a revolution."[23]

When Hiller asserts that it was the criticism "of the pettiness of Marxian sectarian in-fighting" that Toller took from Landauer's *Aufruf zum Sozialismus* (*Call to Socialism*)[24] and not the "romantically constructive, albeit, anarchistic part of this work,"[25] he is making an untenable assertion. We shall see in our discussion of *Masse Mensch* and *Die Maschinenstürmer* that each of these plays is based on a confrontation of opposites, that in each a triangular constellation is presented in which one vertex represents the capitalist, another the "authoritarian" Communist, a third the anarchist position. In *Masse Mensch* the conflict takes place *within* the Woman, and the capitalist vertex is de-emphasized; in *Die Maschinenstürmer* the conflict takes place *externally* and is embodied in three different characters. Here the capitalist position is emphasized at the expense of authoritarian Communism, which recedes somewhat into the background and is diluted by personal, psychological motives. But in both plays (and this is directly contrary to Hiller's assertion) it is the *positive*, anarchist point of view which dominates and about which the action of the play revolves. Hans Marnette, for example, in his dissertation "Untersuchungen zum Inhalt-Form Problem in Ernst Tollers Dramen" ("Studies on the Form-Content Problem in Ernst Toller's Dramas"),[26]traces in detail the extent to which Landauer's *Aufruf zum Sozialismus* influenced *Die Wandlung*.

The "Guidelines for a Cultural and Political League of German Youth," an organization which Toller founded in Heidelberg in November of 1917, provide another example of the ideological nexus between Toller and Landauer. In words which could have been from Landauer's *Aufruf zum Sozialismus* and which exemplify nothing if not the "romantically constructive, yet anarchistic, aspect of this work" (Hiller), Toller writes:

> The League is a community of like-minded and like-intentioned people. We want to be leaders by striding forward, to inflame all of society by being consumed in flames; possessed by the will to turn over the soil, by the unifying idea of the true creative spirit....How can we work in a practical way?
>
> If a sense of urgency is demanded, then we must proceed together in order to gain impetus and join with other movements seeking similar goals. For the rest, however, we want no schematization of individuality. Let everyone interact man-to-man, with soul and spirit streaming forth. Let him spin from his heart bonds of fellowship that will encompass all hearts with a ring of steel....The sense of community we seek can only grow out of an inner transformation of man.[27]

This is not quite the same anti-anarchist Toller that Hiller describes elsewhere, not quite the man who "rejected the doctrine of anarchy for good psychological and logical reasons."[28]

Numerous references in *Eine Jugend in Deutschland* and *Briefe aus dem Gefängnis* testify to the influence of Landauer and his variety of anarchism on Toller. In the same section where he mentions the decisive importance of the *Aufruf zum Sozialismus*, Toller quotes at length from a letter to Landauer which he thrice had reprinted, once in *Der Freihafen* (*The Free Port*),[29] once in *Quer Durch*,[30] and once in *Vorwärts* (*Forwards*).[31] Later on he mentions a visit with Landauer at Krumbach:

> I wonder why, at a time like this...this ardent revolutionary is silent. "I have worked," he says, "my whole life [to insure] that this society, which is built on hypocrisy, collapses; now that I know that the collapse will come...I have the right and the stamina to husband my strength until this time [comes]; when the hour demands it, I will be there and will work."[32]

When the moment came, however, and when the Communists gained control of the *Räterepublik* (Council Republic), Landauer wrote the following words to the Executive Committee on April 16, 1919:

> I have continued to place myself at the disposal of the Council Republic for the cause of liberation and of the good life....You have so far not seen fit to avail yourselves of my services. In the meantime, I have seen you at work, have got to know your propaganda, the manner in which you conduct the struggle. I have seen what your reality looks like, in contrast to that of what you call "phony Council Republic." I interpret the struggle to create conditions that will allow everyone his fair share of the goods of the earth and civilization differently than you. Socialism realized immediately awakens all our creative forces: in your work, however, I see in the economic and spiritual areas that you are no judge of this. I wouldn't in the least think of disturbing the difficult job of defense that you are engaged in. But it pains me deeply that it is only marginally my task, the task of warmth and revival, of culture and rebirth, which is presently being undertaken.[33]

These bitter words call to mind Toller's similar lament, a justification of his role under the Communist-led regime in April and at the same time a self-accusation for taking the path that Landauer had rejected:

> I hated violence and had sworn to myself to suffer it rather than to inflict it. Could I now, when the Revolution was under attack, break this oath? I had to. The workers had given me their trust, and delegated leadership

and responsibility to me. Would I not betray their faith if I were now to refuse to defend it or even to call for a renunciation of force? I ought to have taken the possibility of bloody consequences into account earlier and never accepted a position of leadership.[34]

In *Eine Jugend in Deutschland*,[35] Toller gives an extended account of Landauer's murder in prison by Bavarian soldiers, led by the Freiherr von Gagern, an account which in its brutality rivals and resembles the killing of Jimmy Cobbett in *Die Maschinenstürmer*. In a letter to Maximilian Harden from Niederschönenfeld dated 1920, Toller wrote: "In Gustav Landauer the German Revolution has lost one of its purest men, one of its greatest intellects. But who in Germany knows Gustav Landauer's creative work; who knows his books on Shakespeare, Hölderlin, Whitman?"[36] Toller also quotes Landauer's dying words in his "*Requiem den gemordeten Brüdern*"("Requiem to the Murdered Comrades"):

Do you hear the voice of the brother, of the prophet? It is a stammering, a painful stammering: "Go ahead and kill me! Oh, and you call yourselves human beings!"[37]

Because a strong case can be made for the influence both of Landauer the man and Landauer the anarchist on Toller, we must examine more closely the nature of Landauer's contribution to the various currents of European anarchism that we have sketched in Chapter 3. In doing so, we shall find that Landauer's philosophy is basically a development of Proudhon's and Kropotkin's, but with a mystical element not present in his models, as Eugene Lunn has shown in his study of Landauer, *Prophet of Community*. Indeed, Landauer's book, *Der werdende Mensch: Aufsätze über Leben und Schrifttum* (*Emerging Mankind: Essays on Life and Literature*),[38] contains chapters on "God as Spiritual Bond," "God and Socialism," "Leo Nicholaevitch Tolstoy," "Friedrich Hölderlin in his Poems" (Toller frequently quotes Hölderlin in his prison letters), "Peter Kropotkin," and "Fragment on Georg Kaiser," among others. It is clear from Toller's letters to Harden and from his letter to his nephew Harry that he was familiar with *Der werdende Mensch*.[39] But for our purposes, the most important works by Landauer will be *Aufruf zum Sozialismus* (*Call to Socialism*), and the three pamphlets: *Was will der sozialistische Bund*(*What does the Socialist Bund intend?*), *Was ist zunächst zu tun* (*What is to be done First?*), and *Die Siedlung* (*The Settlement*).[40]

These four works[41] are all connected with the Socialist Bund, an organization that Landauer proposed in May and June of 1908, in a speech before a group of anarchists and socialists from which the *Aufruf zum Sozialismus* grew. The Bund was to bring about a non-violent revolution by first creating anarchist

49

cells within the confines permitted by the present society. These would exist alongside capitalism, but seek to replace it eventually. Each group would be independent; in true anarchist fashion, there would be no centralized direction; Landauer himself would serve only as coordinator and instigator.

The *Aufruf* is, as the title indicates, a passionate cry for revolution and Landauer's brand of anarchistic socialism and, at the same time, a critique of German society. For all its emotion, the *Aufruf* is not without a certain objectivity and logical economic analysis. Landauer begins by giving, in typically fervent prose, a description of the reality with which he had to contend and his intentions: "...we are poets, and we want to dispose of the scientist-swindlers, the Marxists, the indifferent, the hollow ones, those without spirit, so that poetic insight, artistically concentrated creation, enthusiasm and prophecy find a place where they can act, create, build in life, with human beings and for communal life, work, and cooperation of groups, of communities, of people....We advocate no science and no party....The spirit that supports us is the quintessence of life and creates reality and effectiveness. This spirit in other words is called: solidarity; and what we compose [as poets] is praxis, is socialism, is the solidarity of the working man."[42]

Landauer calls his program socialism, but it need not be said how little in common it has with Marxist socialism, either the variety of the *Erfurter Program* and Kautsky or the increasingly revisionist practice of the SPD after 1906.[43] Landauer's criticisms of the Marxists were many and they were specific. But funamentally they define the Marxists' lack of creative spirit, the essential element of Landauer's whole system:

> Have we again arrived at thee, magnificent redeeming one and all—thou, who art as necessary to true thought as to true life, who createst communal life and community and unity and cooperation, who art the idea in the head of all thinking men and the league of leagues in the life of all living creatures throughout all the realms of nature? and whose name is: creative spirit![44]

Although Landauer shares a significant number of economic and social ideas with the Marxists (he rejects capitalism, for example, though not private property), all his differences with the dialectical materialism of Marx and his German interpreters are based on his idealist orientation. And it is this criticism of "authoritarian" socialism, more than all of the various more specific affinities (and they are many), that binds him to Toller: "...if only you [Marxists] knew that it is your task as socialists to help men find forms and communities of joyous work, of joyful cooperative life!"[45] One thinks of the words of the Old Reaper, with which *Die Maschinenstürmer* closes: "...we must help one another and be good...."[46]

In *Masse Mensch* Toller draws a distinction between *Masse* and *Volk*:

The Woman: Stop, you who are bewildered by struggle!
I hold your arm.
Mass should be people united by love.
Mass should be community.
Community is not revenge.
Community destroys the foundation of injustice.[47]
Community plants the forests of justice.

We note a similar distinction in *Die Wandlung*. Friedrich laments: "Abused human beings!...For the sake of the Fatherland...God...can a fatherland make such demands? Or has the Fatherland sold out to the state?"[48] This is quite similar to Landauer's distinction between *Nation* and *Volk*. Charles Maurer states:

Geist, according to Landauer, is inherent in the individual...Landauer made a distinction, however, between individuals having a common historical background, and *Geist* that comes to be an active force in the everyday life of the individuals within a "national" group. Such a group, which is under the influence of *Geist*...Landauer called *Volk*.[49]

He goes on the quote from Landauer's *Beginnen: Aufsätze über Sozialismus (Beginning: Essays on Socialism)*:

"Christianity was a *Volk* in the best and most powerful sense: thorough permeation of the economic and cultural community with the bond of *Geist*!" It has been the active presence of *Geist* at that time that had created a *Volk* out of the Christian *Nation*, and Landauer insisted that *Geist* must be reactivated as a unifying force between individuals so that "economic community, cultural society, can replace the state." The contrast between the concept of the state on the one hand and *Geist* and community (*Gemeinschaft*) on the other remained a basic characteristic of Landauer's thought throughout his life.[50]

Like Kropotkin, Landauer considered the communities of the Christian Middle Ages the best example of what he meant by *Volk*. In fact, an examination of *Die Revolution* reveals that Landauer conceived of the defining characteristic of *Volk*, *Geist*, as a kind of elixir, a magic bond which would accomplish the creation of a cohesive community of members who would remain individuals and yet be able to interact harmoniously. This is the essence of all proposed anarchist societies. He writes:

A level of great culture is reached when manifold, exclusive, and independent communal organizations exist contemporaneously, all impregnated with a uniform *Geist*, which does not reside in the organizations or arise from them, but which holds sway over them as an independent and self-evident force. In other words, a level of great culture develops when the unifying principle in the diversity of organizational forms and supra-individual structures is not an external bond of force, but a *Geist* inherent in the individuals, directing their attention beyond earthly and material interests.[51]

This is exactly Toller's conception of *Geist*. He writes in his speech, "Deutsche Revolution": "A revolution that lacks *Geist* resembles a flame that flares up, only to flicker out uselessly because it lacks the nourishing force."[52] In *Die Maschinenstürmer*, for example, Jimmy appeals to the Nottingham weavers: "And still you can dream!...dream of the land of justice...of the land of communities, joined in work....Not I and I and I! No! World and We and Thou and I! If only you desire the community of all workingmen you will achieve it.... Let each man serve the people; let each man serve the cause; let each man be a leader!"[53] As each worker at the same time serves the greater cause and retains his autonomy, he is at once servant and leader. But such joyfully assumed servitude is by no means slavery. Jimmy tells the industrialist Ure:

The spirit knows no servitude,
No cowardly bondage to the lords of this earth,
The eternal law of spirit, chiseled with letters
Of diamond in the firmament of mankind,
Calls out for faith in truth experienced.[54]

This same faith in the efficacy of *Geist* characterizes Friedrich's vision in *Die Wandlung*. What Friedrich hopes for from the fatherland (and what he does not find there) is just this *Geist*. He exclaims: "The great time will bring us all greatness....The spirit will be resurrected; it will destroy all pettiness, tear down all ludicrous artificial barriers...."[55] He tells the crowd in his famous dithyrambic reply to the agitator:

And now there opens, born of the womb of the spheres
The high-arched gate of the cathedral of mankind.
The youth of all peoples strides aflame
To the gleaming crystal shrine, divined in dreams.
Immense, I behold dazzling visions.
No misery more, nor war, nor hate;

The mothers wreathe the shining youths
For joyful games and dances of increase.
Thou, youth, stride forth, eternally renewing thyself,
Eternally destroying the atrophied;
And thus create life, infused with glowing spirit.[56]

It is evidently this same *Geist* which forms the very center of the Expressionist concept of the new man. If Landauer's anarchism can be termed "mystical socialism," the phrase itself emphasizes the curious and paradoxical combination of worldliness and transcendence demanded of the new man. It was a kind of mysticism, even though in many cases it was without an explicit necessary connection with God (certainly in Toller's case), and this is no doubt what attracted Martin Buber's more religiously oriented mind to Landauer.

We shall see in our discussion of Toller's *Das Schwalbenbuch* that the whole lyric cycle revolves around two ideas which the swallows exemplify: freedom versus coercion, and the community of freely-assumed obligations for one's fellows and mutual aid, in Kropotkin's and in Landauer's sense, versus the society of injustice and artificiality. These ideas are both essential elements of all varieties of anarchism, and thus it is reasonable that the concept of the "new man," in whom all more than merely theoretical anarchists must believe, is intimately connected with these same two concepts.

The connection between Landauer's concept of spirit, his "mystical anarchism," and his critique of Marxist dialectical materialism is evident. Marx had considered dedicating *Das Kapital* to Darwin, and it is in him the positivism, the determinism, the denial of that element essential to all varieties of anarchism, namely individual autonomy founded on spirit, that most disturbs Landauer. He writes of the Marxists:

> ...it is not at all appropriate that on the one hand one claims to know exactly, on the basis of so-called laws of historical development that are supposed to have the force of laws of nature, how things necessarily and irretrievably will evolve without the will or actions of anyone being able to alter this predestination in the least, and that on the other hand one forms a political party that can do nothing else but will, demand, exert influence, act, change details.[57]

We have said that Landauer's criticisms of Marxism were specific as well as fundamental. He claims that history is made, not by processes, but by persons. He accepts the labor theory of value, but rejects the theory that socialism will evolve naturally from capitalism for three reasons. First, he recognizes, like Bernstein, that meliorism will prevent the kind of impoverishment of the proletariat that Marx had envisaged. Second, he denies that the concentration of labor in factories will provide the working class with the kind of education in cooperation and communal work that would lead to socialism, as Marx had suggested. Finally, he regards Marxian socialism as merely an extension of the same exploitation, slavery to the machine, as under capitalism ("Bismarxism," as the anarchist Erich Mühsam called it)—a substitution of political for economic exploitation. Instead of promoting *Geist*, Marxism, too, would further ever-increasing productivity in the interests of the state and against those of the workers. Thus the Communist state neglects the consumer sector to build armaments while the capitalist state sells grain abroad, thus raising the workers' food prices at home. Landauer remarks: "Old women prophesy with coffee grounds. Karl Marx prophesied with steam."[58]

According to Landauer, Marx had ignored the stake the workers had in the capitalist system. But instead of drawing the logical conclusion from this, namely Bernsteinian revisionism, Landauer drew the "illogical" one, mystical anarchism. In an age when the Social Democrats had become increasingly revisionist, he saw his mystical anarchism as the only alternative way to bring about significant change.

We have said that a major difference between Marxism and mystical anarchism was the importance of *Geist* for the latter. In Landauer's opinion, Marxism recognized that it was in its interests to prevent the proletariat from achieving *Geist*. If Marxism were to succeed in this, Landauer felt that the workers would ultimately no longer be susceptible to the spiritual. He wrote: "We have said that socialism need not come as the Marxists believe. Now we say: the moment may arrive, if people continue to hesitate, when one will have to say: socialism can no longer come for these peoples."[59]

Landauer himself felt that his philosophy of mystical anarchism was so closely related to the Expressionist concept of the new man that when in 1918 he was asked to write in the journal *Masken* some notes on the premiere of Georg Kaiser's *Gas* in Düsseldorf, he submitted nothing but notes from his *Aufruf zum Sozialismus*. He considered Kaiser's *Die Bürger von Calais* (*The Burghers of Calais*) a perfect example of his theories, and wrote in *Ein Weg deutschen Geistes* (*One Path of the German Spirit*) that the "new deed" called for a betrayal of the old order. Maurer remarks: "Whoever would perform it must dedicate himself unwaveringly to the community, community not in a political but in a metaphysical sense...."[60] It is interesting to note that when Landauer was murdered, Kaiser contributed nearly all the money he had to fund a memorial to him.

Landauer's feelings about the Bavarian Revolution in its three major phases were ambivalent. It came, as Maurer has noted,[61] too late, and was rather a desperate reaction against the war and the conditions it had produced than a positive, decisive step toward any particular or clearly defined new order.

Landauer's participation (and it should be noted that he at no time, as is often claimed, served as cabinet minister, though he did belong to the Revolutionary Workers' Council) was largely due to the urging of Kurt Eisner, as was Toller's. He opposed the idea of national elections to a new parliament; he supported censorship of the press, stating:"'...now we have a beginning of freedom of public opinion,'"[62] his justification being that right-wing papers had been making spurious claims in order to discredit the Republic. One such report asserted that women had been "socialized"—placed at the disposal of revolutionary males.[63] Although he was opposed to the election of a new Bavarian *Landtag*, he stood for election nevertheless, in order to gain a forum for his views. In January of 1919, he supported a common leftist front including the Spartakists:

> I am not a friend of force, but a friend of misled, honest men. And that is what many workers are who were drawn to the Spartakists like butterflies to a light. Let us form a union of all socialists! A new socialism must arise from the precept of justice and the need of the moment.[64]

These words emphasize a cardinal feature of Landauer's anarchism and anarchism in general—its provisional, experimental character. Landauer's philosophy was in its essentials formed before the war with his reading of Fritz Mauthner's *Beiträge zu einer Kritik der Sprache* (*Contributions to a Critique of Language*)[65] and the publication of *Aufruf zum Sozialismus*, unlike Toller's, which grew as a result of his experiences in the war. Yet both men abjured inflexible dogma where principle was not involved.

We have seen in Toller's case a philosophy which from one point of view appears formless and diffuse, from another is capable of drawing a fine hard line where principle is concerned. That the same problems concerned Toller's friend and mentor we see from the following letter of Landauer's:

> This course [a council government given very strong powers initially] can be followed only if the leaders are as pure as they are strong; this is the point where every revolution is in danger of the most far-reaching corruption. But mankind cannot avoid the fate of having to prepare good from material of evil....[66]

These remarks echo almost verbatim those of Toller in *Eine Jugend in Deutschland*:

> Whoever wishes today to struggle on the political level in the clash of economic and human interests must realize clearly that the law and con-

sequences of his struggle will be determined by forces other than his good intentions; that often the particular form his attack and resistance take will be forced upon him—[a fact] that he must perceive as tragic, and because of which he can, in a profound sense of the word, bleed to death.[67]

Landauer's participation in a revolution he realized was doomed to failure was a kind of leap into faith. Earlier, in *Aufruf zum Sozialismus*, he writes: "Socialism is possible at all times and impossible at all times; it is possible when the right men are there, who want it...and it is impossible when people do not want or only pretend to want it...."[68]

In the concluding chapter of his book on Landauer, Charles Maurer notes that Julius Bab has compared Landauer to Brutus. The comparison is apt, and could as well be applied to Toller. Both Landauer and Toller were reluctantly led by their ideals to support policies in the service of freedom which ended in bloodshed, and for both the ultimate tragedy was not their defeat but the essence of the choice that faced them. It was a comparison Landauer was aware of, as is evident to one who reads his book on Shakespeare. In that work, Landauer writes of Brutus: "Precisely because he lived in an illusion about his surroundings, he maintained the original nobility of spirit, which considers it improper to learn from experience."[69]

Landauer's brutal murder in May of 1919 spared him the necessity of being further disabused of his illusions. Toller was not so lucky, and anyone who compares, as do Dorst and Zadek in *Rotmord*, his final statement before the tribunal in 1919 with that of the Communist leader, Leviné, is struck by the Brutus-like nobility even of Toller's admission that force may be necessary in the service of the revolution. One feels that it is an attempt to accept publicly the last consequences of his thoughts and deeds rather than the serious avowal of force that characterizes Leviné's speech. Yet before his death, Nazism was to teach Toller that such nobility was a luxury in the modern world that Brutus must give way to Cassius.

5

Die Wandlung: Anarchism
and the New Man

I know
The past, and thence I will essay to glean
A warning for the future, so that man
May profit by his errors, and derive
Experience from his folly:
For, when the power of imparting joy
Is equal to the will, the human soul
Requires no other Heaven.

—Percy Bysshe Shelley: *Queen Mab*, III, 6-14

Die Wandlung (*The Transfiguration*, 1919) is an intensely personal statement. It deals with a young Jew, Friedrich, who suffers acutely from a sense of
being an outsider, a pariah in his community. He falls in love with a Christian,
Gabriele, and in order to gain entrance to the world of the "others" he
becomes a fanatic patriot, volunteering to serve in a colonial war to "civilize"
the savages. His decision to enlist precipitates an ecstatic vision of a unified
fatherland.

On a desert battlefield Friedrich first experiences the depredations of war,
encountering wretched and mutilated natives destroyed by his own comrades.
When the cynical front-line soldiers disown the fatherland that Friedrich strives
so mightily to belong to, he begins to realize the truth about the war, but saves
himself from the dilemma by volunteering, as Toller himself had done, for a
dangerous mission.

As the only survivor, Friedrich is brought to a hospital where he hears the
nurse speak of God's support of the patriotic cause and hatred of the enemy.
The nurse's joy at the news of a defeat that cost the enemy ten thousand lives
drives Friedrich to the edge of madness.

After the war, Friedrich, now a sculptor, works on a patriotic statue,
desperately trying to salvage his faith. But a series of encounters brings him
slowly toward a crisis: he is rejected by Gabriele, whose parents oppose the mar-

riage to a Jew, no matter how patriotic. The sight of a wretched beggar woman and her husband wasted by venereal disease finally causes him to smash his statue in a fit of rage.

Having renounced his false faith, Friedrich now, at a workers' rally, achieves an insight into more enduring values. Here he rejects the chauvinistic platitudes of the conservatives, as does the crowd, but he also speaks against the leftist demagogues who call for the masses to rise up in an orgy of destruction. Friedrich convinces the crowd to let him address them again the next day. Slowly his new positive values take shape as he rejects assaults from his dogmatic mother, his materialistic uncle and a doctor who considers him insane because of his idealism. Finally his sister shows him the way to a new and different community—not that of the fatherland but that of humankind itself. At the next rally Friedrich, possessed by the beauty of his vision, succeeds easily in eloquently persuading the crowd of its truth and necessity. With the call for revolution on their lips, they march confidently into the future. One thinks of the new man in Landauer's *Beginnen* who leads by example: "For the first time, however, the watchword had been given: through isolation to community. To the question—where are the human beings who can do no other than create the new forms of union among men?—we answer: the few are there! ..."[1]

The relatively realistic scenes that convey the plot are interspersed with a series of surrealistic ones involving skeletons dancing in a cemetery reminiscent of Georg Grosz's mordant picture "KV" ("Fit for Service"), a workman who murders his insane mother, prisoners, wanderers, and the like. All of these serve to underline the points made in the realistic scenes and show Friedrich his instrumental role in the theater of war.

Toller's *Die Wandlung*, the only one of his plays written before the experience of the Munich revolution, is about pacifism and the senselessness of war, as nearly everyone who has written about this play has emphasized. But more than that, it is a play about the distinction between the true and the false community, and thus about anarchism. It is in the realm of this second, more fundamental theme that Friedrich's Judaism plays a decisive role, but this role is more metaphorically than autobiographically or psychologically significant. Toller was a Jew who suffered from the same sorrows of exclusion and loneliness as Friedrich, as we know from his autobiography. But the fact that the other autobiographical element in the play, Friedrich's transformation into a pacifist, is evidently to be taken quite literally and concretely should not be allowed to obscure the fact that Friedrich's Judaism is a metaphor for something larger than itself—for the need of each man for a satisfying relationship to a larger community, to his fellows, and moreover, a relationship which is based on true mutuality, on taking and giving, community rather than society. Toller shows that the institutions where one might conventionally expect to find such community are frauds. In the religious sphere, Christianity has degenerated into a tool of the church, the state and the capitalists, while Judaism has similarly been transmuted into a caricature of itself, an ossified and institutionalized defense mechanism designed to attract the attention of a hostile environment as little as possible.

In the secular sphere, Friedrich seeks salvation in two directions—the idea of nationhood, Fatherland, and that of love. Both fail. The Fatherland is a fraud which claims loyalty to a fictitious ideal in order to fool the masses and exploit them as cannon fodder, but whose foreign policy (colonial wars) and domestic policy are the handmaidens of a corrupt capitalism. Love, in the person of Gabriele, similarly proves to be a caricature, indeed, the very opposite of what Friedrich seeks. What Friedrich ultimately discovers is that he must build his ideal himself, and that it must be an ideal in which the individual does not enslave himself, prostitute himself to the interests of other individuals and institutions which exploit him. At the same time, it must not be total, egocentric individualism. Friedrich's ideal is mutuality, community plus individual autonomy. It is in fact exactly the kind of *Ich-Du* dialogue that Martin Buber advocates in his *Ich und Du (I and Thou)*.[2] This relationship is, as the title indicates, not one in which the individual is completely submerged into the community, not a *We*, but neither is it a collection of totally unrelated autonomous individuals—neither authoritarian socialism, nor totally individualistic capitalism. On the contrary, its essence is the true community, and in that sense Buber, who is sometimes thought of as a religious existentialist, differs from the individualistically oriented existentialism of philosophers like Sartre. The individual must legislate his own morality, transform himself and accept the responsibility for himself, but he must do it in accord with others. This introduces a messianic elements into Buber's social philosophy, and it is in this that the parallel to his friend Landauer and to Toller's *Die Wandlung* is most striking. For *Die Wandlung* is that play of Toller's in which the messianic, the chiliastic element is felt most strongly. At the same time, its messianism is of this world rather than the next. Katharina Maloof notes correctly: "In the final analysis the solution is not a religious, Christian one. Friedrich follows the path to God indicated by his sister only as far as man. To the question of his sister as to where the path leads, Friedrich replies: 'Farther ...? I am not concerned. I feel as if I were rooted in an infinite sea.'"[3] In *Quer Durch*, Toller writes in a similar vein and altogether in the sense of the lines of Shelly's Spirit, quoted above: "We seek no otherworldly salvation...."[4]

I use the word "parallel" because it cannot be proved from any of the documents currently at our disposal that Buber exerted any direct influence on Toller. Yet the relationship between him and Gustav Landauer, whose influence on Toller was profound, as has been shown, was very close.

Buber's philosophy began to take on its anarchistic elements with the publication of *Daniel* (1913), *Ereignisse und Begegnungen (Events and Encounters*, 1917) and *Ich und Du (I and Thou*, 1923). The concern with anarchism remained central to Buber's thought from the early period on, as we see from his study of the major anarchists, *Pfade in Utopia (Paths in Utopia)*,[5] which contains chapters on Proudhon, Landauer and Kropotkin. The book appeared after the rise of Hitler and Nazism had proved fatal to the hopes (and persons) of other, less hardy anarchists, among them Toller. It is not direct influence I am claiming, but a kind of ambience, a "new spirituality" (to use Paul E. Wyler's phrase),[6] as a reaction to nineteenth century positivism. In all its essentials this *Zeitgeist* corresponds exactly to the ideals which Toller's Friedrich finally sets for himself.

The one significant difference between Buber's social philosophy in the 1920's and that of Landauer and Toller was its religious content. Buber quotes a remark by Leonhard Ragaz as an epigraph in his book, *Hinweise (Hints)*: "Every [kind of] socialism whose compass is more narrow than God and man is too little for us."[7] For Buber, God and his relationship to man are central features of the true community, whereas Friedrich's and Landauer's visions are altogether secular. This was something that Buber recognized: he notes in *Pfade in Utopia* the absence of the religious in Landauer: "'Socialism,' says Landauer (1915), is 'the attempt to join the communal life of man to freedom born of a common spirit, i.e. to religion.' This is probably the only place where the man who rejected all the religious symbolism of our time and all its religious avowals, speaks the word 'religion' in this positive and binding sense—speaks it as the expression for everything he longs for: a joining together in freedom born of a common spirit.''[8] But the absence of religion does not on that account mean the absence of the spiritual, as Buber's remarks indicate and as we have had sufficient occasion to note in the preceding chapter, and it could be argued that the place occupied by God in Buber's social philosophy is very nearly filled by the concept of *Geist* in Landauer's and Toller's.

What is this social philosophy? It is based on two concepts which are central to Toller's first play: *Gemeinschaft* (community) and *Wandlung* (inner transformation). Maurice S. Friedman remarks in his study, *Martin Buber: The Life of Dialogue*: "True community, writes Buber, can only be founded on changed relations between men, and these changed relations can only follow the inner change and preparation of the men who lead, work, and sacrifice for the community."[9] These men, however, are not the statesmen and political leaders; on the contrary, "The really responsible men are rather those who can withstand the thousandfold trembling mouths that time after time demand from them decision."[10] One thinks of the final scene *(13. Bild)* of Toller's *Die Wandlung*, where the exploited and mutilated multitudes gather before the church and demand an answer from Friedrich to their suffering:

> PEOPLE: There he stands, who wishes to speak with us. He says we must wait til noon. But now he must speak. We did, after all, wait.[11]

If we compare Friedrich's answer with Buber's rhapsodic essay, "Was ist zu tun?" ("What is to be done?")[12] written in the same year as the première of *Die Wandlung*, we detect an astonishing kinship. Friedrich cries:

> You, child, go to school and anxiety accompanies you on the way.... But now you [worker] stand in the factory. From morning until evening you push again and again the same lever.... And your breath becomes heavy in the suffocating air and your eyes fill with tears when, through the dusty windows, you imagine the light and freedom and flowers and youth.
>
> I know you, woman, bowed by work and careworn. . . . .
>
> I know you too, man, that horror seizes you at having to go home to your stinking hovel, where misery and sickness dwell....
>
> I know of you, girl, of your nights of hot desire.
>
> I know of you, young man, of your seeking for God.
>
> Of you, rich man, forever heaping up money and despising all, the others and yourself as well....
>
> And you, soldier, forced into a constraining jacket that drains all joy from your life....
>
> And so you are all distorted images of the real man!
>
> You immured ones, you wasted ones, you pent-up ones, you gasping ones, you jaded and bitter ones—
>
> For you have all buried the spirit.[89-9; II, 58f.]

Buber describes a society ripe for renewal in nearly identical language:

> You, encased in the shells into which society, state, church, school, economy, public opinion and your own arrogance have put you, inauthentic *[Mittelbarer]* one among inauthentic ones, break through your shells, become essential, touch your fellows as a human being! The rubbish and mold of centuries is heaped up between men. Form born of reason has degenerated into convention, respect into mistrust, purity of communication into greedy reserve. Now and then people fumble towards one another in anxious intoxication—and miss the mark, for the mountain of mold lies between them.[13]

Toller's Friedrich exclaims: "Thousands of spades are in continual motion, in order to shovel more and more rubbish into the spirit.... The hearts of your fellow men are bell-ropes, on which you can pull at will.... Your lips murmur ossified laws.... Your hands build up walls about you ..." [W 91; II, 59].

Buber replies: "...two lonelinesses are interwoven in your life. Only one of them should you uproot: closing yourself off from others, withdrawing to yourself, confrontation—the loneliness of one incapable of community. The other you should promote, strengthen—the necessary, repeated loneliness of the strong person, who must call home his rays from time to time (in order to store new stength) into a loneliness where he rests in communion with that which is past and that which is to come and is nourished by it, so that he can issue forth with renewed force to the community of being." [14]

But not only in their analysis of what now exists do Toller and Buber speak with one voice. Also in their injunction to man to change himself and thus his world both anarchists agree. Buber writes, for example:

> You should help. Every man who encounters you requires the succor of the soul; each requires your succor.... You should awaken in others the need to be helped, in yourself the ability to help.... Make individuals of the crowds! ...The formless essence has grown out of men, surrendered to impotent abandonment, out of the impotent abandonment of men thrown together—liberate the human being in it, form the formless into communities. Smash the reserve, throw yourselves into the foam; reach out and grasp hands, lift, help, lead, test spirit and solidarity in the crucible of the abyss.... No longer through exclusion, but only through inclusion can the realm be erected. When you no longer shudder and are disgusted, when you dissolve the crowd into individuals, when even the hearts of the crude, the addicts, the wretched beat with your love, then and only then is the new beginning present in the midst of the end.... Silently the world awaits the spirit! [15]

Friedrich concludes with the words:

> Oh, if only you were human beings—unconstrained, free human beings.... Now, brothers, I call to you: march! March in broad daylight! Go now to the rulers and proclaim to them with roaring voices of organs that their power is an illusion. Go to the soldiers and tell them, they should beat their swords into plowshares. Go to the rich and show them their hearts, that had become rubbish heaps. But be indulgent toward them, for they too are poor, lost. Smash, however, the fortresses. Smash, laughing, the false fortresses built of slag, of dessicated slag. March—march in broad daylight. Brothers, stretch out the martyred

hand. Flaming, joyous chord! Stride burning through our free land
Revolution! Revolution! [W 93f.;II, 60f.]

Buber sees true community as "authentic existence" in the existentialist
sense, but one which is also characterized by true communication and mutual
aid. In such a community the presence of God would be realized, but the
duality between the truth of the "spirit" and the realities of life tends to
hinder progress toward this happy state and divide life into two independent
spheres.

To bridge this gap was the task of the Hebrew prophets (Landauer too was influenced by Isaiah and by Ezekiel's call for an inner transformation of man), as
it is Friedrich's, and they attempted it neither by compromising with the
realities of life, the *status quo*, nor on the other hand by completely denying
the earthly. Friedman states: "Never did they decide between the kingdom of
God and the kingdom of man. The kingdom of God was to them nothing
other than the kingdom of man as it shall become. When they despaired of
present fulfillment, they projected the image of their truth into Messianism.
Yet here also they meant no opposition to this human world in which we live,
but its purification and fulfillment."[16] In this sense, to anticipate, Landauer
and Buber did not conceive of their anarchistic socialism as otherworldly
idealism at all; indeed Daniel Guérin has titled one section of his famous study
of anarchism: "Anarchism is not Utopian."[17] And the Naturalist free thinker,
Michael Georg Conrad, begins his book, *Die clerikale Schilderhebung*, with
the words: "This earth is ours. And it suffices even without the otherwordly ap-
pendix, the heavenly dessert. It is our homeland ...on which we can erect the
temple of humanity and realize the reasonably developed program for a human
existence undistorted by socialist phantasies...."[18]

Christ, too, sought to achieve the true community in the here and now. But,
according to Buber, succeeding generations thought of instinct and will not as
forces capable of leading the soul through error to unity and redemption, but
as an evil to be extirpated. Friedman summarizes Buber's views (in an analysis
remarkably similar to Wyler's):

> The state is no longer the consolidation of a will to community that has
> gone astray and therefore is penetrable and redeemable by right will. It is
> either, as for Augustine, the eternally damned kingdom from which the
> chosen separate themselves or, as for Thomas, the first step and prepara-
> tion for true community, which is the spiritual one. The true community
> is no longer to be realized in the perfect life of men with one another but
> in the church. It is the community of spirit and grace from which the
> world and nature are fundamentally separated.[19]

It is this artificial and fateful dualism which produces such evils as nationalism and alienation and the immoral use of power. Buber argues that power in itself is not intrinsically bad. He writes as a Zionist (who endowed scholarships for Arab students at Hebrew University, and whose coffin was followed by long lines of mourning Arabs) an open letter in reply to Gandhi's reproaches: "We do not want force.... We have not proclaimed, as you do and did Jesus, the son of our people, the teaching of non-violence. We believe that sometimes a man must use force to save himself or even more his children. But from time immemorial we have proclaimed the teaching of justice and peace...."[20] In order to delimit one's own rights from those of others power must be continually exercised, but it cannot be exercised to conform to a set of unchanging rules. This means that the constant exercise of individual responsibility in the use of power is what prevents it from becoming evil and arbitrary. In a similar vein, not unlike Schiller's Wilhelm Tell, Toller told his accusers at this trial:

Judges, gentlemen ...I have committed every one of my deeds for objective reasons, and demand that you hold me responsible for my actions.

I would not call myself a revolutionary if I were to say I would never consider altering existing conditions by force. We revolutionaries acknowledge the right of revolution when we see that conditions, in all their ramifications, can no longer be borne, that they have become petrified. Then we have the right to overthrow them.[21]

Here the decision is the individual's, but these words spoken before the court also demonstrate Toller's acceptance of the consequences of his acts, his responsible advocacy of force—the very responsibility that Buber demands.

According to Friedman, Buber's religious socialism developed, like Toller's secular anarchism, immediately after World War I, and was "decisively influenced by the socialism of Buber's friend Gustav Landauer, the social anarchism of Peter Kropotkin, and the distinction between 'community' and 'society' in Ferdinand Tönnies's work, *Gemeinschaft und Gesellschaft (Community & Society*, 1887).''[22]

Buber felt that the industrial age was leading modern man from community to society. This is so under both capitalism and Marxian communism. But such a trend tears man from his origins, imbeds him firmly in the earthly and thus isolates him completely from the spiritual. In consequence a great longing grows within man which modern society is unable to still. Friedman writes: "This longing can only be satisfied by the autonomy of the communal cells which together make up true commonwealth. But this autonomy will never be accorded by the present state, nor by the socialist state which will not renounce its rigid mechanical form in favor of an organic one."[23]

Buber's solution, then, is basically anarchist in nature, and it differs from that of Kropotkin, Toller, Landauer and Proudhon only in its religious element, which, as we have seen, is largely equivalent to Landauer's secular notion of *Geist*. Buber emphasized that such a society *presupposes* the transformation of the individual, his *Wandlung* (transfiguration). Friedman summarizes this well: "Wholly ineffective and illusory is the will for social reality of circles of intellectuals who fight for the transormation of human relations yet remain as indirect and unreal as ever in their personal life with men."[24]

Buber has quoted Comte's characterization of Saint-Simon's program with approval: "a social regeneration based upon a spiritual renewal."[25] Buber continually emphasizes[26] that although society must be reorganized and reordered to make the life of the spirit possible, still the realization of this life depends on a transformation within man himself. In this insight, he echoes Toller's Hinkemann, who tells his drinking comrades, proponents of various political heresies, that all of their theories can at best eliminate hindrances, that a really authentic and human life itself requires more. We shall see that the suffering that is inevitably part of the human condition regardless of social organization is what is symbolically meant by Hinkemann's mutilation, and those critics who protest that it is so bizarre as to be unrealistic, exotic and thus ultimately uninteresting to the rest of us, are consciously closing their eyes to Toller's meaning. Hinkemann's infirmity in its metaphorical sense, far from being rare, afflicts *all* of us, and the most just and perfect human society, the most faithful and loving wife in Hinkemann's case, would still be susceptible and vulnerable to the demands of what Buber calls the unfulfilled longing of the individual. It was in this sense that Toller wrote in *Eine Jugend in Deutschland*: "Even socialism will only solve that suffering which arises from the insufficiency of social systems; there will always be a remainder. But social suffering is senseless, unnecessary, extinguishable."[27]

This same deeply felt conviction appears in a letter on *Hinkemann* to Stefan Zweig:

I wrote this work at a time when I had with great pain recognized the tragic limits of all possibilities of happiness through social revolution, the limits beyond which nature is more powerful than all the human volition of the individual and of society. For this reason, tragedy will never cease. There will always be individuals whose suffering is ineradicable. And if there is an individual whose suffering can never end, then the tragedy of this one individual is simultaneously the tragedy of the society in which he lives. The ancients were familiar with the Promethean hero who believed he could tame fate and suspend all suffering; in our day a whole class has replaced the individual hero. I don't say this out of resignation. Only the weak man gives up when he sees himself unable to lend his yearned-for dream its complete realization. The strong yield nothing of their passionate will, when they gain insight. What we require today are not men who are binded by emotion; we need those who wish—although they know.[28]

Such a conception of tragedy persists in contemporary works. It is personified in the Don Quixote-like figure Bodo Graf von Übelohe-Zabernsee in Dürrenmatt's play, *Die Ehe des Herrn Mississippi (The Marriage of Mr. Mississippi)*; it appears again in his *Theaterprobleme (Problems of the Theater)*.

Earlier, in *Die Wandlung*, Toller has his more naive Friedrich declaim:

My eyes see the path.
I want to walk it, sister,
Alone, and yet with you,
Alone, and yet with all
Knowing about mankind. [W 58; II, 40]

This "wanting in spite of all" accurately describes Buber, writing of the "experiment that did not fail" in *Pfade in Utopia*[29] after the rise and fall of Hitler, but it describes less well the later and more complex Toller of, say, *Hoppla, wir leben!* (1927) and the exile period.

The positive content of Buber's social philosophy, what it is he "passionately wants," can best be judged for our purposes from his attempt (in *Pfade in Utopia*) to come to terms with the concept of "utopia" as applied by Marx and Engels to utopian socialism. He begins by pointing out that what Marx and Engels seem to mean in their condemnation of utopian socialism in the *Communist Manifesto* (1848) is the social philosophies of such thinkers as Saint-Simon, Fourier and Owen who developed their systems before industrialism had evolved to the extent necessary for them to grasp the nature of the proletariat and predict its course. Thus their criticism of existing conditions is largely acceptable, whereas their predictions, systems and theoretical edifices are to be condemned as merely speculative.

Buber suggests, however, that behind this more or less reasonable meaning given to the term "utopian," it had actually acquired the character of an epithet, a weapon of insult used by Marx in an "internal political action" against all varieties of anarcho-socialism which were non-Marxist. He seeks to prove this by pointing out[30] that in his preface to a translation of some posthumous fragments of Fourier, Engels had taken, two years before the

Manifesto, a more positive view of these three Utopians, asserting that what they had been saying twenty and even forty years ago the Germans were only now beginning to discover. Buber that notes that in Engels' anti-Dühring book, only these three men, "the founders of Socialism," are discussed who had, said Engels, "to construct the elements of a new society out of their heads because these elements had not yet become generally visible in the old society." Buber asks: "In the thirty years between the *Manifesto* and *Anti-Dühring,* had no socialists appeared who in Engels' opinion at the same time deserved the appellation 'utopians' and respect, who however need not be conceded those mitigating circumstances, since in their day the economic relationships had already developed and the 'social tasks' no longer remained 'concealed'?"[31]The answer is, of course, yes—Proudhon. Marx and Engels themselves had in their book *Die heilige Familie (The Holy Family,* 1844) found Proudhon's book on property a scientific advance which "revolutionizes political economy and for the first time makes possible a science of political economy."[32] From this it is evident that Marx had begun to apply the term "utopian" to all socialists who disagreed with him and failed to take proper account of him. But quite apart from its perversion by Marx and Engels, the term has potentially a useful message to convey, and to define it is the task of the rest of Buber's book.

A utopia is generally thought of as a fantasy, a "wish-picture," as the word itself (a Greek pun on "no place" and "good place" invented by Thomas More) indicates. But it is a wish-picture that adumbrates what ought to be; it contains the longing for rightness "which is apprehended in a religious or philosophical vision as revelation, as idea, and which, owing to its very nature, cannot be realized in the individual but only within the human community as a whole."[33] All suffering under senseless social orders evokes or at least prepares the way for such wishing. This vision can embody itself in two forms that Buber calls rightness in perfect time or messianic eschatology, and rightness of perfect space or utopia, the "good place." The one looks forward in a religious sense to an otherwordly perfect age in the future and is "creational," the other "remains in its essentials limited to the sphere of society, even if it sometimes includes an inner transformation of man in its perspective. Eschatology means perfection of creation; utopia means the unfolding of the possibilities of a 'proper' order residing in the communal life of man. Another difference is still more important. For eschatology (even if it concedes to man in its elementary, prophetic form a significant active role in the coming of salvation) the decisive act comes from above; for utopia everything is subjected to the conscious will of man; indeed one can almost call it a picture of society that is drawn as if there were no factors other than the conscious human will."[34]

Buber's conception of utopianism emphasizes its fundamental irreconciliability with Marxism, but at the same time its congruence with the philosophy of Toller and Friedrich in *Die Wandlung*—a vision closely tied, as I have emphasized, to this world, to the here-and-now. This is indicated even by the stage direction, "the plot takes place in Europe before the onset of the Renaissance,"[35] with its allusion to a contrast between a medieval period which looks forward in an eschatological sense to a messianic second coming and the Renaissance which succeeds it and tries to construct in this world a "golden age." It is emphasized by Friedrich's rejection of the call:

MAN: Why don't you become a monk? Leave people alone.... I hate you.
FRIEDRICH: Brother, you are deceiving yourself. [W 78f.; II, 52]

We have already seen that, like Friedrich, neither Proudhon nor Kropotkin nor Landauer nor Buber viewed anarchism as a purely theoretical "wish-fantasy" impossible of attainment in this imperfect world. Buber writes:

And what seemed impossible as a concept excites as an image the force of faith, determines intention and plan. It does this because it is in league with forces in the depths of reality. Eschatology, insofar as it is prophetic [and] utopia, insofar as it is philosophical, have a realistic character.[36]

Just as the eschatologial alternative has been robbed of its sphere of action since the Enlightenment, so too has utopia become progressively dominated by technological, "scientific" solutions. Into some of the technologically dominated utopias man's longing for the lost eschatological possibility has transposed a "displaced Messianism." It is these very ("voluntaristic") socialisms which Marx condemns as "utopian" in the pejorative sense of the word. But the remaining technological socialism of Marx, the "necessaritarian" (i.e. historically inevitable and determined) socialism is, according to Buber, not free of utopianism in the larger sense either.

This is because the eschatological has two aspects:

...a prophetic one that places the preparation of [the way] for salvation within the power of decision of each man ...to a degree which cannot be determined at any given moment, and an apocalyptic one, for which the process of salvation has since ancient times been determined in all its details as to time and manner, and for the accomplishment of which men can only be employed as tools: this immutably determined fact can, however, be uncovered, revealed to them, and their function [can be] shown them.[37]

It is evident that the first of these aspects is voluntaristic in nature and lies at the basis of the Expressionist concept of the "new man," and that the second is necessitarian and can be subsumed under the idea of dialectical materialism.

However, the very notion of the "withering away of the state," the post-revolutionary utopia envisioned by the Marxists themselves involves an element of prophetic eschatology even in apocalyptic pre-revolutionary Marxism and, moreover, one which cannot be derived from the authoritarian pre-revolutionary process. Buber quotes several relevant remarks by Paul Tillich: "[these things can] 'in no way be made comprehensible,' 'between reality and expectation lies the abyss'; 'for this reason, Marxism, in spite of its antipathy toward utopias, has never been able to dispel the suspicion [that it contains] a concealed belief in utopia.'"[38] Eduard Heimann, also a Marxist, expresses this idea even more drastically and in words which underscore its relevance to the concept of the new man:

> The withering away of the State is impossible with men as they are. But in counting on a radical and inner transformation of human nature we overstep the bounds of empirical investigation and enter the realm of prophetic vision, where the true significance and the providential calling of man are paraphrased in stammering metaphors.[39]

In examining the utopian element in non-Marxist systems and trying to distinguish it from that in Marxism, Buber detects two distinct elements in it: the schematic fiction, which is predicated on *theory* as in Fourier, and empirical and organic planning, which proceeds heuristically and undogmatically. Buber writes of the mechanism of inner transformation:

> Starting with no reservations from the condition of society as it is, this view gazes into the depths of reality with a clarity of vision unclouded by any dogmatic pre-occupation, discerning those still hidden tendencies which, although still obscured by obvious and powerful forces, are yet moving towards that transformation. It has justly been said that in a positive sense every planning intellect is utopian. But we must add that the planning intellect of those socialist "Utopians" under consideration, proves the positive character of its utopianism by being at every point aware, or at least having an inkling, of the diversity, indeed the contrariety, of the trends discernible in every age; by not failing to discover, despite its insight into the dominant trends, those others which these trends conceal; and by asking whether and to what extent those and those alone are aiming at an order in which the contradictions of existing society will truly be overcome. [*Paths in Utopia*, p. 12][40]

If this is nearly but not quite an exact description of Jimmy Cobbett's sense of the complexity of his task in Die Maschinenstürmer, it does represent that of Toller himself, even the Toller of the 1919 speech before his judges.

It is clear that the variety of socialism with which Buber at the end of his analysis is most in sympathy is the organic (non-dogmatic) utopianism of men like Proudhon and Kropotkin. Both of these elements are central to Toller; indeed his non-dogmatic, heuristic philosophy provides the basis for many of the criticisms leveled at him by Communist critics, as we have seen. Buber's quotation from Kropotkin as a description of his ends could as well be applied to Toller:

...[the most complete development of individuality ought to] combine with the highest of voluntary association in all possible degrees and for all possible purposes: a constantly changing association that bears within itself the elements of its duration and that adopts those forms which at each moment best correspond to the manifold strivings of all.[41]

Landauer had expressed his intention in similar words: "This also means, however: to be on guard against all schematized mapped-out paths; to know that in the life of man and of human community the straight line between two points can prove to be the longest [path]; to understand that the real path toward socialist reality does not issue solely from that which I recognize and that which I plan, but from the unperceived and not-to-be-expected...."[42] Similarly, Proudhon had written in 1849: " 'System ...I have none, I want none, I reject the suggestion explicitly. The system of mankind will be known only at the end of mankind ...as for me, [my task] is to recognize its way and, when I can, to smooth it.' "[43] Eberhard Lämmert begins his article, "Das expressionistische Verkündigungsdrama," by comparing the very detailed description of Odysseus drawing his bow in the 21st canto of the Odyssey and shooting the arrow through the holes of twelve axes with the very different shot into a limitless sky in the Expressionist Sorge's Odysseus. He notes: "The manifold and carefully articulated plot is replaced by a single pathetic act.... There is no goal at all that can be objectively described or delimited—the sharpest contrast to the narrowly circumscribed twelve ax holes on which the Greek proves his skill.... Whatever might lend this deed an individual coloration is rigorously eradicated by the author in order to exemplify as closely as possible the immaterial nucleus of his proclamation."[44] This technique which Lämmert finds characteristic of the Expressionists in general is also that of Die Wandlung. Rosemarie Altenhofer disagrees. She remarks, "The play's greatest

weakness lies in the fact that Toller has not succeeded in representing his utopian ideas forcefully and convincingly...."[45]

In the light of this idea, one can understand why the criticisms like that
quoted in Chapter I that Toller (like most Expressionists) fails to provide a
blueprint of what it is he desires, that he serves up childish vaporings empty of
all content, while in a very real sense correct and well-taken, are essentially irrelevant to his purpose. Toller sought to provide a "stammering metaphor" (to
use Heimann's phrase) that exactly delineates the *direction* man must travel, to
the extent that it can be delineated at all, at least within the confines of a play.

Buber emphasizes the "quantum jump" in Marxist theory, Engels' (and
Schiller's) leap from the realm of necessity to the realm of freedom—the
disparity between centralist coercive means and freedom as an end, between
pre-revolutionary uniformity and putative post-revolutionary multiplicity. Landauer makes the same point in an article in *Der Sozialist* dated June 24, 1893:
"For Marx the way to a non-authoritarian society is through authority, the way
to statelessness is through the state.... That was his great error.... If I want a
society without authority, then I cannot strive for authority."[46] In contrast, the
utopians and anarchists posit no such abyss; their means are in complete harmony with their ends.

The capitalist society is "structurally poor" according to Buber:

> By the structure of a society I mean its social content or community con-
> tent. A society is to be termed structurally rich to the degree that it is
> built up of genuine societies, i.e. of local communes and trade com-
> munes and their step-by-step associations.... No matter at which point
> we examine the construction of such a society, we find everywhere the
> cell-tissue, "society," i.e. a living and a life-giving collaboration, a large-
> ly autonomous interconnection of human beings, shaping and reshaping
> itself from within. [47]

Tendencies toward such a state exist within all societies, and, to the extent that
they are not realized, produce longing in the individual. Buber writes:

> ...the "utopian" socialists have to an increasing degree striven for a
> restructuring of society—not, as Marxian criticism thinks, in a romantic
> attempt to revive stages of development that are over and done with, but
> in league with the decentralistic counter-tendencies evident in the depths
> of the economic and social process and also with the innermost of all
> revolts, the revolt against mass or collective loneliness slowly growing in
> the depths of the human soul.[48]

In this sense, the outcast Friedrich in *Die Wandlung* rejects the false and institutionalized society of Gabriele (and also of his mother and uncle): "But I shall stay ...I too have roots; I too have a country of my own, to which I am bound with my heart's blood, to which I have sacrificed my heart's blood—your country, my country. The whole great Fatherland. You are weak, Gabriele, you are weak" [W 51; II, 37]

Later on, Friedrich replies similarly to his sister (who echoes Goethe's admonition to "die and be reborn"):

FRIEDRICH: I will stay here and yet I will go my way further. Through pestilential streets and across poppy fields, on sunny snow-covered mountain peaks and through deserts, knowing that I am rooted in myself.
SISTER: So one must kill one's self and be born anew in order to discover one's roots.
FRIEDRICH: That knowledge is only a beginning.
SISTER: And where does it lead?
FRIEDRICH: To man![W 87f.   II, 57]

Landauer says very much the same thing in *Skepsis und Mystik*:"...my inner feeling that I am an isolated unity can be false, and I declare it to be false because I cannot be satisfied with this horrible isolation.... I renounce the certainty of my 'ego' so that I will be able to bear existence. I build myself a new world.... The force that is practised by all powerful life, however, has a liberating strength in itself which creates affirmation."[49]

To summarize, then, *Die Wandlung* fulfills Buber's description of organic, prophetic utopian socialism in the following respects. It is a "stammering metaphor" rather than a detailed plan. Like Strindberg's *To Damascus*, it is scarcely a drama at all in any classical or traditional sense in that it lacks external conflict, although it corresponds very well to its own genre, the Expressionist "Verkündigungsdrama." It is at once non-metaphysical and transcendental in that it points beyond the present imperfect society to another, ideal one, which, however, is to be realized in this world and not in the next one. It looks toward a non-collectivist rather than an authoritarian solution. It is voluntarist rather than necessitarian (viz. the conflict between the agitator and Friedrich, which is actually an embodiment of two tendencies *within* Friedrich). It pleads for total transformation and the new man, and it requires that this transformation of the individual precede that of society. It is internationalist rather than chauvinistic. And finally, it does not ignore the realities of the technological age.

It is perhaps not surprising that these two German Jews who grew up in enlightened families in enclaves within a Christian and Polish-speaking environment should be acutely sensible of the problem of the rootlessness of modern man and of his need for true community. Landauer too, in *Der werdende Mensch*, compares his Germanness and his Jewishness to two children of the same mother, loved in different ways but equally strongly. He remarks: "I have never had the need to oversimplify myself or seek a fictitious unity. I accept my complexity and hope to be a unity of even greater complexities than I am aware of."[50] Kafka, in similar circumstances, describes what is at best a highly ambiguous "solution" in *Das Schloß (The Castle)*. Toller and Buber in their vision of what is possible at least are more positive.

Buber saw the revolutionary leader in the context of the Hebrew prophets. He writes, for example:

> Isaiah does not, like Plato, believe in power as man's property. Power is lent to man so that he may fulfill his duty to maintain the state. If he misuses it then it consumes him and in place of the spirit, which also comes to him in order to equip him [to exercise] power, he is now visited only by "an evil spirit." ...It is part of the essence of the leader to be powerless and as a powerless man to step before the rulers and admonish them as to their responsibility, as Isaiah did to Achas.... [51]

It is evident that Buber is here attempting, in the face of the difficulties created by the private nature of truth described in *Ich und Du* and by the belief of each in the justice of his cause, to distinguish the true leader from the false, the kind he refers to in the essay, "Volk und Führer"("People and Leader"), written in 1942:

> In our age powerful changes are taking place through the agency of individuals who are not equal to the tasks they accomplish, are not the sufficient subject of their deeds but through their behavior succeed in being considered the persons that belong to these deeds. In truth they are merely the exploiters of situations. These situations are those of despair, in which the fanatic who rises and hollers: "I will lead the way for you" finds followers and achieves success. He knew no way, he pointed none out; but he set out and the masses followed him. It is easy to understand that the masses see the man who at such an hour arrogates to himself leadership as the tool of history, the man authorized by the tides of fate. It is also easy to understand that the man who is thus believed in gains in strength; but at the core of reality he after all remains the person he is. And the greater the changes the world suffers on his account, the greater does the contradiction between appearance and reality become.[52]

In Toller's *Die Wandlung*, it is the progressive revelation of this contradiction which marks Friedrich's transformation. And at the end he achieves

Buber's insight: ''certainly, that people is unfortunate that has no leader; but threefold unfortunate is the people whose leader has no teacher.''[53]

6

Masse Mensch: Anarchism and Communism

Must the man of action always incur guilt. Always? Or, if he is unwilling to incur guilt, perish?—Ernst Toller: *Eine Jugend in Deutschland*

Not believing in force is the same as not believing in gravitation.—Leon Trotsky: *What Next?* (1932)

Masses Mensch (*Masse and Man*) is a powerful play, and one which is, in a structural sense, I venture to say, very nearly without flaw. Walter Sokel, for example, writes in his article on Toller: "The depth and the tragic content of Toller's *Masse Mensch* raises this drama far above the high-water mark of dramatic high-expressionism and gives it an altogether unique status."[1] Its success in the 1920's was not due solely to Jürgen Fehling's genius, as Julius Bab suggests: "This drama 'Masse Mensch' had a powerful success, but three quarters of this success was that of the director, Jürgen Fehling."[2] On the contrary, it is a work which could well have been performed in 1972, a year in which Enzensberger's *Der kurze Sommer der Anarchie* appeared, in which Yaak Karsunke wrote about the Frankfurt Parliament of 1848, in which Gerhard Kelling wrote a play about Clausewitz ("theme: reforms prevent revolutions"), in which Tankred Dorst's *Toller* enjoyed great success in France and Italy, and in which Heinar Kipphardt's play investigated "the possibilities of a revolution in the face of the superior strength of the means of suppressing it."[3] And the initial stages of the Iranian Revolution of 1978-1979 suggest in a tantalizing way that the tactics of revolution by moral force that the Woman advocates are not perhaps as utopian as critics of Toller's play generally assume.

Sonja Irene L. (referred to in the text of *Masse Mensch* as "the Woman"), the wife of a government official, is organizing a general strike against the slaughter of war and against an exploitative, capitalist system. Her meeting with a group of workers is interrupted by her husband, who attempts to dissuade her from her action, which he sees as a threat to his career. When he suggests that she instead work at organizing charities to help the workers, she tries to explain to him the deeper roots of her activism, her attempt to awaken within all of mankind a sense of brotherhood. The husband is deaf to her arguments and reproaches her for undertaking a course of action certain to harm him, whereupon the Woman for the moment turns aside from her resolve and accompanies her husband home, perhaps for the last time.

At a workers' meeting, Sonja Irene L. (the name Irene, ''peace,'' was added by Toller to the name of the historical model, Sonja Lerch, just as the name of the hero of *Die Wandlung*, Friedrich, alludes to peace) must now ward off the attacks from the left by workers demanding the destruction of the machinery. Factories and machines, she replies, are here to stay, and should be exploited, subordinated to the service of man and not destroyed. She pleads instead for a strike, and carries the workers along with her. At this point the Nameless One emerges from the crowd to agitate in favor of a violent uprising. He argues that a strike is only a temporary expedient. Although he foresees that the uprising will be brutally suppressed owing to the relative weakness of the workers, he supports it nonetheless, feeling that ignominious defeat will radicalize the masses. The Woman sees herself forced to acquiesce in the general wave of emotion, since she feels that she must stand by her comrades in their moment of need, even though in doing so she acts against her conscience.

The next morning it is clear that the predictions of the Nameless One have proved correct. Only when the woman opposes acts of violent reprisal committed by the workers and terms them pure vengeance, does she fully realize that it is only non-violent revolution, spiritual revolution by example, that she can support. The Nameless One calls this treason and by denouncing her as a bourgeois intellectual, he is able to provoke the crowd into placing her before a firing squad. But just then the counter-revolutionary soldiers surround the hall and arrest the workers.

In prison the Woman defines for herself the nature of her guilt in the course of three visits, one by her husband, one by the Nameless One, and one by a minister. Although she is innocent of the crime of which she has been accused, provoking the workers to violence, she realizes that in a more profound sense she has incurred the guilt attendant on all political action when pure theories are to be realized in an imperfect world. She is *schuldlos-schuldig* (guilty owing to the imperatives of her situation), very much in the sense of the dramatist Friedrich Hebbel. Her husband too is edified by her example and begins to see the significance of his involvement in an inhuman economic system that necessarily provokes guilty acts.

The Nameless One appears at this point and urges the woman to escape. However, the price of her freedom would be the stabbing of a guard. This price she refuses to pay, since she realizes that even though the good she would do by living on might benefit millions yet unborn, still killing is never justifiable. After unmasking the minister as a servant of the exploitative state, the Woman goes to her death, in the process shaming and converting two fellow prisoners who were about to appropriate her effects.

If drama is, as the Expressionist Georg Kaiser has asserted, thinking a thought through to its conclusion, then *Masse Mensch* is preeminently dramatic. Moreover, the ideological conflict it deals with is highly relevant to the Europe of today with its new anarchists, with Daniel Guérin, the *Kabouters*, *Jusos*, the new German Communist Party, the *Chaoten* and all the rest. It is not a play which has shriveled to the status of a historical document with the failure of the 1918-1919 revolution. But not only are its ideas still important to us today; very much like Brecht's *Mutter Courage*, *Masse Mensch* exemplifies these ideas in an affecting, concrete way, in spite of all Expressionist abstraction. No one who has read the historical anecdote in *I Was a German* (p. 111) from which it originated will see it simply as an extended example of an ideological fencing match. The Woman's love for her husband and the conflict it represents for her spring directly from Toller's life, and anticipate, for example, the similar conflict in *Hoppla, wir leben!* between Karl Thomas and Eva Berg. *Masse Mensch* contains grotesque humor, e.g. the stockbrokers' dance, but even here we feel a personal sense of commitment and moral outrage which is not present in the same way in similar scenes in other Expressionists such as Georg Kaiser, and which reveals how much more it was a matter of emotional rather than sardonic intellectual outrage in him. Sokel writes:

> Just compare *Masse Mensch* with Georg Kaiser's...*Gas I*....In Kaiser's work the conflict is one of technology and organization; in Toller's it is a moral one. The problem in *Gas I* is whether we should give up industrialization or march along the road of technical progress "from explosion to explosion." Toller's work raises the incomparably deeper and more essential question of whether we may be permitted to sacrifice the ethical principle "thou shalt not kill" to a political goal.[4]

Masse Mensch is important to us here not because it is the most successful of Toller's plays from an artistic, popular and intellectual standpoint, nor because in it we feel that Toller has advanced considerably toward a more realistic and less naive estimation of the problematic nature of revolutionary activities, nor for its stylistic and structural virtues. It is important because it exemplifies the ideological terms in which Toller saw the dilemma of the revolutionary. This dilemma is not restricted to the problem of the justification of violence in the service of revolution, as many critics have claimed, though that is of course the palapable center around which everything else crystallizes. Toller wishes to show not only that the Jesuit apothegm, "the end justifies the means," is unacceptable, but *why* it is unacceptable—the means transform the ends, and thus render *post hoc* distinctions between ends useless. In consequence, the struggle in *Masse Mensch* is not simply one between two socialists who advocate different means to achieve the same result, as he has often been asserted, but one between two fundamentally different philosophies.

It is important to realize that the points at issue go beyond the recognition of the primacy of the individual over dogma (though this in itself is central to the distinction between anarchism and socialism), and also go beyond the struggle between the neo-Kantian ethics and "humanistic socialism" of a Lassalle (or, later, of men like Kurt Eisner or Erich Fromm and the Frankfurt School) and the disciplined authoritarianism of Marx and Engels. The Woman's not fully articulated ideology represents more than simply "humanistic socialism" of the sort which demands that one man never be used as a tool of another, but is willing to compromise with the capitalist state and system of production, as Lassalle was.

Both the Woman and the Nameless One are bitter antagonists of the capitalistic system; *both* wish to destroy it entirely, for they realize that a change in the economic structure of a highly complex organism necessitates a change in all its other aspects as well. But each is also bitterly antagonistic to the other. In order to define the distinctions between their philosophies we must examine the text carefully in order to trace these philosophies as they develop, for *Masse Mensch* is nothing if not a "station-drama" in the manner of Strindberg's *To Damascus*, a series of scenes tied together by the progress of the main character that is based on the passion of Christ. The Woman's philosophy does not spring complete and inviolate from her head, but like Toller's grows out of experience and is constantly measured against reality. Her antagonist does not necessarily represent the incarnation of all evil; he is not a totally unscrupulous and insincere nihilist, but the (albeit ruthless) proponent of a rival revolutionary theory that must be taken seriously. In this sense, Toller does not make the Woman's problem an easy one, and we must assume that the Nameless One is sincere when he argues:

> The cause above all!
> I love those yet to come!
> ....
> Whoever wavers, whoever is indecisive,
> Is aiding the masters
> Who starve us,
> Is our foe[5]

Unlike Ure and the members of the House of Lords in *Die Maschinenstürmer*, the Nameless One's arguments are not merely self-serving justifications, and they confront the Woman with a problem with which she must come to terms: "Can my ideals be realized without using means that taint them?"

Masse Mensch presents this problem in its most dramatic form, and for this reason the Communist criticism of this play is particularly instructive. To anticipate, however, the Woman's and Toller's answer will be *no*. A person whose principle is: "The person who acts may sacrifice only himself,"[6] very nearly condemns himself to inactivity and at best to ineffectualness. In *Masse Mensch* the final scene indicates that although the Woman herself, Moses-like, will not achieve her ideals, perhaps her "progeny," the two fellow prisoners, will be transformed by her example into the "new men" that anarchism demands. In *Hinkemann* and even more drastically in *Hoppla, wir leben!* this slim hope is abandoned. In *Eine Jugend in Deutschland* Toller deals with this problem at length and takes the occasion to refer to Max Weber (whom he had met at the seminars arranged by the publisher Eugen Diederichs at Burg Lauenstein):

> I had failed. I had always believed the socialists, despising force, should never resort to it. And now I myself had used force and appealed to force: I who hated bloodshed had caused blood to be shed. But when in Stadelheim an opportunity for escape had presented itself, I had refused to take advantage of the plan lest my flight should cost a warder his life. What fate awaits the man, I ask myself, who tries to influence the course of the world, that is, who becomes politically active, when he tries to realize the moral precepts he recognizes as just in his struggle with the masses? Was Max Weber right after all when he said that the only logical way of life for those who were determined never to overcome evil by force was the way of St. Francis, that corresponding to the most demanding standards there is only the most demanding path—that of the saint? Must the man of action always incur guilt? Always? Or, if he is unwilling to incur guilt, perish? The masses, it seems, are impelled by hunger and want rather than ideals. Would they still be able to conquer if they renounced force for the sake of an ideal? Is man not an individual and mass-man at one and the same time? Is not the struggle between the individual and the mass decided in a man's own mind as well as being fought out in the social sphere? As an individual a man will strive for his own ideals, even at the expense of the rest of the world. As a mass-man he is driven by social impulses; he strives to attain his goal even if his ideals have to be abandoned. This contradiction seems to me insoluble, because I have come up against it in my own life, and I seek in vain to resolve it.[7]

These are the words of an idealist, but they are also those of a realist, and

79

those who, like Paul Frölich writing in *Pravda*[8] or Martin Reso writing in *Weimarer Beiträge*,[9] reproach Toller for misguided and fuzzy-minded idealism are knocking down a straw man. The poet who in his second play had decided: "This contradiction seems to me insoluble," and had chosen inaction rather than guilt in the events of 1919 can be attacked for his choice but not for his naiveté. Toller's realism is evident in a letter to "F.P.," which, however is no more acceptable to the Marxists on that account, expressing as it does "revisionist" ideas:

> We must finally abandon the bromide that world-capitalism has been shattered by the war. Who could maintain today that in England, for instance, one could justifiably speak of a capitalist crisis?
>
> In particular countries capitalism is shaken; world capitalism is developing to a more concentrated, an internationally stricter form of organization. Whoever fights for socialism must take the long view.[10]

About Toller's relationship to revisionism and Eduard Bernstein we shall have more to say in our discussion of *Hoppla, wir leben!*.

We have seen in Chapter 5 that *Die Wandlung* is important for our theme in that it provides a metaphor for the change necessary to introduce a just and non-coercive society. Nothing less than a total transformation of man's very nature will suffice. Moreover, this transformation must be achieved by the whole of society simultaneously. It will not do to say, as Georg Kaiser does: "...the deepest truth is not proclaimed by you and thousands like you—it's found always by an individual. But then it is so monstrous that it proves totally ineffectual."[11] Halfway measures, reforms such as parliamentary government which merely serve to palliate and narcotize but are in reality tools of a basically exploitative system must be rejected—the *Reichstag* is the figleaf of absolutism, as Wilhelm Liebknecht once put it.[12] This demand for total regeneration of man as a precondition for regeneration of society is, as we have seen, basically anarchist in nature, for it involves a non-dialectical, non-materialistic spiritual process, a quantum jump, a leap from the realm of necessity to that of freedom, quite unlike any sort of socialist projection involving dictatorship of the proletariat as an intermediary stage. The state and all that goes with it must be destroyed, and destroyed at once—not simply replaced by a different state.

Masse Mensch takes this metaphor and tries to give it specific content by showing how men can be brought to such a transformation in a particular instance—a corrupt capitalist society at the end of a disastrous war. Toller shows what must happen when the individual, once transformed like Friedrich in *Die Wandlung*, tries to interact with and lead his fellows to the insight which he as an individual has achieved. The masses must be shown the characteristics of the new man, and this is accomplished negatively, by showing what he is not. The Woman develops her picture of him by trying to steer a course between the Scylla of the capitalist society and the Charybdis of what the anarchists thought of as authoritarian socialism.

Her tragedy (and that of what she represents) results from the fact that there is no such middle course and not from the dramatically interesting but ideologically superfluous fact that she for a moment yields to the arguments of her adversary. For this lapse her personal ethic demands that she atone, and, in doing so, she demonstrates for us in a positive sense the demands the new man will make upon himself, the sense of brotherhood which will voluntarily link him to all other men within the framework of individual ethical autonomy. Paradoxically, the anarchist assertion of the primacy of the individual over party and dogma leads to true community and brotherhood, true service to the common good, *Gemeinschaft* (community) rather than *Gesellschaft* (society), to use Tönnies' terminology.[13] This model suffices in convert the two prisoners to the end and the Woman's husband as well. But whether the Woman's martyrdom does any good for the masses depends solely on a rather subjective decision of the poet to be either an optimist or a pessimist concerning the possibilities of messianism. Certainly past experience has not been encourging.

In *Die Maschinenstürmer* we shall see that Jimmy incurs no such guilt—he at no point assents to the use of force, even though the provocation of his adversaries (in this case a venal and thoroughly corrupt and selfish capitalist society rather than a rival theory of revolution) is possibly even greater than in the Woman's case. The basic conflict, and it is dramatic enough, is rooted in the imperative of the situation, and the resulting tragedy is that of a whole class rather than that of the individual. The revolutionary may remain pure, like Jimmy, and yet he will suffer the Woman's fate.

Whereas *Die Maschinenstürmer* is a play very largely concerned with the economic organization of society and with exploitation of workers, the conflict in *Masse Mensch* is concentrated in the political and ethical spheres. The nature of the Woman's political views becomes clear to us (and to her) in the several confrontations with her husband and with the Nameless One. The husband represents the exploitative, capitalist society and has absorbed its values into his very language:

THE HUSBAND: Consideration, unknown to you, is law for me—
THE WOMAN: Which stamps you and your kind to formulas!
THE HUSBAND: Which demands submission, self-discipline— [MM 12; II, 69]

The Woman represents the individualistic principle with respect to both of her adversaries. In resisting formulas, subordination, and submission to doctrine, she preserves her individuality and thus is the only character in the play who, for example, is named. Her momentary acquiescence in the blandishments of the Nameless One is anticipated in her inability to reject her husband, whom she follows at the end of the first scene even after learning he has betrayed her.

The play is about two kinds of community—the false and the true community. The Woman speaks of her comrades and their feeling for each other:

> *They* need no code of honour
> to be considerate
> If only you could understand them, feel the least hint
> of their need—
> Which is *our* need—must be!
> You have humiliated them;
> And, humiliated, defiled yourselves!
> You have become your own executioners...
> ....
> I am not neurotic,
> Not sentimental.
> And because I'm not, I belong to them. [MM 15; II, 70f]

The Woman describes the world her husband represents, and he in answering only succeeds in confirming her:

> THE WOMAN: Your State wages war,
> Your State betrays the people!
> Your State exploits, oppresses and represses,
> Deprives people of their rights.
> THE HUSBAND: State is sacred—war assures it life.
> Peace is phantom of neurotic cowards.
> War only interrupted truce,
> In which the State, threatened by external enemy
> Threatened by enemy within, endures. [MM17; II, 72]

With the Woman, Toller begins to develop the concept of folk, which is threatened and exploited by the state on the one hand and the mass on the other. The nature of the exploitation from the right is epitomized in the scene at the stock exchange, where the flagging enthusiasm for the war is to be revived through a system of state-run bordellos—Military Recreation Centers, Inc. This scene, which caused Toller and his producers so much trouble, is really the only one which directly demonstrates the depredations of the capitalist society.

The more seductive and more intractable threat to the Woman comes from the left, and thus from within, and it is to this that the rest of the play is devoted.

Toller first adumbrates the exploitation which results from the philosophy of men like the husband, in order to accentuate the acuteness of the Woman's dilemma and motivate her lapse:

THE MASSES: We, eternally wedged into
. Caverns of towering houses,
We, abandoned to the mechanism of mocking systems,
We, faceless in the night of tears,
We eternally severed from our mothers,
From the depths of the factories we call!
When will we live in love?
When will we work our will?
When will we be saved? [MM 30; II, 80]

To those made *faceless* by an exploitative system, and whom the Nameless One (the moral equivalence of the apparently so different opponents is emphasized in German too by similar appellations) wishes to subject to another for the sake of the future unborn millions, the Woman opposes her own solution. It is an anarchist one in the sense that it insists on the moral primacy of the individual, but at the same time insists on unselfishness and true community—"folk" rather than "mass." That these demands are exacting and will require a radical transformation within man, she does not deny; indeed she emphasizes the terrible momentum of the present system. But her solution is at once idealistic and realistic—idealistic in its metaphysical orientation, yet directed at this world and not the next (cf. Georg Kaiser's play entitled *Hell Way Earth* and not, as one might expect, *Hell Way Heaven*); realistic in its recognition that unless such a transformation can be achieved, mankind is headed for destruction. In *Quer Durch* Toller notes: "Our tragedy is different from the Christian tragedy of the Middle Ages, which portrayed want as the way to heavenly deliverance. We don't want heavenly deliverance."[14] Like Kropotkin and Malatesta, the Woman refrains from giving a detailed blueprint for her society, since such would be ideologically inconsistent with the anarchist ideal of a natural equilibrium resulting from an accommodation of various interests. She obviously does not envisage a naive return to nature, an attempt to turn back the clock and ignore the realities of the day:

It is a dream that blocks your vision,
A dream of children, frightened by the night.
For look! This is the twentieth century;
And know:

83

Factory can no longer be destroyed
Scatter the earth with dynamite,
Let a single night of action
Smash the factories,
By the next spring they would
Be resurrected,
And would rage more than ever.
But the factories must no
Longer rule,
And men no longer be
Used as tools.
Let factories be servants
Of a dignified life!
Let the soul of man
Vanquish the factory![MM 31; II, 81]

This is the Woman's vision, and her means of achieving it is the strike. When, however, the Nameless One appears for the first time to argue against striking and for revolution, it is important to realize that he is not merely proposing a different path to the same goal, but a different goal as well. The difference is fundamental and yet it is one that has often been neglected in the literature, which tends to reduce the issue to the justification for the use of force.

Where the Woman speaks of factories as "servants of a dignified life," the Nameless One demands: "The factories belong to the workers! Power to the workers!"[15] Where the Woman speaks of conscience: "Yet my conscience cries *no* to me!", The Nameless One replies:

Be silent, comrade,
For the sake of the cause!
The individual, his feelings, his conscience—
What do they count?
The Masses count![MM 38; II, 86]

—a theme which is taken up again in the fourth scene (*Traumbild*), where the revolutionaries are about to execute their prisoners. The Woman says to the guard:

THE WOMAN: It is *you* who is standing
Against the wall today. Man,
It is you—
SENTRY: Only the Masses count.

THE WOMAN:Only Man counts.
ALL THE SENTRIES: Only the Masses count.
THE WOMAN: I offer myself up
To mankind.
(Malicious laughter from the sentries.) [MM 48; II, 92]

For the Woman the White prisoner of today transforms himself, much like the young Russian soldier in Brechts's *Kalendergeschichte*, "Die zwei Söhne ("The Two Sons"), into the Red prisoner of yesterday, and she recognizes that her comrades, far from defending the revolution, are indulging in the pleasure of revenge. Significantly, it is at just this moment that she withdraws her assent to the use of force in the service of the revolution. Toller, himself, of course had confronted this issue before Dachau in 1919 and again on the occasion of the notorious murder of the hostages in the Luitpold Gymnasium in Munich.

The fifth scene appears to turn largely on the justification for the use of force, and yet here, too, the larger issue appears implicitly, for it becomes clear to the Woman that not only is the use of force always "reactionary," but also that the society envisaged by the Nameless One will be very bit as soulless and authoritarian as the one they are both attempting to destroy:

THE NAMELESS ONE: You avenged your brothers.
The Masses are vengeance for the injustice
of centuries.
The Masses are vengeance!
THE WORKMEN: Vengeance!
THE WOMAN: Stop! You are deranged by battle!
I stay your arm.
The masses should be people bound together
By love.
Masses should be community.
Community is not revenge.
Community destroys the foundation of
inequity.
Community plants the forests of justice.
Humanity that takes revenge,
Smashes itself.
. . . .
This deed is not self-defense,
But blind rage! Not service to the cause.
You are killing people
Are you killing with them

85

The spirit of the state
You are opposing?
I'm protecting the ones outside.
I was ready
To silence my conscience
For the sake of the masses,
I call:
Smash the system!
But you want to smash people.
....
Men, brothers,
I bring humility ....
Smash the foundations of injustice,
Smash the chains of disguised servitude,
Shatter the weapons of rotten centuries![MM 54ff.; II, 95ff.]

She recognizes that a system which is born in force and can maintain itself only by appealing to the base instincts in man is of a piece with the exploitative system it replaces, except that it is a less overt exploitation, a "disguised servitude." The Nameless One argues in essence that two wrongs make a right, and he is able to rouse the mob against the Woman by branding her as a bourgeoise, a middle-class intellectual, thus using a tactic employed by Wible against Jimmy Cobbett in Toller's *Die Maschinenstürmer*, by the engineer against the billionaire-son in Kaiser's *Gas*, by the KPD against Toller himself:

THE NAMELESS ONE: You shield those who grew up with you.
That is your deeper motive:
You traitor!
THE MASSES IN THE HALL: Traitor!
SHOUT: The intellectual! [MM 56f.; II, 97]

In *Quer Durch*, Toller tells how Paul Frölich, writing under the pseudonym of Paul Werner in *Pravda*, attacked him as a counter-revolutionary, a bourgeois intellectual unwilling to use the requisite force in the struggle for Dachau during 1919, a traitor who had come to an accommodation with the Whites. Toller writes:

I want to outline here in a few sentences my position on force. No political revolution can do without force....I believe that the socialist revolutionary never uses force for its own sake. He hates it, he loathes it, and if he uses it, he feels it as a horrible, tragic necessary means....People today believe, especially in Germany, that it is "manly," "revolutionary," "völkisch," to defend brutality and to glorify collective crimes.[16]

This, as we seen, is also the position of Martin Buber. Toller goes on to criticize Frölich's presumption that defeat will increase the misery of the masses, thus radicalizing them and hastening the advent of the dictatorship of the proletariat:

I maintained the position that the defeat that others considered necessary for the forward impulse of the revolution would have just the opposite effect in our situation—that the defeat-theory grows out of revolutionary romanticism, and not revolutionary realism.[17]

One recalls the words of John Wible in *Die Maschinenstürmer*. "We *need* defeats."[18] And in *Masse Mensch*, the Nameless One attacks the Woman as Toller was attacked:

Each one of us bears the sickness of his origin,
You, the birth-marks of the bourgeoisie:
Self-deception and weakness,

....

You lack the courage
To take upon yourself
The act—the hard act. [MM 76ff.; II, 109]

Toller notes in *Quer Durch* of the controversy with Frölich:

I spoke later to Radek about the affair. "You mustn't take these things too seriously with us. It's easier to come by the epithet 'counter-revolutionary' than it is for a whore to come by a lover."[19]

And in *Briefe aus Dem Gefängnis* he writes: "Individuals rarely grow wise through suffering; usually they grow stupid. And through suffering, nations learn to kill their wise men."[20] The theme is all the more important because it symbolizes for Toller not just the bitter disappointment of his inability to reach the hearts of the workers, but because, more fundamentally, it shows the unlikelihood of the transformation necessary to inaugurate the new man, the fact that the ballast of centuries prevents men from recognizing truth when they are confronted with it. What Jimmy and Toller are preaching is precisely the destruction of barriers between men, and the foundation of the classless society of true *community*. What they are forced to recognize is that their adversaries, the Communists, while theoretically advocating the classless society, are willing to exploit prejudices for their own less noble ends quite at variance with their theory (as indeed they did in sabotaging the first Council

Republic in 1919, and later, the republican forces in the Spanish Civil War).

This unwillingness to accept the middle-class intellectual as a true revolutionary, to admit that he might have undivided loyalties, is an issue which transcends the question of the use of force and one which reveals the unbridgeable gap between the two opponents not only in means, but also in ends. Moreover, it is not an issue which has died with the revolution itself. The East German scholar, Martin Reso, for example, writes in 1959: "That the actual problem eluded Toller, and that he treats (instead) primarily the relationship of the intellectual to the revolutionary masses should be mentioned at the outset."[21] The argument is symptomatic of the weakness of Reso's unsatisfactory analysis of *Masse Mensch*, for Reso tries in his paper to show the tragic aspects which inexorably must result from the Woman's philosophy, while at the same time ignoring the problematic aspects of the Nameless One's. The figure that Toller so obviously meant to be a demagogue appears instead as a realist.

Lenin, too, supports the same line of attack: "Whoever attempts to solve the problems of the transition from capitalism to socialism by proceeding from vague clichés about equality, freedom and democracy itself...thereby simply reveals his character as a petty bourgeois, philistine, a clod who slavishly trots along in the footsteps of the bourgeoisie, ideologically speaking."[22]

In his article, "Parteiorganization und Parteiliteratur" ("Party Organization and Partisan Literature"), Lenin specifically denounces "parlor anarchists" such as Toller:

Literature must become party literature. Unlike bourgeois morals, unlike the bourgeois merchant and shopkeeper press, unlike bourgeois literary efforts and individualism, "parlor anarchism,"...the socialist proletariat must assert the principle of party literature, develop this principle and as completely as possible put it into practice. In what does this principle of party literature consist?...literature cannot be an individual matter, which is independent of general proletarian concerns....Literature must become one component of organized, well-planned, unified social-democratic party activity.[23]

It need not be emphasized how far this is from the conception of the Woman and of Toller, who wrote in *Quer Durch*: "Political poetry is only indirectly connected with the daily feature articles of the party [press], with tactical slogans; it is formed by the demands of the idea."[24] Reso remarks with evident disapproval: "Here again, as elsewhere, the denial of the party and the primacy of the idea is proclaimed."[25] Reso also quotes a passage from one of Toller's *Briefe aus dem Gefängnis* to support Lenin's thesis, in the belief that Toller's wrongheadedness will be apparent to all: "People talk a lot about proletarian art these days. It is necessary for us, but it cannot be fabricated on the basis of manifestos. To give shape to the eternal human problems—only that can be the content of proletarian art. It is not the task of proletarian art to toss some partisan resolution or other to the masses; let agitators do that....In the final analysis, even the proletarian writer cannot ignore the tragedy of human existence, which manifests itself in the worker just as it does in the bourgeois."[26]

In all of this, what we have is not so much a falsification, or even a distortion of Toller's view, but rather "transvaluation of all values," a redefinition of morality. Distortion, in fact, would be nearly impossible in a play in which the battle lines are so clearly drawn. In a play so full of *Schrei und Bekenntnis*, sound and fury, the significance and even the truth of the Woman's famous words are hard to mistake:

THE WOMAN: You murder for mankind,
As they, deluded, murdered for their State.
Some even thought
That through their State, their fatherland,
They might redeem the earth.
I see no difference.
Some murder for one country,
And others for all countries.
Some kill for the sake of a thousand men,
Others for millions.
Whoever murders for the State,
Him you call a hangman.
But he who kills for humanity,
Him you enwreathe,
You call him good, moral, noble, great,
Indeed you speak of good, of holy might.
....
It's a strange promised land you're taking us to,
It's the same old land of the enslavement of
mankind. [MM 75-76: II, 108-109]

The enslavement of the one kind of community, the party, is quite different from the kind of anarchistic community the Woman seeks. When the Nameless One argues that rejection of force condemns the revolutionary to inactivity, the Woman replies that more than political revolution is needed—the metaphysical transformation of man:

THE WOMAN: The deed! And more than the deed!

Set free in the Masses their humanity,
Set free in the Masses their community. [MM 74; II, 107f.]

When the Nameless One asserts that where the woman sacrifices unborn generations to the present, he is fighting for the welfare of untold millions whom he loves, the woman explicitly rejects this:

THE WOMAN: No, you do not love people!
....
Whoever calls for blood of men,
Is Moloch.
So God was Moloch.
The State Moloch,
And the Masses—
Moloch.
THE NAMELESS ONE: Then who is holy?
THE WOMAN: One day—
Community—
Free people, working together.
Mankind, freed, working together.
A people of workers.
[MM 76ff.; II, 109f.]

This anarchistic vision, this rejection of the tyranny of the church, of the capitalist state, of the communist "mass" is admitted by Reso, but with something of the air of having uncovered some despicable, heinous offense: "Toller didn't count himself among the anarchists, even though he felt akin to them and subconsciously championed anarchistic ideas....An especial influence of him was Landauer's book, *Call to Socialism.*"[27] Reso quotes from Toller's letter to Landauer:

What I do, I do not simply out of necessity; not simply out of the suffering of brutal daily life, not simply out of a revulsion at the political and social order—these are all reasons, but not the only ones. I struggle (I can say it today, because I feel it is a blessing) because of a vital plenitude....I want to interpenetrate all that lives, in no matter what form it reveals itself. I want to sow it with love, but I also want to smash the ossified, if need be, for the sake of the creative spirit....I do not want someone simply to accept our insights and join us on that account. An insight (as I understand it) must be attained through necessity, suffering provoked by its very fullness, one must have felt one's self "uprooted," must have played with life and danced with death, must have suffered for the sake of the intellect and have overcome it through the creative spirit—one must have wrestled with man.

I do not dream of a sect of a community of creative souls, for everyone contains the creative within himself; the creative spirit can manifest itself in its purest expression only in the work of the individual—however, the feeling of community is a blessing and a source of strength for every creator.[28]

Reso comments: "His words reveal the confusion and ambivalence of his ideas. They make crystal clear the degree of 'maturity' of this man...."[29]

We see here the degree to which Toller's vision goes beyond the economic and dialectic materialism of socialism and approaches the metaphysical. The "spirit" which is here invoked, however, the idealism, is closely bound to this world, to the here and how. This letter indicates, as Paul Edward Wyler suggests in his dissertation, the metaphysical content common to most Expressionist calls for the "new man"—a metaphysics which in very many cases, following a kind of inner law, evolves into a kind of anarchism. Adolf D. Klarmann quotes, for example, from Franz Werfel's *Schlußwort von der christlichen Sendung* (*Summary of the Christian Mission*) in his essay, "Der expressionistische Dichter und die politische Sendung" ("The Expressionist Writer and the Political Mission"):

Our debate [with Kurt Hiller] is the fruit of a differing apprehension of life that drove me a year ago in a critique of activism to declare my adherence to anarchism. I was born in a city [Prague] which, since it was inhabited by Slavs and Jews, has always been a gateway to the East. The accident of our birth is certainly not pure chance, even if a deranged internationalism that is born of the same capitalist irreality dares to claim this....The paradise of laws is a *civitas dei*. Even in your definition the state is something altogether negative. You define the state as the control of the perturbations in communal life produced by elemental instincts. The pessimism of this view is obvious. It denies the messianic potentiality of a community of mankind, united through insight and love. Why do you too preach the state to the German people—the Germans, who would require a magician to free them from the delusion that one can control every aspect of life, that nature can be shaped like some snowball. Germany, the land of millions of organizations, has a great deal of activity but what it lacks is the decisiveness, the devotion, the willingness for self-sacrifice that will make its tormentors pay for a life that has been profaned and disfigured beyond all recognition.[30]

Toller's program amounts in fact to anarchism, both in the political principle of the primacy of the individual it chooses to consider essential and "non-negotiable," and in the economic organization of the society it looks forward to. He writes, for example: "What else could I tell you? That I believe that above all else we must combat war, poverty, and the state (which in the final analysis knows nothing but force and not justice)...and put in its place community, bound together in an economic sense by the peaceful exchange of the products of one's labor for others of equal value, the community of free men which is permeated by creative spirit."[31]

When, therefore, Communist critics of the play reproach Toller for taking the side of the intellectual against that of the masses, they totally misunderstand Toller's argument that truth and humanity are universals, indeed that the true community can exist *only* when it is based on these universals and ignores class distinctions. The extent of this "transvaluation" is, for example, quite clear in Reso's denigrating remark that when Toller wrote *Eine Jugend in Deutschland*, "...he still wrote from the point of view of all-embracing love and 'humanity.'"[32]

When Toller is reproached for ignoring the role of the party as advance guard and defender of the revolution, when the Woman is reproached for placing the masses on the same level with the two concepts she has devoted her life to opposing,[33] the State and God, what Reso actually is doing is pretending that Toller is naive, unclear and confused, whereas he in fact knew very well what the choice was and what its consequences would be. Reso simply prefers to subscribe to the arguments of the Nameless One while trying to disguise this fact by appealing to dialectic on the one hand and Toller's alleged ideological insufficiency on the other. He said, for example: "The separation of individual and mass, of moral ideal and social motivation, introduces vague elements into the whole. The insolubility of the contradiction from which Toller proceeds exists only for the man who reasons idealistically. The Marxist, since he regards the moral ideal and the social situation as mutually independent factors, can do justice to both that which is selfish and that which is altruistic."[34] One is tempted to ask "how." In fact, it is the Marxist and not the anarchist who is solving the problem by self-deception. The problem can only be conjured out of existence in the mind of the man who is capable of postulating an inexorable dialectic movement of history, "the terrible fatalism of history," as the playwright Georg Büchner put it, the inexorability and the fortuitious "correctness" of which exculpate man from any responsibility. The Woman has attempted a similar self-deception in her notion of the malevolent God, who forces man to incur guilt, a concept which will recur in *Die Maschinenstürmer*. But like the lapse in her *behavior*, this *moral* lapse is only momentary, and in the end she is simultaneously guilty and guiltless, accepts her guilt and atones for it with her death. A revolutionary who, like Friedrich in *Die Wandlung*, rejects religious determinism and a church capable of excusing war cannot then invoke it to excuse ''necessary'' bloodshed committed in the service of a more noble cause.

This sort of reproach is not peculiar to Reso, but is characteristic of Communist criticism in general. Alfred Klein, in a sensitive discussion of *Masse Mensch*, says in nearly identical language: ''So long as no moral force is perceived in the mass movement toward socialism, a force that derives its justification from the course of history itself, the claims of [the movement] must, to be sure, appear as comprehensible, but not as necessary. The awareness of guilt is unavoidable for the dabbler in revolution [limited by] bourgeois horizons.''[35]

Interestingly enough, Reso is considerably more positive in his dissertation than in his later article of 1959. He writes: ''Toller emphasized many times that he has never been concerned with questions of party politics. One does him an injustice, therefore, when one reads such a concern into his work.''[36] While Reso's arguments lean clearly toward those of the Nameless One in the later article, in the dissertation he is able to conform to Toller's obvious intentions by seeing the Nameless One in a more negative light. The rather damning criticism of Marxism that one would expect this to involve is avoided by the ideological sleight-of-hand of redefining the position of the Nameless One as anarchism! Reso writes: ''In the name of the masses he is even ready to destroy the masses. His views represent an anarchism that proclaims destruction, even to the point of self-destruction.''[37] Yet it is grotesque to call ''anarchist'' a philosophy which tells the Woman:

> Be silent, comrade,
> For the sake of the cause!
> The individual, his feelings, his conscience—
> What do they count?
> The Masses count! [MM 38; II, 86]

This kind of redefinition occurs again and again in Toller criticism; it is particularly striking in the following passage from the Marxist paper, *Die Linkskurve*. Toller had protested the paper's implication that during a trip to America he had distanced himself from his previous revolutionary views by saying that the quotations attributed to him were false. *Linkskurve* replied:

> The quotations ''attributed'' to Toller were not ''made up out of whole cloth''; on the contrary they were taken from the American press and accepted by us at their face value, since they were in our opinion well concocted—i.e. they fit Toller like a glove [auf Toller zugeschnitten].

The [objections] raised against us do not alter our opinion of Toller in the least. The main thing is that, judging by his past, we consider him capable of everything the American liar ascribed to him.[38]

Of the two chief objections of Marxist critics, the Woman's false values and wrong choice owing to her bourgeois and intellectual origins, and her and Toller's naiveté, Western criticism has adopted the latter. Almost without exception, *Masse Mensch* is criticized because the kind of anarchist solution it proposed won't work within the "real" (e.g. present day) world. This perhaps is true, but it is in a sense irrelevant, for Toller was not so foolish as to assert that it would.

Indeed, and we shall see this again and again (i.e. in *Hoppla, wir leben!*), perhaps the chief merit of Toller's work is that it shows us the nature of the terrible choice which confronts the revolutionary. For this task, the abstraction of the Expressionist form proved to be admirably suited, and for this reason Toller and the Expressionists of his philosophical persuasion forebore from postulating specific blueprints which would only distract from "the spiritual in art," as Kandinsky put it in his famous book of 1912. The English anarchist Herbert Read remarks in his *Poetry and Anarchism: The Philosophy of Anarchism* (London: 1940): "I am not concerned with the practicability of a programme. I am only concerned to establish truth" (p. 17).

Walter Sokel emphasizes this in his article on Toller.[39] He points out the dialectic structure (in this he resembles Jost Hermand), in which, for example, the Nameless One's accusation: "Your activity is high treason!" represents a thesis which is countered by the Woman's antithesis: "Your state wages war," a rejoinder that raises the argument from a political to an economic level (in that it hints at economic causes of the war). This in retrospect alters the interpretation of the thesis by calling into question the concept of state and thereby implies a synthesis. Betrayal of a state which can only exist by the economic mutilations of man and society engendered by war, far from being reprehensible, is a necessity. Thus Toller combines Georg Kaiser's notion of "thought-play" (a notion akin to Einstein's "thought experiments") with Strindberg's "dream-play."

According to Sokel, the dialectical, the rhetorical and the abstract combine in a highly effective and powerful work:

Toller's Expressionistic dramas have often been reproached for this language which, poor in metaphor, manipulates abstract concepts. It runs the risk, of course, of sounding rhetorical, propagandistic, dry and bombastic. But one ought not to underestimate Toller's dramatic power, which fills these abstract definitions with ecstatic rhythm and propels them forward. An ethos that is brought to a fever pitch in the best parts of *Masse Mensch* transforms abstract rhetoric into true poetry.[40]

Katharina Maloof's interesting dissertation[41] typifies both the strengths and weaknesses of Western criticism. Maloof does not feel constrained to perform the kind of mental gymnastics required of Reso and even Alfred Klein; still less does she resort to the basic dishonesty exemplified by the passage quoted from *Die Linkskurve*. Nevertheless, at the end of a fine textual analysis of the play, she makes a number of criticisms which appear to judge it by irrelevant standards, and finds Toller wanting for not achieving what he in fact never set out to do. It is instructive to deal with these criticisms individually.

Maloof, recognizing like Sokel the importance of the rhetorical in the play, compares it unfavorably with Schiller's *Maria Stuart*. Except that each play deals with the conflict between political expediency and certain ethical standards of the heroine at variance with this expediency, the differences between the two plays seem to me to outweigh their similarities. The conflict between power and justice, politics and morality is of course far more complex for Elizabeth and Mary than for the Woman, but no more painful on that account. In *Maria Stuart* private motives of jealousy reinforce the demands of reasons of state, whereas the Woman suffers from no such ambivalence. Naturally, this ambivalence lends Schiller's play added dimensions. But to draw from this the conclusion: "Toller on the other hand, is not able to portray such a characteristically multi-faceted figure as the Queen"[42] seems to me in the first place unjustified and in the second place a mistaken application of criteria suitable for classical drama to an Expressionist play. Maloof makes the same sort of criticism of the characterization of the Nameless One: "If we compare the Nameless One with her [Maria Stuart], then we have to admit that the Nameless One is drawn as an extreme, lacking in all humanity. Toller can only think in extremes; he cannot represent the ordinary man."[43] Quite apart from the fact that there are plenty of compromisers in others of Toller's plays such as *Pastor Hall, Hoppla, wir leben!, Nie wieder Friede (No More Peace)*, this reproach is misdirected at a play about which Toller said: "The sensual fullness of the experiences was so strong that I could only control them through abstraction, through dramatic highlighting of those features that determine the basic issues."[44] And we have already noted that this abstraction, important as it is in its function of reducing the issues to the essential and eliminating topical distractions, is not absolute. It has, for example, been pointed out that even the Nameless One's position, brutal as it is, is depicted as one which the humane revolutionary must take seriously and come to terms with, and not simply reject out of hand.

Maloof concludes: "From these comparisons we see that the idealist Toller

95

cannot solve the real problem of political activity in his *Masse Mensch.* He sees the problem only in the constrasting of power and pacifism, i.e. only in black and white extremes....But can't the [politically active] man be drawn as a practical politican who possesses enough courage to act, but also the courage to accept the consequences of his deeds? Just how does Toller, the idealist, conceive of the solution of the political problem?''[45]

The fact that certain problems have no solutions may be hard to accept. Yet it is this very fact that Toller is intent on impressing on us in *Masse Mensch*: "This contradiction is still insoluble for politicians today, and it was this very insolubility that I wanted to show."[46] And in *Briefe aus dem Gefängnis*, Toller writes:

> The ethical man: exclusively satisfies the law of his being. The political man: fights for rules of society which can serve others as the foundation of a higher form of life. Fights even when to fight is opposed to the law of his being. If the ethical man becomes the political man, what tragic path is spared him?[47]

It was certainly not beyond Toller's capabilities to portray pragmatic politicians, and he has done so in Kilman and even in Albert Kroll in *Hoppa, wir leben!* and at the same time has shown us in vividly explicit terms how little of the mission of Friedrich remains in such temporizers. But that was not his task in *Masse Mensch*. He has presented us with extremes because that is the way the problem presents itself to the revolutionary. If one cannot be 37 percent pregnant, neither can one accept the philosophy and methods of the Nameless One and still retain one's innocence.

7

Die Maschinenstürmer: Anarchism and Social Darwinism

He who despairs over an event is a coward, but he who holds hope for the human condition is a fool. —Albert Camus: *The Rebel*, Ch. I

Die Maschinenstürmer (The Machine Wreckers, 1922) is set in Nottingham at the dawn of the industrial revolution. The play begins with a prologue which provides a "cosmic framework" for the action to follow and introduces the spectator to the misery and suffering of the weavers by the indirect expedient of presenting a debate in the House of Lords. Lord Castlereagh argues for a bill restricting the rights of workers to organize themselves and providing the death penalty for weavers convicted of wrecking weaving machinery. He is opposed by Lord Byron, who argues that the workers have no legal alternatives, and who opposes the notion that poverty and exploitation are simply manifestations of a natural law.

The play proper opens as Jimmy Cobbett returns to his native city. He is telling a fairy tale to a group of starving, wretched children when he is interrupted by a band of striking workers who are hanging strikebreakers in effigy. The workers' leader is John Wible. Jimmy sees immediately that the workers lack a far-sighted leader in their struggle against exploitation and the threat to their jobs posed by the new mechanical looms. In gaining the trust of the workers, however, Jimmy alienates John Wible, who conspires with Ure, the factory owner, and Henry Cobbett, the factory foreman, who is Jimmy's brother; the three plan to provoke the workers to violence and use that to suppress the workers' movement and to eliminate Jimmy.

Jimmy however preaches non-violence and patience to the workers, pointing out to them that the weaving machinery is there to stay. He urges Ure to re-hire the workers he has fired. But in the meantime, Wible, jealous of Jimmy, incites the workers to smash the machinery, thereby providing Ure with an excuse to suppress the revolt with the utmost brutality. Wible succeeds in convincing the workers that Jimmy, brother of the parvenu and unscrupulous opportunist, Henry Cobbett, is guilty by association and therefore a tool of Ure. When Jimmy appears during the ecstatic climax of the workers' destructiveness, he is attacked and killed by his fellow workingmen. Wible flees and the revolt is suppressed.

It has been claimed[1] that, from an ideological point of view, Die Maschinenstürmer adds very little to the problems which are the focus of Masse Mensch. In a sense, this is true. Both plays involve enlightened leaders, redeemer-figures, who point the way to a new society. This new society is recognizably the same in both plays and is compared to two extreme alternatives, both of which are rejected by the author but not by the masses. The extremes are incorporated in two figures in each play who compete for the favor of the masses. The problem of violence is central to both plays. And finally, each play ends with the apparent defeat of the redeemer and what he stands for, but also with the ambivalent indication that this defeat may not prove final, that his example may eventually inspire future generations to follow him.

But there are also important differences between the plays. Whereas in Masse Mensch the Woman compromises herself and then must atone for this failing, Jimmy in Die Maschinenstürmer remains throughout the pure revolutionary whose fate appears on that account all the more inexorable and existentially necessary, and thus tragic. Jimmy's martyrdom is for this reason even more impressive than the Woman's, and we shall see that it too has its effect on his comrades. And yet, whereas in Masse Mensch we feel perhaps a definite though realistically skeptical hope for future regeneration, in Die Maschinenstürmer that hope is very much attenuated. For if Ned Lud is brought by Jimmy's death to be tending toward Georg Kaiser's view of the essentially private nature of to be tending toward George Kaiser's view of the essentially private nature of regeneration: the messianic pre-war drama Die Bürger von Calais (The Burghers of Calais, 1914) has given way to the mordant cynicism of Gas II (1920). Friedrich and the multitudes of Die Wandlung have given way to Jimmy Cobbett and to the Woman. There the agitator is defeated easily by Friedrich's eloquence; here his counterpart is victorious.

Conversely, the Nameless One in Masse Mensch is the pure authoritarian revolutionary, who exists only to the extent that he embodies a particular ideological position antagonistic to the Woman's, and who has no other, personal, motives for opposing her. John Wible on the other hand is a humanly interesting and highly complex character in a psychological sense. It is obvious that Toller took some pains to develop his personality and motivations. He is in fact proof that Toller is capable of transcending mere black-and-white characterization.

98

In the final scene, where Jimmy is killed, Ned discovers that he, Brutus-like, has been encouraged by Wible to strike the first blow while Wible is careful to keep his own hands clean:

JOHN WIBLE: Do something, you cowards! Tear his tongue from his mouth, his eyes from their sockets!

....

NED LUD: John, why didn't you hit him?

JOHN WIBLE: I struck the first and last blows behind his neck.

NED LUD: You're lying.

....

JOHN WIBLE: His eyes! Did you do it?

NED LUD: You weren't even looking!

JOHN WIBLE: I--I-----

NED LUD: Ah, now I understand! You cowardly punk! (Ned Lud takes John Wible by the collar and drags him to the corpse).

JOHN WIBLE: I--can't stand the sight of blood--oh--oh------oh.[2]

Wible's cowardice is certainly at work here, and we have had occasion to see it also in the scene where Wible forces Lud to hide the strike funds instead of doing it himself, an act explicitly forbidden by the bill debated in the prologue. Yet in spite of his weakness and even base rancor, one does not feel that Wible sets out with the purpose of doing evil. The Wible of this final scene is to some extent counterbalanced by the Wible of II, 2, who replies when his son remarks:

TEDDY: Father, there's a molehill in the yard. Shall we catch the mole?

JOHN WIBLE: Let the little fellow live.

[MS 34; II, 137]

Egoism is at the focus of his character, and ultimately motivates both his longing for luxury and a better life for himself at the expense of both his comrades and his wife (who is in consequence reduced to prostitution), and his more significant betrayal of Jimmy, and thus of the future. His injured self-esteem, his longing for power, are distilled into an urge for revenge at all costs when he sees himself replaced by Jimmy as leader of the workers. Wible's commitment to his fellows proves weaker than his egoism. This fact is interesting because it shows Toller's insight, gained during his years in prison, into the pettiness and selfishness of his fellow revolutionaries. It vividly brings home to us the inertia against which the new order must fight. But most important, it underscores how drastic a transformation is necessary to bring about the birth of the "new man," a kind of *coincidentia oppositorum*, for he must be at once an individual who retains his moral freedom and a communal being who voluntarily submits his will to the service of the community.

Soergel and Marnette[3] have emphasized the ideological affinities between *Masse Mensch* and *Die Maschinenstürmer*. On the other hand, Dorothea Klein and Walter Sokel[4] emphasize the elements in it that point forward to *Hinkemann*. Klein writes: "In Toller's dramatic development, this play is rather a transitional form between the conceptually abstract mode of representation characteristic of *Die Wandlung* and *Masse Mensch* and the more complex characterization of *Hinkemann*, which proceeds from the sensual."[5]

We can see why if we recognize that the philosophy that Jimmy represents is anarchist in nature. It is evident that anarchism is essentially political (or more precisely, anti-political) rather than economic in its orientation. It attempts to maintain the sanctity of the concept of individual freedom, a concept common to Godwin, to Proudhon (with his notion of "respect"), to Bakunin, and to Kropotkin. It does so by allowing only those non-coercive economic systems compatible with the notion of freedom of the individual. Now in *Die Maschinenstürmer* Toller emphasizes for the first time not the metaphysical nature of the transformation in the redeemer himself, the "epiphany" of *Die Wandlung*, not the philosophical context, the crystal-hard choice that the redeemer must make, as in *Masse Mensch*, but instead the economic reality which forms the background of his choice. We are shown the pernicious effects of international competition, of the introduction of machinery, of strike-breakers, of economic exploitation and dislocations of all kinds, very much as Gerhart Hauptmann portrayed the same kind of impoverishment (to use Marx's term) in *Die Weber*, set nearly thirty years later. To do so, it was necessary for Toller to abandon the abstract austerity of *Masse Mensch* in favor of a more traditional five-act tragedy with a large cast of characters who are named, and behind whose names more or less fully developed personalities stand.

This psychological depth is developed to a surprisingly high and sometimes rather subtle degree. I have already referred to Wible's ambivalence, weakness and egoism. That his treachery is not totally self-serving is evident from the following remarks he makes after he agrees to betray his rival:

URE: Yes, Wible, they talk of a gulf between owners and workers. Nonsense! Take a father's love, for instance. What difference is there? When our children are sick we feel their pain as if it were our own. You as well as I. Good day, Wible.
JOHN WIBLE: (alone) You bloodsucker! The one dies of hunger; the other starves him. Is that a difference? One child wallows in the lap of

luxury; the other never even sees white bread. Is that a difference? Scum, all of you, scum! And if you think, Ure, that I came creeping to your money-bags like a louse to your belly—bah! Me, a traitor? Horse shit! Workers have to be driven forward with ox-whips. Blood is the whip that will wake the bums up! [MS 51f.; II, 147]

A psychologist analysing these lines might see weakness, compensation, self-delusion, self-contempt ["like a louse"], but not unalloyed wickedness. With almost Shakespearean appropriateness, Wible attempts to convince himself at the moment of his act of betrayal (but before the deed is done) of his loyalty to his comrades.

This psychological finesse is of a degree of subtlety that we have not yet encountered in Toller's first two plays. We see it in so abstract a figure as the one-armed beggar—a kind of Shakespearean fool who is like a subdued version of Bertolt Brecht's Azdak—cynic and raisonneur, but at the same time a deeply humane and decent man. The beggar warns Jimmy against inordinate trust and idealization of the workers:

Do all men keep their word, are all men brave, honest, unselfish, true? No. Then why should all workers be? Because they're "workingmen"? I think you see them the way you would like to see them. You've created new gods for yourself called "holy workers".... Open your eyes and see that you're struggling alongside of mere men—well-intentioned, malicious, greedy, unselfish, petty and generous—and try your luck with them anyhow! If they win with your help and they change their nature in the fight, I'll take off my hat to you ...if I ever get one! [MS 93; II, 174]

The beggar has learned of the workers' betrayal of Jimmy and does not intend to warn him. In his sober, matter-of-fact view of Jimmy's vision as an illusion, he believes that Jimmy can only create more misery than he can cure. But when the depth of Jimmy's ardent concern for his fellow man becomes evident, the beggar is so touched that he reveals his secret (without omitting to ask for permission to take Jimmy's shirt after he is killed):

JIMMY: If only we could save the children! Holy little children, abandoned to a brutal fate! This future generation's rotten to the core.

....

Stillness

BEGGAR: Jimmy ...Friend ...Tonight your workingmen are planning to smash the machines.

....

BEGGAR: Take care, buddy; take care! If they don't believe you any more, they'll hang you.... And if they feel they've done wrong, then they'll really hang you.... May I keep your shirt, Jimmy? [MS 95f.; II, 175f.]

There is an interaction on the psychological level which prompts the beggar to reveal his secret in the first place and which lends the events a degree of poignancy and immediacy far beyond that of *Die Wandlung* and *Masse Mensch*.

This was necessary if Toller was to portray the "situation of the working class in England" (and if implication, in Germany). This is the only one of Toller's plays set in the distant past, and one of three plays based on historical themes (the others being *Feuer aus den Kesseln* and *Wunder in Amerika*) and we know from Toller's own remarks[6] and from the researches of Furness and Marnette[7] that he actually used Engels' *Lage der arbeitenden Klasse in England* (*Situation of the Working Class in England*)[8] and Marx's *Das Kapital* in its composition.

In his use of historical data and psychological realism, Toller was attempting to present a broad panorama of the economic conditions and imperatives with which the "new" proletariat had to contend. To do so, he needed people, not abstractions or embodiments of ideologies, and they had to be people about whom we care. He wrote: "How my play will turn out, I don't know yet. I'm taking paths that are new to me. I use the world of the senses as a point of departure more than ever before."[9]

What results from this are mixed characters, a fact which lends the play added depth, but which is not an unmixed blessing. To the degree that philosophical conflict yields to economic conflict and abstractions gives way to realism, the ideological waters become muddied. To see this we can turn to the characterization of John Wible, one of the vertices of the triangular ideological constellation: Ure-Jimmy Cobbett-Wible. Wible corresponds in a sense to the Nameless One in *Masse Mensch* in his capacity as the danger from the left, the authoritarian socialist, but only to a degree, since his very psychological depth introduces personal resentments into his behavior. He is no longer the pure revolutionary. When he says, therefore, to Jimmy:

We *need defeats*. Only the deepest misery breeds rebels. Give them their bellyful, give them their schnaps and they'll fart on your insights and wallow in the trough like fat sows. [MS 53   II, 148]

it is very difficult to unravel his true motivations. We ask ourselves to what extent this represents his true beliefs, and to what extent it is self-justification for his sell-out (in the immediately preceding scene) of the workers, the consequences of which will be a brutally suppressed rebellion, as he realizes full well.

102

That these sentiments are by no means so extreme as to be beyond the capabilities of real revolutionaries is clear from the following remarks of Paul Nikolaus:

> Proletarians, I weld you together with hate, which binds more ardently than love; for I must teach you to hate in order to be able to lead you to love.... . I teach you hatred against those who scorn you, against your slanderers, against your masters.... Hate surmounts all obstacles; no enemy can withstand hate.... Let hate be your slogan: Hate the bourgeois![10]

In *Eine Jugend in Deutschland*, Toller wrote of the situation at the end of April, 1919:

> The Communists also know that our situation is untenable, but they press for a military decision.... They hope that defeat will provide powerful revolutionary stimuli; they believe that the proletariat will become more mature and more active through defeat.[11]

In words that echo Jimmy's, Toller continues: "Misery, suffering and oppression are only useful as revolutionary stimuli when they arouse in men the conviction that they are suffering unnecessarily and that it is within their power to alter things for the better."[12]

Toller tries to retard this blurring of the ideological conflict that results from the increased psychological depth and the consequent personal motivations in two ways. First he gives the fully-developed characters certain ideological burdens to carry in addition to their functions as living, breathing representatives of various traits of bourgeois and proletarian social groups. Ure is a real person, a wealthy man struggling with his conscience and inventing the same sort of self-delusions and justifications as Gerhart Hauptmann's realistically-drawn Dreissiger. But at the same time he represents on a more abstract level ruthless capitalism quite unconcerned with the effect of its actions on human beings and capable of arguing in the *mask* of Lord Castlereagh (as the stage directions indicate) for "reductions" in the population to avert the dire consequences predicted by Malthus. One thinks of the masks that Brecht had certain of his characters wear. It may well be that Toller was thinking here of Shelley's lengthy poem, "The Mask of Anarchy," (1819). The poem, which Godwin's son-in-law wrote in response to news of the "Peterloo Massacre," contains the verse:

> I met Murder on the way—
> He had a mask like Castlereagh—

Very smooth he looked, yet grim;
Seven blood-hounds follow him:[13]

Ellsworth Barnard describes the circumstances of the massacre in his Shelley edition in words that underscore its resemblance to the events in Nottingham of 1811-1812, seven years earlier.

> England was full of social unrest, caused by the persistent economic depression which followed the Napoleonic wars and by the reactionary domestic policies of the Tory government. Popular agitation for long overdue Parliamentary reform became so strong that the government was frightened into severe repressive measures; on August 16, 1819, a mass meeting in St. Peter's Field, Manchester, called to further the cause of reform, attended by several thousand workingmen, and conducted in a completely orderly manner, was charged by a force of cavalry with drawn sabers. Nine persons were killed and several hundred injured. The Tory leaders publicly approved the wanton attack.—Shelley's comment to Peacock on hearing "the terrible and important news of Manchester" was: "The tyrants here, as in the French Revolution, have first shed blood. May their execrable lessons not be learnt with equal docility!"[14]

Shelley's connections with anarchism are, of course, many and significant, dating from the early (ca. 1810) and prolonged influence of Godwin. He felt (as did Buber) that a total inner transformation of man was necessary to achieve social justice, and that this must occur before the revolution.[15] Shelley writes in his *Address to the Irish People*: "Before restraints of government are lessened, it is fit that we should lessen the necessity of them. Before government is done away with, we must reform ourselves."[16]

One thinks of Toller's acute empathy for the suffering of his fellow human beings, of his remarks on famines in China, for example, when one reads lines like the following of Shelley's:

Me—who am as a nerve o'er which do creep
The else unfelt oppressions of this earth—[17]

And one thinks of Toller's conception of the mission of the poet, when one reads Shelly's words:

Most wretched men
Are cradled into poetry by wrong,
They learn in suffering what they teach in song.[18]

The less fully developed characters in *Die Maschinenstürmer*, on the other hand, are given an even more overt and symbolic function, and here it is interesting that many of them derive from Toller's own life, notably the Old Reaper, who seeks the malevolent God that he may shoot Him with his cane as retribution for His hatred of man, and "Louis with the cart," based on a pathetic figure from Toller's childhood.

Toller's second means of mitigating the blurring of the ideological lines of his play is a series of stylistic devices that serve to remind the spectator constantly of the points at issue. One such device is antithetical effect. By the expedient of artifically producing the crassest conceivable contradiction between language and poetic reality, a sense of excitement, of outrage, or of tension is produced. A typical example of this technique occurs in the prologue, when Castlereagh says of the bill which would hang labor activists: "This bill is a tribute on the altar of Justice!" [MS, 9; II, 122]. One more example of this technique will suffice; Wible denounces Jimmy in the following words:

> The rat who betrayed us and became Ure's henchman is Henry Cobbett.
> Jimmy Cobbett is his brother! [MS 105; II, 182]

and the implication is clear to the weavers—just as clear as the magnitude of the discrepancy between implication and reality to the reader and spectator.

We have already noted how some figures achieve a degree of psychological three-dimensionality, while others serve either abstract or symbolic roles. Among the former, certain relationships realize their full significance only when their connections with each other are emphasized. Thus, for example, Ure and Jimmy form two extremes on one level, for each is completely convinced of the harmony of his own ideology with the laws that govern the universe—Jimmy believes completely in brotherhood, whereas Ure believes that his actions are justified by such maxims as the survival of the fittest.

Another level is inhabited by Wible on the one hand and Henry Cobbett on the other. Each of these is too weak to conquer the selfish impuses which drive him to hypocritical opportunism. That Wible believes neither in the ideals he professes nor in the justice of his act of betrayal, I have already indicated. Similarly Henry Cobbett is very well aware that all the claims to moral superiority he bases on his newly acquired social status rest on quicksand, that he will never really be a member of the establishment and that his position is maintained only by force and artifice. He is not sincere in his elitist posturings, and we have already seen that his denials of his proletarian origins have the ring of a hollow psychological compensation mechanism. This becomes particularly evident when these origins reach out after him in the person of his brother to threaten his precarious position, and he reacts by forcing his mother to choose between a refuge in her old age and her older son (and not between himself and his brother). He must employ the bludgeon of material comforts to preclude an honest choice. This hypocritical-opportunist level is underscored by a dual exploitation: Wible exploits Henry's relationship with his brother for his own purposes, just as Henry exploits Wible's wife Mary.

If we now examine the connection between this dual exploitation and the workers, a highly interesting situation emerges. For both of these unnatural and depraved relationships arouse the workers, but each arouses them in such a way as to appeal to their lowest instincts, to those very instincts which Jimmy asks them to overcome. Mary's prostitution incites the lust for revenge in the workers and blinds them to human weakness, from which, as Ned Lud points out, they all suffer. Similarly Jimmy's relationship to his brother is seen by the weavers as treachery and impels them to murder, and murder of a particularly savage sort. This discussion of the details of Toller's techniques of characterization leads naturally to a discussion of the ideological content of the work.

There are three important ideological confrontations in *Die Maschinenstürmer*. The first occurs in the prologue, and, like the "Prologue in Heaven" of *Faust*, it sets the cosmic framework for what is to follow and anticipates the economic philosophies at the root of the more specific debate to come. The function of the state as handmaiden to the economic interests of the bourgeoisie, its "executive committee," is underscored by the fact that Ure appears in the mask of Castlereagh, just as Jimmy in the mask of Byron represents the Expressionist poet's mission to cry out the demands of humanity—"Lengua sin manas, cuemo osas fablar?" ("Tongue without hands, how dare you to speak?" we read in the *Cid*). The essence of Byron's role (based on a famous speech that Byron actually delivered in the House of Lords) is explicitly recognized by Castlereagh, who rejects it:

> He spoke like a poet, and not a statesman. But politics is the business of hard men. [MS 81; II, 121]

The defeat of the poet Byron in the prologue anticipates Jimmy's rejection by the children in the first scene—a scene which in turn foreshadows the brutal ending of the play. Jimmy tries to awaken the children's perceptions with a tale of social injustice, and they react by quarreling over a scrap of bread. Elsewhere, in *Das Schwalbenbuch*, Toller compares the poet to the bird who brings all that is beautiful and valuable to man, only to be rejected and persecuted.[19] He is rejected by the right as a danger, because as Gustav Landauer says, poetry leads to revolution.[20] And he is also rejected by the left as ineffectual, because as Lukács puts it:

> And the Expressionists? They are ideologues. They stand between leaders and masses; they are subjective, usually with honorable (though ordinarily immature, unclear, confused) convictions. At the same time however,

they are deeply imbued not only with those uncertainties to which the immature masses were subject as well, but also with all possible reactionary prejudices of the epoch, which make them more than vulnerable to the most various anti-revolutionary slogans; abstract pacificism, the ideology of non-violence, abstract criticism of the bourgeoisie, anarchist fads, etc.[21]

Interestingly enough, the kind of revolutionary elite which, according to Lenin's writings of the period from 1902 to 1904 ought to lead the masses, was to be composed of intellectuals drawn from all classes. And, indeed, several of the staff members of *Linkskurve*, which so vociferously denounced bourgeois revolutionaries and reformers like Toller, Tucholsky, Döblin and Heinrich Mann, were themselves of non-proletarian origins. Johannes R. Becher was the son of a lawyer, and Ludwig Renn descended from a Saxon noble family.

Just as Jimmy's rejection by the children at the beginning of the first act points to his betrayal by their parents in the last, so Jimmy's rejection by his mother and brother at the beginning of the second act anticipates the collapse of his hope for a true community, a family of all mankind. This hope, which achieves its most eloquent expression in Jimmy's encounter with Ure, is first expressed in the second important confrontation, his speech to the workers as the end of Act II in words that recall Martin Buber:

> JIMMY: *Your guilt is that you gave up without a struggle,* that you didn't stand shoulder to shoulder together! That you don't *live* for the sake of community, that you don't work to build the house of justice! ...And yet you can dream! ...of a land of communities united in solidarity ...of mankind united ...of creative, joyous, constructive work ...Brothers, unite! Begin! Begin! Not I and I and I! No! World and we and thou and I! [MS 43   II, 142f.]

When Wible rejects these words as mere phrases and demands power for the workers, i.e. the vote, Jimmy in true anarchist fashion disdains the vote as a tool of a totally corrupt society, which must be rebuilt completely: "We need more than votes. All land to the workers, not the parasites!" [MS 44; II, 143]. Once again he preaches a voluntary community of enlightened individuals; "Each of you serves the people, each serves the cause. Each of you a leader!"[MS 45; II, 144], whereupon the workers carry him off on their shoulders. John Wible, the stage direction notes, "remains behind."

That Jimmy's belief in the worker and in his own capacity to lead them is an act of will, a kind of *Philosophie des Als-Ob* (philosophy of "as-if," albeit in a different sense than Vaihinger's), we recognize at certain moments that reveal an element of prescience which antedates the beggar's revelations. He tells Wible: "They are workingmen-ignorant, misled workingmen."[MS, 531; II, 148]. Later on, the following exchange occurs:

OLD REAPER: Do you believe in the kingdom of God, ...the kingdom of peace?
JIMMY: I fight as if I did. [MS 55; II, 149]

We see this secular faith in action in the third great confrontation, that of Act IV between Jimmy and the industrialist Ure. In a scene which can be compared to the meeting of the Marquis Posa and Phillip II in Friedrich Schiller's play, *Don Carlos* (1787), Jimmy pleads the cause of the workers and begins by describing their misery and exploitation. In doing so, he does not aim, as Gerhart Hauptmann did in *Die Weber*, at primarily awakening a sense of sympathy in the specator, a sense of conscience and a desire to mitigate the weavers' want. In Hauptmann one feels that the entrepreneur Dreissiger, for all his callousness and cruelty is neither a depraved nor an evil man, but simply one who like Ibsen's heroes is too weak to do good. In his dealings with the tutor and theology student, Weinhold, we observe quite clearly that he is intelligent enough to have to delude himself in order to live with his conscience. But the situation seems to be one that calls for feeling rather than willful ignorance, Christian charity rather than callousness. The structure of society itself is not called into question.

In *Die Maschinenstürmer*, however, Jimmy's description of the workers' misery does not aim primarily at awakening sympathy—either in Ure or in the spectator. Instead he delivers a ringing indictment of the system itself, an attack which is nothing less than a call (to Ure, who is in Jimmy's eyes its victim as much as the least of his employees!) for revolution:

JIMMY: Out of the cruel fountain-head of war
Still runs the heart-blood of Europe's lands.
Misery cries aloud in prisons of despair.
Here men go hungry, there the granaries
Are choked with mildewed corn. Here there is no coal;
The people freeze, and there, above the pits,
The coal stands mountain-high. The hauling stops,
Because a brutal system, sanctified by you, would have it
So. [MS 72; II, 160]

The "brutal system" that Jimmy would destroy is not simply to be replaced by a fraudulent parliamentary democracy, as we have seen from Jimmy's categorical rejection of suffrage, nor is some sort of dictatorship of the proletariat based on coercion and gratuitous force acceptable:

JIMMY: Is every violent act an altar, before which mankind's knee must worship? The senseless act is the delight of cowards and fools! [MS 53; II, 148]

Later on Jimmy reproaches his fellow workers "What do you want? To tyrannize like the masters ...slaves!" [MS 113; II, 187].

It can be shown that Castlereagh, in the first great confrontation, and Ure, in the third, represent the philosophy of Social Darwinism. Castlereagh says:

Poverty is a law of nature, always with us. Compassion can have no place in Parliament. Reverend Malthus showed us that hundreds of thousands too many live in England; nature denies these masses food. We see misery ...it is God's weapon, before which we must bow in silence. Every year wars, squalor, vice rid the earth of excess population. Are we to oppose this God-given natural law? That would be immoral! We must accept it and do all in our power to aid it. [MS 81; II, 122]

Darwin, of course, was inspired by Malthus' theory that the geometrical growth of population would outstrip the arithmetical growth in productive resources and lead to periodic disasters, and he advocated that the "weaker and inferior" members of society refrain from marrying and bearing children as frequently as the sound. From this orientation, and based on such notions as natural selection, survival of the fittest, and the struggle for existence, the Social Darwinists conceived of human societies as organisms that evolve in a manner similar to that of animal species. In the struggle for supremacy, the ruthless and efficient ones will be successful and survive, and the inefficient and flabby ones will perish. There is indeed some support in Darwin himself for theories of this sort; one thinks of passages like the following:

We civilized men ...do our utmost to check the process of elimination; we build asylums for the imbecile, the maimed, and the sick, we institute poor-laws; and our medical men exert their utmost skill to save the life of every one to the last moment.... Thus the weak members of civilized society propagate their kind. No one who has attended to the breeding of domestic animals will doubt that thus must be highly injurious to the race of man.[22]

What Social Darwinists themselves, men like Herbert Spencer, were able to make of this is evident from Spencer's *Principles of Sociology*:

Not simply do we see that in the competition among individuals of the same kind, survival of the fittest has ...furthered production of the higher type; but we see that to the unceasing warfare between species is mainly due both growth and organization. Without universal conflict there would have been no development of the active powers.[23]

All of this was intended to demonstrate to would-be reformers the futility and wrong-headedness of their task. If they could be made to realize that society is an organism fully as complicated as any example of natural evolution described by Darwin, they would bow before its complexity and give up their childish hopes of rapid transformation. Like Castlereagh, Spencer concludes:"...there cannot be more good done than that of letting social progress go on unhindered; yet an immensity of mischief may be done in the way of disturbing and distorting and repressing, by policies carried out in pursuance of erroneous conceptions.''[24]

What subtleties there were in Spencer were lost on men like Spencer's friend Andrew Carnegie and John D. Rockefeller. Richard Hofstadter quotes Rockefeller, appropriately enough, from a Sunday school address:

> The growth of a large business is merely a survival of the fittest.... The American Beauty rose can be produced in the splendor and fragrance which bring cheers to its beholder only by sacrificing the early buds which grow up around it. This is not an evil tendency in business. It is merely the working out of a law of nature and a law of God.[25]

The philosophical position that Ure represents, then, is clearly that of Social Darwinism. It remains to show that this Anglo-American mutation of Darwinism was a significant force within Germany. This question is dealt with by Georg Lukács in his book, *Die Zerstörung der Vernunft (The Destruction of Reason)*,[26] in the chapter "Social Darwinism, Theory of Race, and Fascism." Lukács begins by noting the enormous influence of Darwinism itself on the continent and pointing out that owing to its scientific nature, to its expression of a kind of dialectical development in nature, it is fundamentally an anti-bourgeois theory fully consonant with Marxism, and was recognized as such by the establishment.

Nevertheless, the potentialities of such a theory as a justification for the exploitation perpetrated by capitalism were soon recognized. Lukács remarks:

> If capitalism is to be justified as the best economic and social system conceivable, if sociology ...is to lead to a reconciliation with the capitalist system and persuade vacillators of its unsurpassable perfection, then the contradictions, and especially the inhumane aspects of capitalism may no longer be ignored and obscured; on the contrary, the apologia must take these as its point of departure.[27]

110

The class struggle, the economy as the motor of social change, the labor theory of value—all these are debased by a "Darwinism transformed into platitudes" and explained as consequences of the "struggle for existence." Of the sociologists who propounded these views Lukács regards Ludwig Gumplowicz[28] as the most important. Gumplowicz saw Darwin's explanation of natural evolution as an exact analogue of social evolution. This equation was opposed, interestingly enough, by Ferdinand Tönnies,[29] Buber's mentor, whom Toller had met at the Diederichs' seminars at Burg Lauenstein.

Gumplowicz claims that all idealistic and messianic movements, whether Christianity or the French Revolution, are doomed to fail because they are "contrary to human nature." The natural inequality of man requires the state as the only possible agency capable of creating order. Thus anarchism is rejected.

That such theories were anathema to Toller is clear, and it may well be that *Die Maschinenstürmer*, written in the winter of 1920-1921, was conceived of as a response to them, for we read in a letter of this same period to Tessa: "For some months now I have been working again on practical studies; I occupy myself with economic, political and sociological works."[30]

As indicated, there is in Darwin a certain justification for extrapolations such as those of the Social Darwinists. Yet Darwin himself felt uneasy about the way in which he was being exploited. He writes to Sir Charles Lyell:

> I have received in a Manchester newspaper rather a good squib, showing that I have proved "might is right" and therefore that Napoleon is right, and every cheating tradesman is also right. [31]

In fact, *The Origin of Species* admits of sociological models diametrically opposed to those of Spencer. Peter Kropotkin's *Mutual Aid* (1902) was written in direct response to what he considered to be an unjustifiably narrow inference from Darwin, and to T. H. Huxley's essays, "The Struggle for Existence" (in *Nineteenth Century*, February, 1888) and "Evolution and Ethics" (1893). Kropotkin did not deny the concept of "survival of the fittest." He states: "Life *is* a struggle; and in that struggle the fittest survive."[32] Rather, he asserted that the concept of "fitness" was not axiomatic and begged a crucial question, one which required definition. His own answer, based on his scientific studies and research conducted during expeditions in Siberia, was that "those animals which acquire the habits of mutual aid are undoubtedly the fittest."[33] Those feelings which "induce human beings to unite for attaining common ends by common effort"[34] were to be fostered. This is exactly the position of Lord Byron in *Die Maschinenstürmer* and of Jimmy Cobbett.

It is important to realize that while Jimmy (and by implication Toller) represents Kropotkin's philosophy in almost unalloyed purity, he does not on that account propound a "utopian" solution. On the contrary, he sees quite plainly the necessity for years of suffering and self-abnegation on the part of the oppressed. Like the children of Israel, required to wander for forty years in the desert, the new man is to be born slowly and amid great pain. And like Moses returning with the tablets of the law to find the people he had been leading toward freedom worshipping the golden calf, Jimmy laments before his death:

> O comrades ...I thought you free and you were slaves! You will always be slaves! Your women bought by the masters, and you cringed before them ...slaves! Pressed into uniforms, you cheered, and your deed is the deed of a slave who rebels. What do you want? To tyrannize like the masters ...slaves! ...The man who flogs you along the road to freedom: he's the one you follow! [MS 113; II, 186f.]

Toller's epigraph to the *Gedichte der Gefangenen (Poems of the Prisoners)*[35] describes Jimmy's situation exactly:

> He who prepares the way
> dies on the threshold.
> But before him,
> Death bows in awe.

Jimmy's eloquent and very moving words on the tactics of revolution are not so much directed at the abstract political and philosophical discussion of the primacy of the individual over the claims of party of the sort described in *Masse Mensch*. Rather, it is the ethical aspect of the question which so interests and saddens him. The two are of course sides of the same coin. Rosa Luxemburg in her essay, "Leninism or Marxism," remarks in true anarchist fashion: "The self-discipline of Social Democracy is not merely the replacement of the authority of the burgeois rulers with the authority of a socialist central committee. The working class will acquire the sense of the new discipline, of the freely assumed self-discipline of Social Democracy...."[36] This political question is dealt with in the more abstract *Masse Mensch*, but it is the individual ethical implications of it that are central to Jimmy's speech.

We fell very palpably that the servitude of which he speaks is not the political domination of a centralized Leninist or Blanquist elite over the masses, but the self-imposed spiritual servitude of an outworn coercive mode of thought and feeling, which the workers are too weak to discard.

Moses was able to see into the Promised Land; Jimmy can only find what comfort he can in resignation:

Forgive me.... It was passion that spoke.... My poor brothers, slaves....
There was no one who taught you otherwise.... You fought against the
wrong enemy! O brothers, if the workingmen of England abandon their
holy mission ...if the workingmen of the continent, of all the earth fail to
join in the great work of mankind, ...to erect the world-wide community
of workers, then, brothers, you will remain slaves until the end of your
days! [MS 113; II, 187]

Jimmy regrets his anger, but he does not retreat from his insight: "My poor
brother-slaves." One feels in these last desperate words a kind of self-delusion,
for there *was* someone to lead the way into the Promised Land, Jimmy himself,
and the promise was rejected. We can see this clearly, not only in the average
worker, but especially in the person of Ned Lud. Lud has been inspired with
conviction of the rightness of Jimmy's vision and yet had been the first to turn
against him and yield to Wible's demagoguery, even though earlier he had
been clear-sighted enough to show the women persecuting Wible's wife for her
prostitution the error of their ways. "Think with your heads for once, not with
your guts!" [MS 66; II, 156]. One is forced to conclude that Lud's words at the
end of the play represent at best a kind of private insight, at worst self-delusion
of the same sort which had deceived Jimmy in spite of the beggar's warning

Others will come . . .
Wiser, more devout, more courageous than we.
Your kingdom totters, masters of England! [MS 117; II, 189]

Katharina Maloof does not agree. She writes:

Die Maschinenstürmer is more optimistic than *Masse Mensch*, since the
masses are regretful and are ready to repent. The material misery is the
result of an intellectual and spiritual atrophy in man himself. The fault
lies not in the mechanization of the world, for man retains his power over
it. What is wanted is insight into the force of humanity and the will
toward brotherhood....[37]

Toller himself wrote in *Eine Jugend in Deutschland*:

How easily the masses are even now swayed and diverted by whims, by
promises and hopes of self-advantage. Today they cheer their leader,
tomorrow they abandon him.... I came to know the social conditions
which underlie this spiritual instability, the great want of today that cripples strength of purpose—the dependence of mankind on the labor
market, on machines. I used to think that the power of reason was so
strong that he who had once seen reason could not but follow it. But ex-

perience is soon forgotten; the path of the people is laborious. The greatest harm comes to the people not from their opponents, but from themselves.[38]

Jimmy's disillusionment resembles that of the anarchist Proudhon, who wrote in 1852:

How many times in these last five years have I caught the people in adultery, in indifference, in imperialist complicity, in ingratitude toward its teachers! Ah, the people have not deceived me; but cowardice even when anticipated, is always hideous to see.[39]

This impression of total futility is confirmed by the appearance of the Old Reaper, for whom in death the malevolent God he had been pursuing in order to kill Him assumes once again an infinitely benign and benevolent aspect. But it is too late; now He is dead:

I have lived long enough to see this deed ...and too long ...how tired one becomes of life ...I would like to die.... Ah, thou poor, dear God. *The Old Reaper bends, sobbing, over Jimmy's corpse and kisses him.* [MS 118f.; II, 190]

For the Old Reaper, God, the demon, had been identified with the machine, the technocratic society that enslaves man. Jimmy's death finally transforms this God-demon-machine into a benevolent deity, a servant of man, but it is only at the moment of his death that he is able to achieve this insight, and it is a highly subjective achievement, for it has meaning only to one man—the Old Reaper.

Corresponding to the movement from the abstraction of *Masse Mensch* to the relative psychological realism of *Die Maschinenstürmer,* from clashes of philosophical principles to individual ethical imperatives, is the movement from the political aspect of anarchism in *Masse Mensch* to its economic aspects in *Die Maschinenstürmer.* I have already shown that the conflict between Castlereagh-Ure and Byron-Jimmy represents in concrete terms the conflict between Social Darwinism and the communist anarchism of Peter Kropotkin. There is in this conflict, however, an arresting ambiguity, which must be dealt with before we go on to examine Jimmy's vision in more detail.

In its Spencerian incarnation, Social Darwinism seems to involve a curious ambivalence. On the one hand it is invoked in support of one of the most coercive and repressive systems of economic enslavement the world has ever known, and to that extent is, logically enough, a fit and appropriate adversary for Kropotkin's anarchism. But on the other hand, the philosophy of laissez-faire, the doctrine of absolute noninterference of the state in the affairs of the in-

114

dividual itself contains elements of anarchism. Hofstadter writes of Spencer:

> He called for a return to natural rights, setting up as an ethical standard the right of every man to do as he pleases, subject only to the condition that he does not infringe on the rights of others. In such scheme, the sole function of the state is negative—to insure that such freedom is not curbed.[40]

William Graham Sumner sees the choices in stark terms and places Social Darwinism on the side of liberty:

> Let it be understood that we cannot go outside this alternative; liberty, inequality, survival of the fittest; not-liberty, equality, survival of the unfittest. The former carries society forward and favors all its best members; the latter carries society downwards and favors all its worst members.[41]

It is true, there is an undeniable flavor of anarchism here, but it is the anarchism of Max Stirner rather than that of Bakunin or Kropotkin. We have said that the common denominator of the various varieties of anarchism is political—the primacy of individual liberty, and that they admit of economic models only to the extent that these comport with this principle. But within this constraint, various economic models are permissible. One of them, implicit in Stirner's variety of anarchism, looks very much like Social Darwinism.

But while the sincerity of Stirner is not open to doubt (particularly in view of the fact that in his own impecunious life he was very far from defending a privileged economic position from collectivist incursions), the same cannot be said of men like Ure. Ure's philosophy is quite evidently less a motivating force behind his behavior than a justification of it. This hypocrisy is placed in its proper perspective in the second scene of Act V, where the visitor to Ure's factory, a representative of the government, is simply lied to.

Moreover, in the case of the Nottingham of 1811-1816 (and the Germany of the first part of the twentieth century that it is a mask for), the coercive economic arrangements already existed. For the state then to claim not to be interfering with economic competition in the international sphere while at the same time it actively prevented "mutual aid" and workers' associations in the domestic sphere amounted to intervention every bit as incompatible with all varieties of anarchism as the most strictly planned economy.

Die Maschinenstürmer begins with the arrival of Jimmy in Nottingham. His appearance serves two functions. The episode with the children referred to above anticipates Jimmy's betrayal later on, and Jimmy's questions to Ned Lud provide an occasion for exposition. Jimmy, like the outsider in Ibsen and like Moritz Jäger in Gerhart Hauptmann's *Die Weber*, serves as catalyst whose presence decisively alters the course of events, though he cannot control them. Unlike Jäger, however, Jimmy, with the insight of a higher level of consciousness, is prompted to preach restraint—to place spiritual strength and humility above physical retribution and more conventional worldly dignity. In this sense there is something to Toller's (otherwise rather lame) protest: "Jeder Vergleich mit den 'Webern' hinkt."[42] There are a great many more or less superificial similarities between the two plays: the women who are more zealous than their husbands, the entrepreneur who is physically confronted with starving and exploited children, the alliance of Church, State and bourgeoisie, the moral depravities of the workers in which they find their only solace, the former worker become parvenu who is more brutal than the manufacturers themselves, the pious old worker, the workers who stand in almost religious awe before the God-machine that they had been bent on destroying. Many of these elements, which we may call "clichés of the genre," are common to works such as Germinal (1885), L'Assommoir (1877), Gas (1919) and even Hard Times (1854), all of which depict the impact of the industrial revolution on human relationships. But where works like Germinal are ultimately defeatist (as the Marxists claim), Toller for all his pessimism adumbrates the possibility of a solution, the conviction that a solution is conceivable, if not realizable by man in his present state of consciousness. This solution lies in Jimmy's anarchistic vision, a vision which revolves around the concept of the true community of men. He tells Ure:

Within our hearts there is a bud unfolding,
Whose petals conceal wonder upon wonder—it is
the THOU; the THOU that
Lifts the biblical curse of toil;
What now is torment, the stigma of the ostracized
Will once again become our holy, inspired task. [MS 76; II, 164]

In almost classical purity the positions of Spencer's Social Darwinism and Kropotkin's communist anarchism confront each other in the arguments of Ure and Jimmy:

URE: Young man, the dreams you dream are dangerous visions.
You walk this earth like a blind man.
Life thrives in the struggle of all against all.
The strong stag thrusts his weak rival aside,
And sires a noble, powerful race.
The victor propagates his kind, not the weakling!
The harmony of this world springs from the
Brutal clash of interests.

He who stays on top, stays there in accord
With timeless laws of nature,
Which our poor human faculties will never fathom.
And only thus does culture develop.
JIMMY: But if a foe attacks the weaker stag,
The stronger one protects his frail brother,
Stands at his side and lends to him his strength.
You speak of freedom, speak of the clash of interests,
Of force that remains victorious according to
The law of the strong.
Freedom for all, you shout. What freedom is
Left for the workingman?
....
Just take a look at nature! Where is there an
Animal that lives alone?
The eagle, calmly circling in the aether
Spies dead game. With a loud cry, he
Proclaims it to his brothers.
Together they fly to the meadow, peacefully
Sharing the discovered prey.
The sated ant gives of his food to his
Hungry fellows . . .
....
The Negro, the savage shares peacefully with his
Brothers a community of cheerful, wonderful life;
No barriers of class divide brothers of one tribe.
Only the free, the civilized man is deaf to grace;
To THOU, deaf to the divine: EACH OTHER. [MS 74; II, 162f.]

Choosing the same examples from the animal realm later used by Toller, Kropotkin writes in *Mutual Aid* (translated into German in 1904 by Toller's friend Gustav Landauer) of the reindeer and ruminants: "Their watchfulness over the safety of their herds against attacks of carnivores; the anxiety displayed by all individuals in a herd of chamois as long as all of them have not cleared a difficult passage over rocky cliffs; the adoption of orphans ...could be mentioned."[43]

Of eagles he writes: "From this and like observations, Syevertsoff concluded that the white-tailed eagles combine for hunting; when they all have risen to a great height they are enabled, if they are ten, to survey an area of at least twenty-five miles square; and as soon as anyone has discovered something, he warns the others."[44]

Of savages he writes: "A savage who is capable of living under such a complex organization, and of freely submitting to rules which continually clash with his personal desires, certainly is not a beast devoid of ethical principles and knowing no rein to its passions."[45]

It is worth noting at this point that this same imagery is employed in Toller's lyric poetry, particularly in *Das Schwalbenbuch*, where it stands for the same conception of mutual aid that is at the center of *Die Maschinenstürmer*. Most striking is the following passage which shows the swallows uniting to protect themselves against a brutal predator:

On the breezes of the morning, spreading the might of his wings,
Splendid, hovers a hawk.
I hear shrill cries of frolicking swallows.
From all sides sallies of swallows fly near.
Who sounded the signal to attack?
With the force of arrows they plunge at the royal bird,
Who holds in his talons a swallow, so young.
O, my brothers, my brave sparrows!
But what an unequal struggle.
Calmly, with a quickened beat of his wings, the victim
resists,
And scarcely does he heed the tiny pursuers.
Poor sparrowhawk!
Again and again the swallows attack the aggressor,
Harass him with fiery passion.
....
In blissful arcs, the swallows proclaim the triumph of
Brotherhood.[46]

It is plain that the aggressor, the royal bird, and the swallows who celebrate the victory of community are to be taken symbolically—the former is the rapacious exploiter, the Ure of the animal world, the latter form the kind of ideal community with which Jimmy attempts to inspire the weavers. In a similar sense, it is not gratuitous information when Toller tells us:

The swallows have come back again.
They will stay! They will stay!
My cell looks to the East!
To the East![47]

In concrete terms, the light of the rising sun provides warmth for the birds (and we know from the various descriptions of the swallow episode in *Justiz. Erleb-*

nisse, Eine Jugend in Deutschland, and *Briefe aus dem Gefängnis* that the swallows did nest in cells which faced east), but in a more abstract sense the rising sun is that of the pre-Stalinist Russian Revolution.

The bird motif appears, naturally enough, in countless prison poems throughout literature as a symbol of freedom, but here Toller means it to point to more than just physical freedom. He asserts, for example, in another cycle, *Gedichte der Gefangenen (Poems of Prisoners)*:

> Comrade
> in every city, in
> every village a prison
> accompanies you.[48]

and in the second edition he goes on to ask:

> Who can say of himself that he is not imprisoned.
> Even though no bars rob him of his sky
> And no walls circumscribe the earth for him?[49]

In *Das Schwalbenbuch* as in the *Gedichte der Gefangenen*, the two central concepts are freedom (in this broadened sense of noncoercive, individual spiritual freedom) and community. In the latter cycle, the longing for community reminds one of Buber: "...We only know that the hands of man/Harm one another. That no bridge of help/Connects the streams I and Thou."[50] Elsewhere in the cycle, Toller speaks of "A pilgrim who has lost the way to his friend...."[51] Or he emphasizes that freedom from coercion does not mean total egoism. He says of the prisoners:

> They hate one another because they are so pitiably alone; because they are submerged in the chaos of their egos....[52]

For the prisoners in *Das Schwalbenbuch* the opposite of community, the world against which Jimmy Cobbett struggles, is represented as it is in *Die Maschinenstürmer*:

> They entrust it [their life] to an idol who wears a
> Uniform-hat, who arranges it, catalogues it, prescribes
> Duties, writes birth certificates, military certificates,
> Marriage certificates,
> Death certificates, places a cross after their played-out
> Names,
> Carries the filled volume to the registry office.
> That's how it must be; that's how one serves God,
> For ever and ever, amen.[53]

There is not the slightest difference between the coercive society described here, the prison without walls created by the state against which the anarchist fights, and the order within the actual prison that Toller describes in *Das Schwalbenbuch* in the following words:

> ...They carry
> Whips in their hands. Men call them whips of justice.
> The whips of this house are: Solitary confinement.
> No bed No food No exercise No pen or paper
> No talking No singing No reading No light
> Strait-jacket.[54]

Against this coercive, mechanized society in which each man, within and without actual prison walls is reduced to a number, Toller places the flight of the swallows, true and responsible freedom combined with the notion of mutual aid:

> Let Europe chant the praises of her aeroplanes,
> But I, Number 44,
> With all the silent music of my heart
> Will praise the flight of swallows.[55]

Martin Reso recognizes the anarchistic nature of these poems. He says of one passage: "...the statement remains unreal, since its realization must be characterized as confused and unsuccessful ...primarily owing to the complete indefiniteness and anarchical character of the statement."[56] Although Reso sees, curiously enough, in *Das Schwalbenbuch* a "precious jewel of German lyric poetry,"[57] he is forced to admit:

> All idealism leads—and this is inherent in its character—to the glorifica-
> tion of an aristocracy of the intellect. If now a humanistic tendency is ad-
> ded to this, [such a] humanism must be dreamlike and abstract, must
> consist completely of the proclamation of self-perfection, of regeneration.
> Toller does indeed try to deal with this fault through an awareness of the
> necessity of social change, but he nevertheless remains mired in the ideal
> and the vague.[58]

This significant passage shows clearly the gap between the anarchist conception of an ideal society that requires a radical transformation of man himself
and the communist conception that proceeds instead from social engineering
and social revolution. We note that in *Das Schwalbenbuch* Toller has depicted
this same abyss (Reso calls it a fault) between the same two theories of social
change, and that moreover he uses similar imagery, no doubt drawn from

Kropotkin.

In *Die Maschinenstürmer* the conflict is expressed ideologically and dramatically; in *Das Schwalbenbuch* Toller employs the *topos* of the animal that is more humane and noble than man. He writes:

Men call you brutes,
And there is pride in their voices when they pronounce
the word, brutes.

....

Until men rediscover the source of their
Brutishness,
Until they are-*are*
Their struggle will only be worth renewed struggle,
And even their most holy transformation
Will require yet another transformation.[59]

He asks:

"When, oh when, animals, will you unite/ Against humankind?"[60] and his words echo Jimmy's approach:

Your guilt is that you gave up without a struggle, that you didn't stand shoulder-to-shoulder together! That you don't live for the sake of community, that you don't work to build the house of justice! [MS 43 II, 142]

The struggle between Jimmy's workers and their oppressors and between the swallows and their persecutors is that between Swift's Houyhyhnms and Yahoos. Toller notes in *Briefe aus dem Gefängnis*: "It is part of the arrogance of the educated man to babble about the 'ascent from the inorganic to the organic' when reverent silence is called for."[61] In another letter, he employs the same sort of metaphor:

Our theater lacks men ...who [can] create [on the basis of] the new communal life, to which they are as inextricably bound as the branch is to the tree. Our dramatists belong to a bourgeois society. Since bourgeois society has lost its organic unity, since it has crumbled, leached out in the chaos of superannuated, feeble forces, receiving light and warmth from no star, its dramatists too present a picture of senile confusion![62]

Like Kropotkin in *Mutual Aid*, Toller regards the simple and the natural as the humane, beneficent order toward which man should strive, and the sophisticated alienation of modern society as an aberration which distorts his basically unselfish impulses.

121

We have outlined in this chapter the ideological content of Jimmy's vision. In all respects, insofar as it is developed in this play, it is identical with Kropotkin's communist anarchism. We have seen that Jimmy's is an idealistic philosophy, that he struggles as if it were possible for what is rationally conceivable actually to be realized. And such is the strength of his vision that the wish nearly becomes father of the fact. Ure admits in wonder: "I feel it—you believe what you are saying...." [MS 75; II, 163]. Yet he is not able to convert Ure, nor is he able even to convert his fellow workers. What Jimmy learns, as Hinkemann will learn later, is the essentially private nature of truth. T. S. Eliot wrote:

Between the idea
And the reality
Between the motion
And the act
Falls the Shadow.[63]

8

Hinkemann: Anarchism and Psychology

I see too deep and too much.—Henri Barbusse: *L'Enfer*

Toller's *Hinkemann*,[1] which was written in Niederschönenfeld during 1921 and 1922, was a popular success, to judge from the number of productions and performances. Spalek lists 127 reviews of productions in Vienna, Dresden, Hamburg, Frankfurt, Berlin, Stuttgart, Jena, Leipzig, Basel, New York, London, Tartu (Estonia), Helsinki, Riga, Warsaw, Moscow, Leningrad, Belgrade, Ljubljana, and Buenos Aires.[2] The play caused such a sensation that it was prohibited in several cities, among them Oldenburg, in part owing to scandals caused by rightist students at the productions in Vienna and Dresden.[3]

The plot of the play that provoked all of this furor bears a distinct resemblance to that of Büchner's *Woyzeck*. Hinkemann, emasculated in the war, returns home to find that he can no longer endure the cruelty of civilian society. When his mother-in-law blinds a goldfinch to make it sing better, he sees in this a parable of man's inhumanity to his fellow suffering creatures. Unable to find work as a laborer, and afraid that he is an object of derision to his wife, Grete, he becomes hysterical but is soon convinced of Grete's love. Hinkemann is so touched by her devotion to him that he secretly finds work as a carnival geek, biting through the necks of rats and drinking their blood for the delectation of the public. In the meantime, Grete has been seduced by Grosshahn, a comrade of Hinkemann's, who then takes her to the carnival where she coincidentally sees her husband at work. She realizes the magnitude of love so great that it causes Hinkemann to abase himself and act against his most sacred principles, and rejects Grosshahn immediately to return to her husband.

Hinkemann goes to a bar, the patrons of which represent various leftist and religious sects, each bitterly opposed to the rest. He takes issue with the vacuous optimism of a doctrinaire socialist, and asks what the social engineers will be able to do to cure those awful spiritual tortures that result from other than economic and material causes. Just then, Grosshahn, drunk and wounded at Grete's rejection of him, enters and reveals Hinkemann's infirmity to all, maliciously and inaccurately claiming that Grete finds him ludicrous.

Hinkemann rushes out, collapses and is brought home. He loses all control of himself in a fit of insanity, which, however, dissipates when he looks into Grete's eyes and sees in her a tormented creature, as helpless as he is in a cruel and soulless world. He is once again convinced of her love and her repentance, but no longer has the strength to go on. Grete, unable to bear Hinkemann's despair, commits suicide.

Of those who received *Hinkemann* unfavorably, the major criticisms of western critics seem to be its "bad taste,"[4] an alleged fragmentariness and lack of dramatic consistency,[5] and its putative implication that the apparently formidable but actually impotent Hinkemann was to be seen as a symbol of postwar Germany.[6]

The first of these criticisms will not concern us in this post-Arrabal age, though as late as 1959 Werner Gilles found it "a ghastly play, in spite of all of the love of mankind it attempts to teach—disgusting and unbearable."[7] The unusually vociferous denigration of *Hinkemann* by rightist critics is all the more ironic, as John Spalek points out, in view of the fact that it is the one play by Toller that explicitly calls into question the claim that Communism has the solution to all of the world's problems, just as the one play that depicts a successful revolution untainted by the "defeatism" that mars Toller's later plays in the eyes of the BPRS, *Die Wandlung*, has had to be rejected by them owing to its anarchist orientation. Spalek remarks: "The imperceptiveness, or the complete inability of the critics to be objective about Toller, was never demonstrated more clearly."[8] The third line of criticism was lent some support by the title of the first edition (1923), *Der deutsche Hinkemann*, the second impression of which (1924) was already changed to *Hinkemann*. All subsequent editions (four impressions of the second edition, and the third edition) are simply titled *Hinkemann*.

Modern western criticism follows the trails blazed by the earlier reviewers, as Dorothea Klein notes.[9] Both Maloof[10] and Willibrand[11] complain of the lack of psychological motivation and question whether a simple worker like Hinkemann is capable of expressing the complicated thoughts he does, or whether he would be likely to buy and pray before a statue of Priapus, as he does at the end of the last act. On the other hand, Walter Sokel claims:

> In *Hinkemann* Toller attains in both a thematic and a formal sense a new dramatic level, and with it, the sharpest definition of his craft....With this drama, Toller completes the decisive transition from the caricaturing [typical] of Expressionism to the individualization of realism in the Shakespearean tradition; the consequent technique of characterization carries him far beyond the topicality of Expressionism into the universal and the timeless....While *Masse Mensch* refers only to revolutionary

situations and today (at least in the west) seems old-fashioned, *Hinkemann* will retain its currency so long as man consists of drives and spirituality, selfishness and love.[12]

We shall see that *Hinkemann* does indeed achieve a more than topical significance, though not solely for the reasons that Sokel adduces. What is interesting here, however, is that he detects in the making of this play the very psychological skill and complexity that Willibrand and Maloof find wanting. The many comparisons of Toller's play with *Woyzeck* also implicitly acknowledge elements of psychological realism, as do the (less frequently noted) resemblances with Gerhart Hauptmann's *Fuhrmann Henschel* (1898) and *Rose Bernd* (1903).[13] The parallels with *Woyzeck* are quite striking, and indicate a definite influence. To cite only one example, *Erster Handwerksbursch* says in *Woyzeck*: "...And in conclusion, ladies and gentlemen, let's just piss over this cross, so that some Jew will die!"[14] And Hinkemann says to Knatsch, "If two people [piss] over a cross—a Jew will die."[15] Further parallels are cited in Dorothea Klein.[16]

The early Marxist criticism of the two Russian productions (Moscow and Leningrad) is surprisingly favorable in view of Toller's announced intention to demonstrate the limits of socialism:

> As to your doubts whether Hinkemann is a tragic figure or not, I have nothing to say. I wanted to show in Hinkemann not only the indelible tragic sorrow of a man typical of many others, but also the tragic limits of a society, and where it can no longer help the individual.[17]

This benevolence is generally accomplished, for example, in the review by Sergei Gorodetskii,[18] by interpreting the play in a completely individualistic, personal and realistic sense, and then arguing that the consequent pessimism may apply to someone with such a bizarre wound as Hinkemann's, but that it has no more general significance in the cosmic scheme of things. Other Russian critics[19] are less indulgent and find this pessimism defeatist and sentimental.

The modern Marxist criticism exhibits the same curious dichotomy. Hans Marnette speaks of "a deep *political and philosophical pessimism.*"[20] Martin Reso recognizes this pessimism but, like the earlier Soviet critics, contrives to detect no danger to the Marxist ideal in it. He writes:

> What remains of this play? There remains an unprecedented outraged protest against the inhumanity of the social order; there remains an appeal to the human qualities of the individual; there remains the certainty that a new society, yet to be created, can and must prevent such misery. The reservations that have been leveled at the play from all quarters are

not invalidated by these observations. The goal Toller had set himself, namely to show not only "the tragic sorrow of a man typical of many others, but also the tragic limits of society," could not be reached with this subject. And so there remains simply a protest of despair.[21]

This interpretation of *Hinkemann*, both of the western and of those Marxist critics inclined to be favorably disposed toward Toller, has been achieved in both cases by emasculating and trivializing the play. Hinkemann is surely more than a man mutilated in such a unique and unusual way that his experiences are significant for other more normal beings only because they underscore the brutality of war. In closing one's eyes to this symbolic dimension, one blinds one's self to Toller's purpose as well. It is of course true that Toller does not claim that the inner transformation of man that he so vividly depicted in *Die Wandlung* is objectively impossible or inconceivable. Hinkemann says indeed:

> All of us: one soul in one body. To think there are people who've forgotten that! In the war they suffered and they hated their masters and obeyed orders and killed each other. And they've forgotten everything—They'll soon be suffering again, and hating their bosses again, and obeying orders again—and killing each other again....That's the way people are. They could be different if they wanted to. But they don't. They mock the spirit. They sneer at it and disgrace the spirit and crucify it. Again and again.
>
> How senseless it all is! They impoverish themselves when they might be rich and do without the kingdom of heaven. The blind! [H 60-61; II, 246]

Man could be otherwise, could transform himself, but he will not. This seems to be the inescapable conclusion of Hinkemann's words, for he says them with a rope in his hands (in the second edition), over the body of Grete and amid the ruins of his life. One may be permitted to doubt that a "new, yet to be created society can and will prevent such misery," as Reso claims. Indeed, we may interpret Hinkemann in his impotence as a representative of the political poet in post-war Germany, who cries: "I write. But he, against whom I write, can not read."[22] This interpretation may seem somewhat daring, for we are told of Hinkemann: "Hinkemann speaks neither 'glibly' nor sentimentally. His language always exhibits the inarticulateness, the torpor of the simple soul" [H 1; II, 195]. Yet in the decisive fourth scene of the second act, in the bar, Hinkemann's protestations of inarticulateness have the self-deprecatory air of one who recognizes the hollowness and inadequacy of his adversaries' arguments, in spite of their facility.

Hinkemann (answering Unbeschwert): Maybe it *is* simple. Perhaps you're right....A lot of what you said about woollen shirts and silk shirts is right. People can't be good when they don't have enough to eat—Maybe I'm just too dumb to figure it all out, to see it clearly, the way it is like you—. You're a party worker and you understand faster....[23] [H 26; II, 217f.]

Toller is using here the technique of Shakespeare, whose King Lear sees only when he is blind, or of Sophocles and his Oedipus and Tiresias, who, though blind, are the only ones who recognize the horrible truth. Whereas Hinkemann laments here that perhaps he is too dull to see clearly, later he exclaims to Max Knatsch:

You wander through the streets, day after day, like a blind man. And then, all of a sudden, you *see*. Knatsch, what you see—it's terrible. You see the *soul*. And you know what it looks like? Dead....Have you ever put out the eyes of a goldfinch? [H 46; II, 234]

This interpretation of Hinkemann as a symbol of the impotent political poet is supported by Toller's irony in presenting him as a slow, weighty speaker whose very inarticulateness achieves an eloquence so powerful as to silence all others, as well as by his deprecatory references to himself as dim-witted and blind to reality when in fact, it is only he who sees the truth. The theme of the blinded goldfinch also supports this interpretation, for the bird has been mutilated by Grete's mother (as Hinkemann has been mutilated by the war):

HINKEMANN: Your mother. Your own mother. a *mother*! Imagine a mother putting out the eyes of her own goldfinch because some newspaper says that blind birds sing better.... [H 2; II, 195f.]

The evident connection between Hinkemann and the goldfinch is more than a simple identification with another suffering creature, whose suffering Hinkemann now understands, though before his wound he would have been blind to such misery. It is a symbol for the poet whose eyes are opened by pain. He tells the side-show concessionaire, who stands for all that exploits man's worst instincts, for the society that prostitutes its poets and saints:

HINKEMANN: No, sir, it was all worthwhile. They've opened my eyes for me. I see it all now, down to the bottom, down to the very bottom. I see men for what they are. I see what the world is. It's war again, sir. People are killing each other and laughing. Killing each other and laughing! [H 38; II, 228]

And in his delirium at the end of the play, Hinkemann recalls the vision he had of Grete and her eyes while he had been at the front:

HINKEMANN: I've known your eyes so long now. I saw them first at the works—and then in barracks—and in hospital—and in prison. The same eyes everywhere. The eyes of hunted, beaten, tormented creatures—. Gretchen, I thought you had everything, and now—you're just as miserable and helpless as I am. [H 56; II, 242f.]

Although Hinkemann ultimately comes to believe Grete—believes that she loves him, that she does not find him ludicrous, that she has not ridiculed him, still he kills himself. Ridicule, the rape of another's personality—this is the worst crime to Hinkemann, as we see in the parable of the desertion of Hinkemann's mother by his father. He says of his mother:

That was the worst thing of all—that he laughed at her when her soul writhed helplessly. Good God, didn't you hear her? Are you satisfied? [H 51; II, 238]

But here it is no longer enough for Hinkemann to know that his mother's fate is not his, that he has been ridiculed by the person who means the most to him. That indeed his self-abasement for her sake, his humiliation, have converted her. For as we have seen again and again in Toller, even though the individual may be transformed, yet he is only an individual. Mankind will go on producing Grosshahns and concessionaires to exploit it, and will willingly acquiesce in its own exploitation. Hinkemann tells Grete:

I came home and I saw grotesque faces—wretchedness, just the senseless, endless wretchedness of blind creatures. I don't have the strength to go on. I don't have the strength to dream. A man who doesn't have the strength to dream has lost the strength to live. That bullet was the fruit of the tree of the knowledge of good and evil—. All that I see, I understand; all that I understand tortures me. Once suffering made me want to go on—I no longer want to. [H 58f.; II, 244f.]

We have already noted Toller's letter to Stefan Zweig,[24] especially poignant in view of what we know of subsequent events, in which he avers that only the weak give up when they are unable to realize their dreams. The strong are able to carry on in spite of all disillusionment. What is wanted, Toller claims, are men not blinded to reality by their emotions who are strong enough to carry on in spite of all. The relevance of these words to Hinkemann is obvious. He, the poet, sees plainly the kind of strength that is required to endure this brutal world, and at the same time he sees his impotence—how far he is from possessing it. He is no longer able to strive in spite of his knowledge, no longer able to pursue an ideal so manifestly impossible of realization. In not having the strength to dream, Hinkemann allows the stuff of his dreams, which might, as

Landauer suggests, have through an act of will remained an ideal, to be transformed into an illusion. The eating of the fruit of the tree of knowledge of good and evil has robbed him of the possibility of paradise. The possibility, which objectively exists ("Making themselves poor when they could be rich"[25]), exists only for those whose faith in the spirit is strong enough. Thus he laments: "Any day could bring paradise; any night, the deluge." [H 61; II, 247]

Toller realizes that the dilemma of *Masse Mensch* can only be resolved if man is transformed, if the new man is born. Only then can the new, non-coercive society be created without employing means which vitiate its ideals. In the light of this insight, it becomes necessary to reject authoritarian socialism in favor of anarchism. The question then becomes: is this anarchism realizable, and the answer hinges on the possibility of the transformation of man, and thus on his commitment to *Geist* (creative spirit). When Hinkemann speaks to his comrades during the political discussion in the bar, we are not to take his use of the word "soul" in its narrowest sense as mere indemnification, recompense for lack of sex, companionship:

And that woman—how shall I put it—. You'd hardly think it was possible—but that woman loved—as you might say—his soul. [H 31; II, 222]

Sokel's interpretation unnecessarily circumscribes the theme and thus trivializes it. He says:

The problem is thus not a philosophical, ideological one, as it is in *Masse Mensch* and in *Die Maschinenstürmer*. It is rather an individual and spiritual problem. The community we are concerned with is not [composed of] the people of a nation or of mankind, but is rather the most intimate and deepest of all ties: that of two human beings that love one another....The question is much more intimate and therefore also universal: can a woman love her husband as a human being even when he has ceased being a man, and can the husband believe in such a love. In posing this question, we are inquiring into the very nature of love itself.[26]

Hinkemann's infirmity, when it is interpreted in the broader sense indicated above, proves to be not a lack in him, but one in the rest of us. The impotence of the Expressionist poet, of the anarchist, of the man who calls upon all to live for the spirit, has its origins in a defect of his listeners. Hinkemann characterizes himself with the following words:

I'm as absurd as this world—as miserable and ridiculous as this world.

The world has lost its soul and I have lost my sex. Is there any difference? [H 58; II, 244]

These words point clearly to the meaning we are to attach to Hinkemann's mutilation. Hinkemann's call goes beyond mere alterations in economic systems in order to make it possible for man to be good. It is in this sense that we are to interpret his repeated questioning of such superficial reformers as Singegott and Unbeschwert:

HINKEMANN: when the new order comes, there may be cripples there. How are they supposed to be happy?

....

UNBESCHWERT: That's another of those questions. A damned tough question. [H 29; II, 220]

When Toller describes his purposes in writing *Hinkemann* in the passage quoted above, it is clear that he intends more than a mere investigation of the nature of love, as Sokel claims. He wishes "...to show also the tragic limits of society and where it can no longer help the individual."[27] It is significant that Toller speaks of the limits of society, not simply those of socialism, though Hinkemann's interlocutors in the tavern represent various types of socialists. For Toller, all society is inadequate; only community can meet man's needs. It is in this sense that he writes to Tessa:

The socialist economic order does not result in a few men of different political origins directing the social organism. The socialist order is a communal economy; it is active communal life. Or to put it plainly: it is the elimination, to the greatest extent possible, of all tendencies toward oligarchy.[28]

Although Toller uses the adjective *sozialistisch* here, it is clear he is talking more about a philosophy like Kropotkin's communist anarchism than he is about the socialism of any of the established German parties of 1921. This is expressed even more unmistakably in the letter, "to a worker," which speaks, significantly enough, of the necessity for political literature in the true, non-dogmatic sense of the term and pleads for the place of aesthetic values in proletarian writing:

Isn't beauty a lesson? Do we not become more human, better men by contemplating beauty?...Have we lost our dream of a community which no longer wears itself out in the petty skirmishes of politics, indeed, a community freed from the professional politician as a social phenomenon? Of a society without hunger and anxiety, devoted to noble happiness and to noble suffering.[29]

The nature of Hinkemann's injury, his emasculation, has provoked a good deal of controversy in view of Toller's assertation that he had intended it to represent that suffering that remains after all Socialist solutions have been applied—the suffering that no social system can eliminate. The genetic interpretation, that the injury implies the capitalist war that caused it, is inadequate in the eyes of leftist writers, since with the eventual victory of the proletariat and the withering away of the state, there will be no more wars. Still, Toller, who in 1921 had not yet had the chance to witness wars between Communist powers such as Vietnam and China, could have had Hinkemann injured, say, in a traffic accident but chose not to. Rosemarie Altenhofer, in her fine study of Toller's plays, suggests that Hinkemann represents the "undeveloped state of consciousness of the proletarian in a non-socialist society, for whom love is the only area 'where he is free.'"[30] She goes on to suggest a different sort of socialist interpretation: "Improved social conditions will be accompanied by a higher state of consciousness of the proletarian, and certain socially determined demands and norms will be eliminated such as a questionable concept of masculinity that rests on potency alone. The possibility of creating new values through enlightenment and schooling, the increased intellectual capability of relativizing traditional norms will not eliminate the suffering but they will provide the presupposition for finding a new 'anchor' which may not lead to happiness but which will give life a certain sense."[31]

Such an interpretation, it seems to me, omits entirely the important laughter-motif that dominates the play from the scene between Hinkemann and his mother to that where Grosshahn holds Hinkemann up to ridicule. If Hinkemann is seen as the bearer of political message, a poet, then his sexual impotence is symbolic of a much larger kind of impotence, the inability to beget the "new man," and the laughter that he encounters represents a much more pervasive resistance to the demands of humanity than those suggested by the immediate situation. To convey this sense of impotence, of the unwillingness of even the workers to be converted, a sexual symbol was necessary. Indeed, the anarchist psychoanalyst Otto Gross, who lived in Munich in the last days of the War, and maintained close contacts with a number of Expressionist and leftist writers such as Leonhard Frank, Franz Jung and Franz Werfel, also sees sexuality as a metaphor for man's reaching out to his fellows, for mutual aid. In his essay, "Über psychopathische Minderwertigkeiten" ("On psychopathic Inferiority Complexes," 1909), he theorizes that when the demands of society and social organization are internalized by the individual, they result in psychic conflicts such as aggressive tendencies in men and sexually unconventional tendencies in women. These can take the form of crime, kleptomania and other sorts of antisocial behavior. A kind of antinatural selection results, since those women who reject the monogamous family and chose independence do not attract husbands, and thus do not reproduce. Later on, Gross moved further away from Freud and redefined his notion of aggressive tendencies to include the defense of the sanctity of the individual against collectivist incursions, and his notion of sexuality to include a reaching out for physical and psychic contact with one's fellow human beings. He says in "Protest and Morality in the Unconscious," (1919), "This sovereign predisposed-social and innate-ethical propensity...has already been made known to us in the discoveries of Krapotkin: the inborn '*instinct to help each other.*' By means of a comparative biological proof of this instinct, Krapotkin has begun to establish the basis for a *genuine ethics* as both a genetically-founded and normative discipline."[32] Thus the laughter of Hinkemann's comrades is all the more devastating since it implies a brutal rejection of the very same heightened level of consciousness that Altenhofer foresees.

Of the figure of political significance in the play, two advocate anarchist solutions: Max Knatsch, who represents anarchism in its nonproblematic aspect as a criticism of both capitalism and socialism, and Hinkemann himself, who represents, as we have seen, a vision of a society of both noble happiness and noble sorrow. Knatsch is presented as a clear-sighted radical who refuses to compromise his principles. He recognizes, for example, that the idealization of the proletarian (and thus the Marxian conception of the proletariat as a monolithic class) is a myth of the socialists. Unbeschwert launches an attack against the anarchists:

UNBESCHWERT:...But those who think they can skip the logical historical stages—those radical fanatics and dreamers from the east, who want to replace scientific fact with faith—

It is Knatsch who replies:

MAX KNATSCH: Will be solemly denounced from the pulpit. I know, I know—you've got your little formula....If men aren't ready for revolution, then all your historical developments and social conditions won't help them! And if they are ready for revolution, then the new age will begin, whatever the conditions. [H 25; II, 216f.]

In this, Knatsch represents Landauer and also Toller himself, who wrote in *Quer Durch:* "The German Revolution did not fail because the people weren't ready for it. All that talk of the necessity of the readiness of the people for socialism is dialectical tight-rope walking....No one becomes ready through knowledge alone; he just needs to be given the opportunity to march; then, in spite of all obstructions and detours, he will arrive at his goal.''[33] Michel Unbeschwert, who reproaches Knatsch [H 25; II, 217] (''...You're an anarchist—Someone who doesn't belong to a party doesn't accept responsibility.''[34]), later on (p. 35) laughs at Hinkemann, just as Immergleich responds to Hinkemann's hypothetical question with laughter—the same laughter which serves as a leitmotif for soullessness and brutality:

> HINKEMANN: ...Supposing—(he swallows nervously) someone—who had been in the war had lost his—manhood, for example. Supposing *that* had been blown off in the war—what would become of him in your new socialist state?
> (Peter clucks and sniggers softly) [H 28; II, 219]

It is the anarchist Knatsch who feels an instinctive kinship with HINKEMANN: ''That sort of thing makes you feel like crying, but not like laughing.'' [H 28; II, 219]. Yet Knatsch, too, is unable to offer a solution, and in the decisive moment, when Grosshahn describes the geek who is actually a eunuch, he laughs with the others. Like Ned Lud, he has faltered.

Hinkemann and Grosshahn represent two vastly different proletarian figures. Grosshahn, although a socialist, is the total cynic, willing to use and exploit people every bit as selfishly as any capitalist; Hinkemann is the skeptic who could survive only if he were able to extinguish his feelings, his sensitivity to others' suffering. The poet and the revolutionary who has seen to the very core can no longer return to ignorance. When Niekisch refused to admit the suprapersonal significance of Hinkemann's suffering in terms of the political poet's mission, Toller reproached him:

> It surprised me that you, like the newspaper critics, saw the superficial ornamentation, but not the essence....A deep sense of necessity drove him to demolish man's illusions. Yet experience has to lead the way, the experience of insight.[35]

9

Hoppla, wir Leben! —Anarchism
and Revisionism

We have not had a revolution in Germany, but we have had a counter-revolution. —Kurt
Tucholsky: *Gesammelte Werke*, I, 407

As Jost Hermand points out in his book *Unbequeme Literatur*
(*Uncomfortable Literature*),[1] Toller is remembered today, insofar as he is
remembered at all, primarily as the author of *Die Wandlung, Masse Mensch*
and *Die Maschinenstürmer*, which are treated by many critics as emotion-laden
but poetically weak effusions typical of the early phases of Expressionism.
Toller is seen by critics like Felix Hollaender, Herbert Ihering, and Hans
Siemsen as an ambitious but mediocre writer, whose early plays are of some
historical interest, and whose later plays have rightfully vanished into oblivion.
Julius Bab, for example, remarks, after telling the story of Toller's imprisonment:

> This is what one has to know in order to understand the success of these
> plays, which cannot otherwise be understood solely in terms of the
> political topicality of their themes and certainly not in terms of their ir-
> resistible poetic power. For hard as it is to say something unfriendly about
> this doubtless pure and emotionally honest author—his inherent creative
> power is minimal....This Toller was a very nice—dilettante.[2]

Toller, it should be noted, returned the compliment, calling Bab "the most
wretched example of German critical fault-finding."[3]
Of Toller's later plays, only *Hinkemann* appears in both the 1961 Hiller anthology[4] and the 1961 East German Uhse-Kaiser anthology.[5] The latter includes also (for hagiographic reasons, one supposes) *Feuer aus den Kesseln*.
Both omit *Der entfesselte Wotan, Hoppla, wir leben!, Wunder in Amerika,
Die blinde Göttin, Nie wieder Friede* and *Pastor Hall*. This neglect of Toller's
later works has created, as we shall see, a distorted view of both his literary and
his political development. In the case in question, *Hoppla, wir leben!* (1927),

134

the neglect can be justified neither in terms of dramatic success nor in terms of literary quality. *Hoppla, wir leben!* was, as Spalek indicates,[6] performed in Hamburg, Leipzig, Vienna, Frankfurt, Moscow, Copenhagen, Leningrad, Stockholm, Aarhus, Tallinn (Estonia), Moscow, Mannheim, Tiflis, London, Dublin, Cambridge, Rostov, Helsinki, Tashkent and Essen—all within two years of its successful premiere at Piscator's new Theater am Nollendorfplatz in Berlin on September 3, 1927. Piscator describes the event in his book, *Das politische Theater*, which also gives a detailed account of the production of the play: "As the curtain went down after the prison scene and the last words of Mother Meller: 'There's only one thing left to do—hang one's self or change the world,' the young proletarians spontaneously struck up the 'International,' which all of us sang, standing, until the end."[7] These words, by the way, do not appear in the printed edition of the play, which otherwise follows Piscator's version of the ending,[8] and it is unclear whether they were inserted in the stage version by Toller himself or by Piscator. Many of the critics who were impressed by the performance ascribed its success more to the genius of Piscator than to the play itself. Typical are the remarks of Felix Hollaender in the *8—Uhr—Abendblatt* of September 4, 1927: "Is it poetry—is it drama—is it horrid song, because it's politics? [Hollaender paraphrases a character in Goethe's *Faust*] To these and many other questions the bitter answer is: paper, nothing but paper....How extraordinary Piscator's power must have been, if it was able to ignite such an unsuitable object to such a brightly burning flame that we left his theater deeply moved in spite of all our critical reservations."[9]

These comments (and others, like those of Herbert Ihering in a similar vein in the *Berliner Börsen-Courier*, No. 44 of September 5, 1927) are somewhat disingenuous in view of the enormous worldwide success of the play indicated by the other productions noted above, none of them directed by Piscator. In the successful Leipzig performance was supervised by Toller himself. A number of writers, most recently Rosemarie Altenhofer ("Ernst Tollers politische Dramatik") and Thomas Bütow (*Der Konflikt zwischen Revolution und Pazifismus im Werk Ernst Tollers*) have emphasized the violence done by Piscator's staging to the spirit of the play—Altenhofer, for example, remarks that Piscator "staged it to pieces" (p. 179). Spalek lists more than 271 reviews in his bibliography,[10] among them nine in *Die rote Fahne* alone, which evidently found it necessary to deal with the work at some length.

In view of this considerable, one might even say sensational, popular success, one is forced to ask oneself why a work discussed with such fervor in 1927 has almost totally disappeared from the scene. It is clear why a play that so savagely attacks the hypocrisy and corruption of Weimar Germany in the tradition of *Der entfesselte Wotan* and of Carl Sternheim would meet with the disapproval of bourgeois liberals, not to mention the automatic opposition of rightist circles to anything written by Toller. The following exchange, for example, between the banker and his son could very well have been written by Wedekind or Sternheim:

FINANCIER: How long will Kilman hold out?
....
FINANCIER'S SON: He's passé. You may as well fling your Kilman into the general bankruptcy of democracy. Just sniff the atmosphere of the industrial world! I'd advise you to put your money on a national dictatorship. [HL 33; III, 31]

Or, one thinks of such similar scenes as the "Discussion evening of the Study Group of Intellectual Brain-Workers," or the scene in which Graf Lande, having planned Kilman's assassination, repairs to an assignation with Kilman's daughter, only to be put off with the following exchange:

LOTTE KILMAN: Well, perhaps you men disgust me. Perhaps you're beginning to bore me.
COUNT LANDE: But darling—.
LOTTE KILMAN: Only women can be tender in bed. I don't deny that I'd like to seduce the little doll. [HL 105; III, 89]

The mordant satire of a thoroughly corrupt society offered in the Grand Hotel scene reminds one of the third act of Wedekind's *Die Büchse der Pandora* (*Pandora's Box*), where Alwa and Schigolch go through the pockets of Herr Hunidei, while he is being entertained by Lulu in her room and find nothing but gloves and a book of homilies:

SCHIGOLCH: This guy seems to be a total reprobate!...This race is done for. This nation has seen its best days....The jerk doesn't even have a silk scarf. And we Germans grovel before these guys.[11]

Jost Hermand draws a highly instructive parallel between the "Americanized" Weimar Republic and the America of Toller's *Reisebilder* in *Quer Durch* in his description of the scene in the Grand Hotel in the third act, where

...the parasitical Weimar and Stresemann cronies, the cabinet ministers, bankers, nobility and bourgeois philosophers of culture ply themselves with oysters and champagne and at the same time expatiate in pompous words on democratic self-sacrifice. It is only a small step from this to the *Amerikanischen Reisebildern* of 1930, in which Toller confronts the hypocritical liberalism of the "American Dream" with social realities like

Prohibition, puritanical prudery, religious intolerance, junky films, lynchings, garish advertising, brutal greed for profits, and suppression of socialists and blacks, in order to reveal the superficial character of this conception of democracy.[12]

Hermand characterizes the Marxian and Socialist criticism aptly with the following words: "On the basis of this chauvinistic chorus of hatred from the rightists one expects from the Communists either effusive praise or at least leftist solidarity. But once again, the old law, 'The enemies of my enemies are not necessarily my friends' proves true."[13] Bruno Kaiser complains, for example, of Toller's "doubts of the justification for decisive, partisan, revolutionary action."[14] Alexander Abusch, writing in *Die rote Fahne* of September 7, 1927, reproaches Toller for not asserting the exclusive right of the KPD to lead the proletariat, although his view of the play is not totally negative.[15] Similarly, Frida Rubiner condemns the play as defeatist and counter-revolutionary.[16] Fritz Hampel complains of the play's "pacifist-anarchist bias."[17] Ernst Steckel considers the play poison for the ideologically innocent proletarian.[18] These few remarks will suffice to show the main lines of the attacks to which the play was subjected.

It seems, in view of the discrepancy between the public reaction to *Hoppla, wir leben!* and the tenor of the remarks quoted, that to a large extent the negative criticism is based on ideological differences rather than any objective evaluation of the work on a dramatic or even on a philosophic basis. The reason for this discrepancy, it is suggested in Hermand's article, is a distorted interpretation of the playwright's intentions caused by a mistaken identification of Karl Thomas with Toller. The reasons why such an identification might arise are obvious enough. Toller, like Thomas, was imprisoned for his role in the events of 1919 and removed from society, though not for eight years. Toller, like Thomas, joined the revolution out of moral conviction: "There are always only a very few, who are driven by inward necessity" [HL 16; III, 18]. Toller, like Thomas, had had occasion to be examined by psychiatrists.[19] Karl's tale of his conversion to pacifism during the war [HL 62ff.; III, 55ff.] resembles almost verbatim similar descriptions in *Eine Jugend in Deutschland* of Toller's experiences in the Bois-le-Prêtre.[20] Toller, like Thomas, broke off his studies. Moreover, others among the characters are patterned on historical figures. Fritz Hampel calls Kilman "one-hundred percent a Braun-Severing."[21] Dorothea Klein notes: "Ernst Heilborn points out convincingly that the election of the Minister of War, Wandsring, in the play refers to the election of Hindenburg in 1925...."[22] She identifies the other two candidates as Wilhelm Marx and Thälmann.[23]

In spite of these similarities, it is clear that Karl Thomas can be said to speak for Toller only to a limited extent. Hermand, and before him, Martin Reso, Dorothea Klein, Katharina Maloof and others emphasize the distance between creator and creature, and see in it a kind of objective self-criticism on the part of the author of his own political ideology. Hermand views Toller's method as something akin to dialectic, in the manner of Brecht's *Der Jasager*, which he willingly transformed in *Der Neinsager* in 1929-1930 (about the same period as *Hoppla, wir leben!*) in order to explore all the possibilities of the dramatic idea, to "think the thought through to its conclusion," as Georg Kaiser put it. Hermand writes:

> While *Die Wandlung* still is directed toward and culminates in a great prophetic scene and thereby corresponds in an almost paradigmatic fashion to the typical Expressionist drama, here Toller proceeds in a significantly more dialectical manner. In *Hoppla, wir leben!* no manifestos are proclaimed; no sermons are hurled at the public; rather, a series of basic stances toward revolution is examined in a highly antithetical manner in the form of dialogue....In sharp contrast to propagandistic theater and to empathetic [Aristotelian] theater, here there is no "hero"; [there are] simply representatives of ideas who either complement one another dialectically, or lead one another *ad absurdum* intellectually.[24]

One thinks of Buber's concept of dialogue as a device for achieving truth within a social context. The Marxist Reso also emphasizes the distance from which Toller sees Karl Thomas. He writes:

> The human being, Karl Thomas, perishes because in a world he no longer understands he wishes to bring about something that is impossible....His experiences after being released from prison indicate to him that he is the only one still true [to his ideals]—which isn't true, since his friends and comrades are behaving altogether honorably....Because he is right in his estimation of *one* of his acquaintances, Kilman, he generalizes his experiences and condemns his friends, because he, as Toller puts it, "equates motivation and deed."[25]

According to this view, Toller examines the behavior of his "hero" with an objective and unjaundiced eye, and far from using him as a mouthpiece, judges him against Kroll, Eva Berg and Mother Meller and finds him wanting. It is therefore unfair to criticize Toller for the "defeatism" or for the ideological deficiencies of Karl Thomas, as Malzacher, for example does: "If one wants to achieve a political effect through one's writing, if one wants to speak to one's time, uncover abuses and sound an alarm—and Toller wanted to do all of these things!—then one has to begin with clear ideas and know how to formulate them."[26]

Such criticism amounts to setting up a straw man and then knocking him down, because it attributes views and purposes to Toller which are not his at all. Dorothea Klein refutes such passages as the above: "Toller certainly *did* have clear ideas, and he formulated them in *Hoppla, wir leben!*. He simply didn't do it in the form of a pure propaganda-play. It was just by juxtaposing various points of view that Toller hoped to cause a reasonable spectator to recognize the point of view that he considered correct as the only valid and appropriate one."[27]

This view, which to some extent agrees with and prefigures Hermand's, is also that of Katharina Maloof, who emphasizes the extent to which Toller regards Thomas critically: "This ruin of the hero reveals more than the concession of Karl Thomas' inability to distinguish between appearance and reality in the political sphere; the author also answers the question of the possibility of a humane community—a question that had occupied him in all his works—with a 'no.'"[28]

Toller's own discussion on the variant endings of his play in *Quer Durch* confirms both Maloof's sense of the pessimism and despair inherent in all the variants as well as the theory that Toller regards Karl Thomas critically:

> In my first version Thomas, who doesn't understand the world of 1927, runs to a psychiatrist in an insane asylum, realizes in the conversation with the doctor that there are two kinds of fools—those who are incarcerated in solitary confinement, and the others, who are inflicted on mankind as politicians and military men. It is then that he understands his former comrades who promote their ideals through onerous, routine work. He wants to leave the insane asylum because he has achieved the mature man's relationship to reality, but now the psychiatric authorities are no longer willing to let him go, for now he *is* "dangerous to the public" whereas before he had only been an inconvenient dreamer.[29]

This was a view that Toller had come to even before he wrote *Hoppla, wir leben!*, as numerous similar passages in his prison letters and prose writings demonstrate. He writes to Henri Barbusse for example: "In this age of the decline of capitalism, which tempts in different guises the soul of all of us, which persecutes all who rebel against it, it is certainly not particularly easy for a man to raise his voice untiringly in an unending struggle."[30]—an exact picture of Kilman's regime.

In 1923, in a letter which highlights both the anarchistic aspects of Toller's conception of his ideal society and the hard work necessary to achieve it, he remarks: "True democracy is uncomfortable; it requires the intensive participation of the people in public life, self-determination, readiness on the part of each individual to assume responsibility. True democracy is the form of government in which the individual can develop most fruitfully."[31]

And finally, he writes in *Quer Durch*: "There is only one form of propaganda that is not permitted the artist, and that is the tendency toward black-and-white portraiture, which paints adherents of one party as devils and those of the other as angels."[32] Words which are paraphrased by Karl Thomas himself, who tells Kilman: "I've never claimed that the bourgeoisie was raven-black and the masses snow-white" [HL 47; III, 42].

Before we proceed in our analysis of Toller's techniques of characterization, it will be expedient to summarize the plot. *Hoppla, wir leben!*, written three years after Toller's release from prison, begins with a prologue. Six revolutionaries are awaiting execution, among them Karl Thomas, Eva Berg—a young girl who is in love with Thomas, Albert Kroll, Mother Meller, who faces death with calm dignity, and Kilman, who ridicules a frightened fellow prisoner, even though he himself has scrupulously avoided danger and in fact has been able to strike his own deals with his captors. Finally the death sentence is commuted to further imprisonment, whereupon Karl Thomas goes mad and is delivered to a mental hospital.

Eight years later, he is released and visits Kilman, who has in the meantime become Minister of the Interior. Thomas encounters in Kilman a ruthless compromiser, a tool of the industrial and banking classes ready to engage in any chicanery to prevent worker participation in the national election, including sending out goons who manhandle Mother Meller. Eva, since fallen out of love with Thomas, has now resolved that only the totally unemotional day-to-day routine work of radical organizing bears any promise of success. She is fired from her job while organizing worker resistance in the chemical works.

Meanwhile, Thomas has found work as a writer in the Grand Hotel, which serves as a microcosm for all the depravity and corruption of the Weimar society of the twenties. He is appalled that his old friends have given up their hopes and dreams of a radical transformation of society, and on learning that the reactionary Minister of War has been elected president, and on seeing Kilman sell out to various bankers and industrialists, he determines to assassinate him. Although Thomas is anticipated by an anti-semitic student who regards Kilman as a leftist, he is arrested for the murder and imprisoned along with his former friends. An interview with the psychiatrist convinces him that the world is insane, and unable to bear a situation to which he sees no solution, he kills himself. As if to confirm Karl's insight, a statue to Kilman is unveiled by the man who hired his assassin.

It is clear that Toller has developed from the period of *Die Wandlung* and that his dramatic purposes are no longer the same, a fact which Malzacher in the passage quoted above refuses to recognize. *Hoppla, wir leben!* is no longer a pre-revolutionary play written for a pre-revolutionary period, one which proceeds from ethical ideals and principles to reality, but rather very much a post-revolutionary coming-to-terms with political realities. Toller states in *Briefe aus dem Gefängnis*: "We must finally abandon the platitude that world-capitalism has been shattered by the War."[33] In the working out of his "dialectic," Toller proceeds by bodily lifting Karl Thomas out of time and lending him the status of an extraplanetary observer who views the post-revolutionary situation in terms of its justice and its effects, rather than in terms of causes and the justifications which have been adduced to excuse each little compromise along the way. Toller noted in a letter from his prison cell to Alexander Bloch of January 5, 1923:

> What is happening outside I learn from the newspapers; and I have the feeling that I, observing from my island the visage of these times, see its outlines more clearly, more impressively, less blurred than if I were outside, influenced by transitory events which, though they seem important, only obscure the view because one doesn't immediately recognize in them their exaggeration.[34]

He does this in order to examine critically the basis of two kinds of revisionism: the perverted and self-serving variety represented by Kilman, and the honorable and frustrating variety represented by Albert Kroll, Eva Berg and Mother Meller.

Dorothea Klein points out[35] the carefully delineated political spectrum of characters through which Toller represents the various shades of accommodation with capitalism. Graf Lande and the student assassin of the right correspond to the radical anarchist Thomas on the extreme left. These radicals are united in their isolation and in their respective plans to achieve their goals by destroying violently the representatives of the existing order.

A second group, which also seeks to alter radically the existing order, but through more or less legal means, is composed of two factions: Kroll, Mother Meller and Eva Berg form the left wing; the conservative nationalists, Baron Friedrich and Wandsring, form the right wing. Between these groups and mediating among them stands Kilman.

The characterization of Kilman is quite subtle. We see him in the prologue as more or less totally reprehensible, a coward who manages to extricate himself at the last opportune moment. In spite of his betrayal of his comrades, Kilman is able to affect great indignation when the sixth prisoner asks to see a priest

before his execution: "You call yourself a revolutionary? You twerp! You want
to see the chaplain! 'Dear God, make me good and let me go to heaven!'" [HL
13; III, 16]. When Karl Thomas suspects the truth (even here displaying a kind
of clearsighted realism that escapes the others, for all their subsequent matter-
of-factness), we witness the following exchange:

KARL THOMAS: Or—did you beg for mercy? Then swear at least that
you'll keep quiet.
WILHELM KILMAN: Why do you guys let him insult me? [HL 12; III,
15]

When we see Kilman at work however, in the second scene, it is obvious he is
extremely competent, as he himself avers and as even his enemies confirm. Yet
this very competence shows all the more clearly the bankruptcy of his revisionist
philosophy (to the extent that it is sincere in the first place). He believes, he
tells Thomas, that the masses are incapable in this technological age of independent action; that they must be led by a kind of avuncular elite. He claims
to aim at bettering their conditions by working within the democratic system.
He tells Thomas: "In our goal we agree. It is only in the choice of
means...."[HL 49; III, 43]. An interesting counterpart to this was provided by
another, more honorable revisionist, Eduard Bernstein, who said: "This
aim...is nothing to me, *the movement everything.*"[36] Toller writes to Max Beer
in pejorative terms of the revisionists: "The active wing has always been
isolated and suppressed by those who exhibit their revolutionary talents on
Sundays in commemorative articles and who on weekdays ally themselves with
the class they pretend to fight."[37]

But the picture of Kilman we get from the prologue is corrected somewhat in
the scenes following. We have seen that in response to Thomas' assumption:
"Your cabinet post is just a smoke-screen, right?" [HL 44; III, 39]. Kilman
tries to create the impression of a man working for the same revolutionary
goals, but through other, evolutionary, means. He says of these means: "We
reject the notion of a struggle of brute force. We've tirelessly preached that we
intend to win with moral, spiritual weapons only. Violence is always reactionary." [HL 46; III, 41]—words which one can well imagine coming from
Toller's own heart. When Kilman tells Karl Thomas: "Life doesn't unravel according to theory. We learn from our experience" [HL 44; III, 40], we feel
justified in accepting this as Toller's considered verdict, for it seems clear from
his remarks on the first version of the ending (quoted above) that Thomas is to
be seen as an exemplar of the revolutionary who has not learned from his experience, and thus is doomed to ineffectuality, whereas Kroll, Meller and Berg
have drawn the necessary conclusions and altered their tactics to fit the post-

revolutionary circumstances. If compromise corrupts and absolute compromise corrupts absolutely, then it is evident that Karl's planned assassination is the futile act of a romantic, for on the one hand, whoever takes Kilman's place, even if as a tactic, will be corrupted, and on the other, in such an obviously disillusioned and politically dormant post-revolutionary situation, such a deed will not serve as a *Fanal* (a torch, to use the language of *Die Wandlung*). Toller notes in one of his prison letters of the post-revolutionary period (1921):

> Whoever fights for Socialism must take the long view....Sometimes I feel that I ought to denounce these times, if only to free myself from the living nightmares that swirl around me in a terrible swarm of brutality, of orgies of hatred, of complete disregard for life, of soullessness. The catastrophe seems to be inevitable.[38]

Erich Mühsam, for example, describes the situation in an article "May Day" in the May, 1927 issue of *Fanal* (Jg. 1, Nr. 8, May 1927, pp. 113-114):

> What great good luck. May Day falls on a Sunday! Just imagine the joyous celebration—everyone can march along out to the countryside, the red and black-red-gold flags decorated with the lovely ornaments of a young springtime, and the measured tread of battalions of workers, melodiously accompanied by the rattling of baby carriages, moves in exemplary order to the celebration, where families can brew coffee, and commemorative speeches and flirting are followed in the evening by dancing. "May has arrived!" resounds though hill and dale; we do *not* preach hatred of the rich, only equal justice for all! Grassman, however, removing his clenched fist from his pocket and banging it on the lectern which is draped in red and resplendent with the green of spring, assures the joyful couples who, hand in hand, are transfixed by the speaker's mighty moustache, that he will tell Steigerwald where to get off; that the emergency labor law is a disgrace to the German social system; that the bourgeois parties had better not push us around, for the colossal participation in this year's May Day events shows that the workers stand foursquare behind their proven leaders, firmly determined to fight for the eight-hour day with their ballots in their hands, true to their battle-tested, million-man strong organizations, to their party and to their unions, now and forever, until death—for victory will be ours in spite of all! And now Grassman waves to a worker who in spite of the lucky chance that the first of May falls on a Sunday this year is unable to help celebrate, for he has to keep an essential service in operation and in his capacity as taxi driver take the devoted labor leader to the next village to struggle against exploitation and the bourgeois parties for peace and the

people's spring—Oh, May of Mays!''

John Willett, in his fascinating *Art and Politics in The Weimar Period*, describes a meeting called by the editor of *Die Aktion* and attended by Franz Jung. After being told that it was up to each individual to make the revolution, Jung records: "There was a moment of silence. The meeting, where a moment before everyone had been shouting at one another, dispersed as if touched by an icy breath" (p. 44).

The year 1927 is plainly not the time, nor Karl Thomas the man that the words in *Die Wandlung* refer to:

...A brother, who bore within him
The will to build temples of ecstatic joy,
And open wide the gates to noble suffering,
Who formed the glowing, crystal cry:
The way!
The way!
O poet, lead us.[39]

The abyss between these words and those of Eva Berg and Albert Kroll (even from a stylistic point of view) is immense. Karl asks Eva:

KARL THOMAS: What is...sacred to you?
EVA BERG: Why use mystical words for human things? Why are you staring at me? I see as I speak to you that the last eight years, when you were "buried" have changed us more than a century would have in normal times.
KARL THOMAS: Yes, sometimes I think that I come from a generation that has disappeared.
EVA BERG: What the world has gone through since that episode!
KARL THOMAS: How can you talk about the Revolution like that?
EVA BERG: That Revolution was just an episode. It is past.
KARL THOMAS: What is left?
EVA BERG: We are. With our urge for honesty. With our strength for new work. [HL 57; III, 51-52]

If we regard Eva and her friends and Kilman as two varieties of revisionists, then it is this honesty which serves to distinguish them. It is not immediately clear to what degree Kilman sincerely believes in the intrinsically reasonable arguments he adduces to prove his good will. The scene in the Grand Hotel indicates at least that he can't be overtly bribed. And when the comic figure, Pickel, at the end of a long and diffuse spate of blather asks the more or less rhetorical question: "Your Excellency, what will become of the world?" [HL

51; III, 45] Kilman, obviously plagued by his conscience, evades the question:

WILHELM KILMAN: What will becomes of the world?
PICKEL: What do you want to make of it, I mean, Your Excellency?
WILHELM KILMAN: Let's have a cognac first. Do you smoke?
PICKEL: Too kind of you, Your Excellency. Indeed, I have always said to
myself: you simply need to stand face to face with the Minister and....
WILHELM KILMAN: The world—the world—! H'm. It's not so easy to
answer that. [HL 51; III, 45]

Yet the question of Kilman's sincerity, while interesting, is in a sense irrelevant. Whether he is sincerely laboring under the delusion that he is acting in
the best interests of the working man, or whether he is cynically exploiting
them, the result is the same. Old ladies are beaten for distributing pamphlets,
strikers are fired and arrested, districts are gerrymandered, students are disenfranchised, and the power of the state is exloited for the benefit of various
private financial interests. Kilman tells Karl Thomas that life does not unravel
according to theories, that one must learn from one's experiences. What
Kilman has learned, apparently, is total abandonment of principle; deceit and
corruption under the guise of striving for the betterment of workers—another
example of what Erich Mühsam called "Bismarxism."

Karl's reaction to this situation, his plan to assassinate Kilman, is obviously
chimerical, if only because the presuppositions for a successful revolution are no
longer present as they were in 1918/1919 (if, indeed, they were then). And, in
fact, events prove this, for when Kilman actually is eliminated, it is the instigator of his death, the reactionary Graf Lande, who emerges to unveil his
monument.

We have seen that in the case of Kilman Toller's avowed intention to avoid
black-and-white caricatures has been realized, but we have also seen that we are
in no doubt as to how we are to regard Kilman's actions from the point of view
of usefulness to the working class. Toller once wrote of the Kilman-type politician:

I think there was no socialist who was not enraged when he read the
names Auer, Timm, von Haller at the bottom of this proclamation ("Call
for the Establishment of a Civil Guard," December 27, 1918). In a
revolution whose most significant aspect is the struggle between
capitalism and socialism, two revolutionary cabinet members and one
high revolutionary bureaucrat ally themselves with representatives of
capitalism who must, with every fiber of their beings, be enemies of
socialism. There can be no community of interest between the reactionary

bourgeoisie and the proletariat for the protection of the Revolution. Whoever considers such a community of interest possible or necessary is either naive or stupid—in either case, he is no socialist.[40]

What Rosa Luxemburg had warned Bernstein of has actually happened to Kilman: his means have so transformed his goals that there is nothing left of them, at best a caricature of a kind of welfare state. When Bernstein protested that capitalist Germany did, after all, contain certain anarchical elements, Luxemburg replied: "Capitalist society—to speak with Marx—is like that foolish virgin whose child is 'only very small!'"[41] And, as Leon Trotsky remarked in his *History of the Russian Revolution*: "In practice a reformist party considers unshakable the foundations of that which it intends to reform" [Part III, Ch. 5].

The quixotic aspect of Karl and his plan is underscored by the comic figure, Pickel. As Dorothea Klein shows, he is a kind of distorted image, a caricature of Karl Thomas. Altenhofer sees this as Toller's criticism of his own earlier political stance. Although Pickel's place in the economy of the play seems to have been generally misunderstood (he is considered superfluous by nearly all critics), he proves crucial to the interpretation when seen in the proper light. We have already noted the difficulties Karl has in making himself understood to Eva Berg, difficulties which are also characteristic of Pickel. Karl Thomas tells Kilman: "We speak different languages."[42] and Eva Berg similarly complains to Karl, "Again you're using expressions that no longer apply" [HL 58: III, 52].

Both Karl and Pickel are at variance with their milieu because of their isolation—Karl's years in an asylum, Pickel's origins in "Holzhausen, Bezirk Waldwinkel" [HL 50; III, 44]. Pickel absently blabbers his purpose to the first person he meets, the banker, just as Karl Thomas concentrates solely on his guiding star and refuses to be diverted by the mundane and banal realities of life. Klein notes: "Pickel blunders through the different acts and scenes: no one has time for him; everyone regards him as a burdensome nuisance."[43] The same could be said (naturally with corresponding changes in accent) of Karl Thomas, who, for example, is rejected by Eva and kicked out of her apartment, as he is rejected by Kilman and even Dr. Lüdin in the printed version of the play. Finally, both Karl and Pickel are suspected of the murder, whereas in fact both represent impotence and ineffectuality.

That Thomas represents the anarchistic alternative to the revisionism of Kilman on the one hand and of Kroll, Berg and Meller on the other has been recognized and emphasized by a number of interpreters. Toller's director, Piscator, who had conducted almost daily discussions with the author during the summer preceding the premiere, wrote: "The theme does not trace the path of a wavering revolutionary....Thomas is actually an anarchical, sentimental man, who quite logically fails. He shows us how we ought not to behave [he is a *reductio ad absurdum*]. What he demonstrates is the folly of the bourgeois social order."[44]

This view is essentially correct. Thomas is an anarchist not because he advocates the "propaganda of the deed" of the 1880's (he doesn't advocate it for others, nor in the end does he go through with it himself), but because he is conscious that the society he finds, if it is to be altered in any way that will make a difference, must be altered from the bottom up. Like a true anarchist, Thomas rejects the organized political party outright. In a passage that expresses Toller's sympathy with this view, but at the same time his doubts, he laments to Tessa:

> Your doubts of the possibility of reaching people through the party politics of our day have long since been my doubts, too. Will the parties (organizations of cliques) be able to create socialism? But how else?[45]

It will not do to modify society in the evolutionary way foreseen by Kroll. We see the conflict quite easily in the following exchange:

> KARL THOMAS: What courage! You're really cowards, all of you, all! all! If only I'd stayed in the lunatic asylum! My own plan already disgusts me! What's it all for? For a pack of cowardly, bourgeois dupes!
> ALBERT KROLL: You seem to expect the world to be a sort of fireworks displays set up for your own benefit, with rockets and flares and battle cries. You're the coward, not I. [HL 77; III, 66f.]

What Kroll demands is the kind of routine, hard work propounded by the Trade Union Congress in the Mannheim Agreement of 1906, in which the SPD in effect surrendered the revolutionary goals of the radical Erfurt Program of 1891 to the meliorism of the trade unions. Peter Gay quotes from this agreement:

> It is to be hoped that the frequent ructions between the party and the trade unions between 1905 and 1906 will have a lasting good effect in that the complete cooperation which now exists will never again be endangered by theorists and writers who attach greater value to mere revolutionary slogans than to practical work inside the labor movement.[46]

According to Gay, this alliance with the working man and his immediate aims, natural as it was for the SPD, spelled the end of the party as a revolutionary force long before this fact became evident to all in the fateful events of August, 1914. A party must choose between revolutionary action and parliamentary "boring from within" in the pursuit of electoral majorities—there is no middle way, and this is essentially the "dilemma of democratic socialism," to use Peter Gay's phrase.

Reso, too, recognizes this individualistic anarchistic center in Thomas, though like Piscator he condemns it, and believes that Toller also does. He claims:

> In Thomas is fulfilled the fate of a man who lives too much in the realm of ideas and overlooks the actual realities. He wants a world that is pure, free and humane and in which the old mistakes aren't made any more....He leaves not a trace behind, since he wants to conduct his struggle divorced from other people, without any ties to classes or social groups.[47]

Reso of course means that Thomas does not recognize the primacy of the KPD. But it is not true that Thomas rejects the help of like-minded comrades; it is rather the case that such comrades no longer exist. Karl's discussion of his dream (his vision), one which constantly recurred during the years of his treatment, during which he was able to view society from a distance, is instructive:

> KARL THOMAS: The edge of a forest. The brown trees reach towards the sky like pillars. Beech trees. The woods vibrate green with a thousand little suns. So delicate. I wanted to enter, I longed to. I didn't succeed. The tree-trunks bent out angrily and flung me back like a rubber ball.
> PROFESSOR LÜDIN: Hold on! Like a rubber ball. Interesting association. Listen to me; your nerves can bear the truth. The wood is the isolation cell; the tree-trunks represent the padded walls, rubber walls of the highest quality. [HL 24; III, 24f.]

This interpretation, like the doctor's perverted image of man in Georg Büchner's play, *Woyzeck*, is the polar opposite of what actually plagues Thomas. The woods, with their thousand suns and trees which reach for heaven represent the true *Gemeinschaft*, the ideal society, the community that Karl so desperately seeks, but which eludes and ultimately repels him in the next act, to which this scene is a prelude. The doctor tries to convince Thomas that his ideals are chimerical by gratuitously defining his world as a madhouse, whereas in fact it is potentially (in Karl's vision, at least) a place of unparalleled beauty. This is also evident in the chilling scene between Karl and the two children, Fritz and Grete. Unlike the old woman's tale in *Woyzeck*, where the children's illusions are brutally shattered by the adult, here it is the children as symbols of future who destroy the adult Karl's hopes utterly:

> KARL THOMAS: You don't know anything else about the war?
> FRITZ: That's enough for us.

GRETE: And how! The last time I got an F because I mixed up 1916 and 1917.
KARL THOMAS: And—what do you know about the Revolution?
FRITZ: We don't have to learn so many dates about that, so it's easier.
KARL THOMAS: What do the suffering and insights of millioris of people mean, when the very next generation is deaf to them? All experience flows into an abyss. [HL 61; III, 54f.]

Toller wrote to Tessa in a similar sense: "Your words slip into a void, no one is there to receive them. The emptiness forces its way into you; you want to become aware of your own voice. Then, when you *are* aware of it, you are horrified: your words have lost their life and sound and fall from your mouth, dead.''[48] And after Karl has related the gruesome experience in the war which has opened his eyes and transformed him, which has led to his revolutionary activities, he is forced to see that it will work no such change in this coming generation:

FRITZ: Were there many of you?
KARL THOMAS: No, the people didn't understand what we were fighting for, did not see that it was for them that we were struggling.
FRITZ: Were there many on the other side?
KARL THOMAS: Very many. And they had money and hired soldiers.
(pause)
FRITZ: And you were stupid enough to think that you could win?
GRETE: Yes, you sure were stupid.
KARL THOMAS: (stares at them) What did you say?
FRITZ: You were *stupid*....We've got to go now, Hurry up Grete! [HL 64; III, 57]

This scene occurs after the disillusioned and weary Karl, rejected by Kilman, asks Eva to flee with him from reality into a kind of Gottfried Benn-like South Sea paradise. Eva rejects such escapism and leaves for work. The scene with the children, then, represents a last attempt by Karl to break through the "walls of rubber" into the community he longs for, a last attempt at renewal of his flagging conviction. For this reason, his failure is all the more devastating—a failure reinforced by the fact that Eva immediately returns. She has been fired for her rabble-rousing activities because of the machinations of the erstwhile leftist, Kilman. The bankruptcy of routine, hard, daily agitation could not be more impressively demonstrated.

This little object lesson teaches us that although Jost Hermand is correct in a sense in calling attention to Toller's complexity, to the fact that Thomas is not unreservedly his mouthpiece, that Toller presents us with a whole spectrum of possible modes of political behavior, each of which has its merits, still it appears that Toller ultimately comes down on the side of Karl. One feels that indeed Toller in an intellectual sense thought that the task of the anarchosocialist in 1927 was routine agitation, as the many remarks from *Quer Durch* and elsewhere quoted above indicate. In this he was no doubt guided by the same clear-eyed common sense and acuity that informed Eduard Bernstein's classic text of revisionism, *Die Voraussetzungen des Sozialismus und die Aufgaben der Sozialdemokratie* (*The Presuppositions of Socialism and the Tasks of Social Democracy*).[49]It was obvious that the predictions of the Erfurt Program were faulty, that the bourgeoisie was not disappearing, that capitalism could recover even from such crises as the inflation of 1923, that the proletariat was not growing increasingly desperate, nor was it ripe for a revolution. Bernstein argued that the SPD had in fact become revisionist in spite of the assertions of the Erfurt Program and ought to recognize that fact. He said: "I set myself against the viewpoint that we have to expect a collapse of the bourgeois economy in the near future, and that Social Democracy should be induced by the prospect of such an imminent catastrophe to adapt its tactics to that assumption."[50] In the ensuing debate, Karl Kautsky rejoined: "If Bernstein believes that we must have democracy first, so that we may then lead the proletariat to victory step by step, I say that the matter is just the other way around with us: the victory of the proletarist is the precondition of the victory of democracy. Does anyone believe that this victory is possible without catastrophe? I desire it, but I don't believe it."[51]

In spite of all this, however, one cannot but feel that Toller's sympathies do lie with Karl Thomas after all. Toller saw the justice of the revisionists' arguments, but he also saw the force of Kautsky's and Karl Thomas' arguments. *Hoppla, wir leben!* is nothing if not a tale of unrelenting futility and oppression and the lesson of the scenes with Karl and Eva and Karl and Fritz and Grete, as well as all three variant endings, leaves no doubt that *both* Karl's and Kroll's paths lead to failure. This conclusion is as inescapable as the logic of the little syllogism with which Kilman regales Eva:

WILHELM KILMAN: You have been inciting the women at the Chemical Factories to refuse to work overtime?
EVA BERG: I've only been exercising the rights the Constitution gives me.
WILHELM KILMAN: The Constitution was planned for peaceful times.
EVA BERG: Aren't we living in them?
WILHELM KILMAN: The State rarely knows peaceful times.
[HL 29; III, 28]

Hermand, Maloof and Klein are certainly right to indicate that Toller meant Kroll to represent the realistic revolutionary in 1927; yet it seems clear that with another, no less realistic and logical part of himself, Toller realized that this path as well was futile (as indeed events have proved: only a few years after Bernstein's death, Hitler seized power).

In *Masse Mensch*, Toller was concerned with identifying the dilemma that faces every humanist, every ethically motivated revolutionary who seeks power to realize his ideals. There the danger was from the left, from a philosophy in which dialectics and determinism had rendered ethics superfluous. Here, in *Hoppla, wir leben!*, we see that in spite of Toller's intentions to depict the whole political panorama in all its shades of gray, what we are left with after all is another, different dilemma, another black-and-white situation where the choice is just as stark and the solution just as elusive as in *Masse Mensch*. Only here the challenge is from the right.

In *Hoppla, wir leben!*, Karl Thomas stands for the ideals for which Toller has always stood. It is a little disingenuous to ask, as Walter Sokel does, what Karl has to counter Eva's arguments and then answer; "...an ideal that's vacuous and intellectually refutable and has only subjective emotional meaning for someone who was left behind the times and stunted in his own development [owing to] his emotional instability."[52]

The unpleasant fact is that the ideals of Thomas, the anarchist, which promise the best of so many worlds, will be realized *neither* by the revisionism of Eduard Bernstein nor by the starkly pragmatic Marxism of Kautsky. One reads the brilliant essays of Bernstein and Luxemburg with the uncomfortable feeling that each is right. And yet their philosophies are mutually exclusive.

We do not know whether the words with which Mother Meller rang down the curtain at the premiere: "There is only one choice: one must hang one's self or change the world,"[53] were inserted by Piscator or Toller. At least, in view of their close collaboration and Toller's later remarks, we have no reason to assume they were added against Toller's wishes. But in any case, the irony is evident. The crowd which heard those words and sang the "International" as the curtain fell left the theater to change the world. For Toller, however, the revolutionary's spectrum of choices had again shrunk to two, to a black-and-white "dilemma of democratic socialism," and it was the other alternative that he ultimately chose.

10

Conclusion

Wandering between two worlds, one dead,
The other powerless to be born . . .—Matthew Arnold: *Stanzas from the*
Grande Chartreuse[1]

Of Toller's twelve full-length plays, it is the six that deal with the relationship between bourgeois and proletarian figures that are most useful in defining his political ideology. The remaining plays sometimes contain social criticism, like *Wunder in Amerika* (1931) and *Die blinde Göttin* (1933), but it is not criticism which implies or grows out of any sort of coherent political philosophy. *Die Rache des verhöhnten Liebhabers* (1925), "an amorous puppet play adapted freely from a story by Cardinal Bandello," is generally regarded as uniquely frivolous amid the canon of Toller's otherwise deeply serious plays. *Bourgeois bleibt Bourgeois* (1929), written with Walter Hasenclever, is an adaptation of Molière's *Le Bourgeois gentilhomme*.

In the Toller literature to date, the emphasis has indeed been on the early plays, probably because these were the basis of Toller's celebrity. Toller's one wholly optimistic play, *Die Wandlung*, written immediately before the revolution that it urged on Germany and performed immediately after this revolution had become reality, made Toller famous. The four plays written in Niederschönenfeld by the political prisoner, *Masse Mensch*, *Die Maschinenstürmer*, *Hinkemann* and *Der entfesselte Wotan* made Toller one of the most notorious writers of the Weimar Republic. When he was released in 1924, the scandals and polemics in the press that attended the performances of these plays were if anything surpassed by those following his first play written after his release, *Hoppla, wir leben!* The disappointing response to Toller's late plays, written under the shadow of Hitler's seizure of power in 1933 or in exile was not wholly a consequence of a rational assessment of their artistic merits. Theaters and producers who had witnessed the riots arranged by the Nazis at performances of *Hoppla, wir leben!* were unwilling to stage them. After 1933, of course, Toller, whose books were among the first to be burned, shared the fate of all the exiled German intellectuals, robbed of their language, of an audience for their ideas, of publishers and of theaters. Some of Toller's later works, like *Pastor Hall*, appeared only in English translation; some, like *Wunder in Amerika* were written in collaboration with other writers (in this case Hermann Kesten), or like *Die blinde Göttin* translated and adapted by English dramatists and produced in versions bearing little resemblance to the originals.

Of course, it is entirely possible that the later plays, marked as they were by a deepening sense of hopelessness owing to the evident collapse of all that Toller believed in and devoted single-mindedly to the analysis of human frailty, Nazism, the susceptibility of the masses to delusion and fraud do in fact represent diminished artistic powers. Certainly Toller himself feared that this was so. Recent critics, however, have made a case for the artistic importance of these later plays, just as other writers have rediscovered the certainly unjustly neglected prose works.

Some of these claims (I am thinking of Altenhofer's remarks on *Feuer aus den Kesseln* in particular) are quite convincing; others, like her analysis of *Nie wieder Friede* are less so.[2] What can be said with some degree of assurance is that there is a far greater degree of unity to Toller's work than we have so far realized: he is concerned here as before with the question of man's moral regeneration and whether what is conceivable is objectively possible, with human weakness and blindness, with the potentialities and seductions of leadership and power. However, these themes are treated in the later plays more as psychological problems than as political and tactical ones. Like Elias Canetti, Hermann Broch, Theodor Adorno and countless other exiles, Toller probed in these works the vulnerability of his society and his fellow men to barbarism.

In *Feuer aus den Kesseln* (*Draw the Fires*, 1930), a "historical drama" about the growth of revolutionary sentiment in the German navy from 1916-1918, there are anarchist features, but of a marginal sort. They appear in the person of Köbis, if not the "hero," at least one of the crucial characters of the historical panorama, and the one among the sailors who sees their plight and defines it in abstract and general terms. Weber says of him "Alwin is reading his learned books again."[3] What these books are, we learn when he quotes what turns out to be a remark of the anarchist Max Stirner: "I hope for nothing. I rely on myself alone."[4]

That these are words not mere idle posturing, but actually define his philosophy we learn from subsequent events. He tells the court that tries him:

> I kept silent when they accused me of threatening to blow up the *Prinzregent*. I kept silent, and I wanted to. I had no intention of defen-

ding myself in front of you. I despise you! ...We were much too stupid and too cowardly to do what you accuse us of! Today I wish we had done it. We hoped for great things from the Reichstag, the Deputies, the newspapers, the Independent Socialists. But nobody helps you if you don't help yourself.[5]

Feuer aus den Kesseln, Toller's anticipation of the "documentary theater" of the 1960s, deals not so much with a particular naval revolt (as does, for example, the anarchist writer, Theodor Plievier's *Des Kaisers Kulis*) as with the question of "judicial murder," the possibility of justice—a theme that one encounters everywhere in Toller's opus from the very first pages of *Eine Jugend in Deutschland* to the *Briefe aus dem Gefängnis,* to *Justiz. Erlebnisse,* to *Die blinde Göttin,* to the sections of *Quer Durch* dealing with race problems in America and Tom Mooney. Toller's writings on crime and punishment in fact constitute a German counterpart to Kropotkin's analyses in his *In Russian and French Prisons.*

As Altenhofer points out, the Marxist critique of *Feuer aus den Kesseln* is in fact justified in the sense that Toller examines an exceptionally egregious case of judicial murder (one comparable in its scope and implications to the Haymarket executions or to the condemnation of Sacco and Vanzetti) completely within the standards of bourgeois society.[6] He does not claim, as do his Marxist critics, that no justice is possible until the exploitative capitalist society is eliminated, for this would at least provide the Weimar establishment an explanation, if not exculpation. Here too, then, we note that Toller in true anarchist fashion affirms the claims of the individual against the rival demands of collectivism.

In the plays dealing with the rise of National Socialism: *Der entfesselte Wotan* (1923), *Nie wieder Friede!* (1934), and *Pastor Hall* (1936), the subtleties of political theory understandably recede into the background owing to *das Gebot der Stunde,* the exigencies of the day. Toller's faith in the goodness of man, his resolve to abjure the use of force in the service of humanitarian aims, his commitment to education, example, and the word as motors of social change—all of these crumbled in the face of Hitler and Nazism. Pastor Hall, in the play of the same name, is willing to employ means that the Woman in *Masse Mensch* was not—he flees, and in doing so causes the death of the guard, Heinrich Degen. Yet in the end he too dies, just as the Woman had died. When Hall enters the concentration camp, he is still capable of claiming:

Today I believe the only course is through understanding. There's not a question on earth that's so tortuous and muddled that it can't be solved without the use of force.[7]

But his fellow prisoner Hofer's description of the brutal torture and death of Erich Mühsam, and his own fate soon teach him otherwise. And Toller himself, at the end *Briefe aus dem Gefängnis*, asks:

Are there still any pacifists left who believe that the ruling powers of Europe could make the dream of peace come true? Do they hesitate at the thought of the journey? If only they would decide![8]

To Walter Fabian he writes from prison:

Believe me, these walls are no protective ramparts. You outside are grieved by the knowledge that men have learned nothing, nothing at all from the course of these last years; have gained no insight and have no strength to plan sensibly; that they remain barbarous in their feelings, and that the more barbarous they are, the more heroic they believe themselves to ·be; that political parties have failed which had a world to win; that catastrophes will destroy Germany, destroy Europe, catastrophes to fight which our good functionaries arm themselves with pamphlets. [You are grieved by all this.] The man in prison is grieved even more, for he lives without the distractions of everyday work.[9]

Political parties fail, and the new man does not appear—these two insights demonstrate the extent of the despair of the anarchist, for whom the party means prostitution of the individual and subordination of means to ends, and for whom the only alternative, the hope in a new man, proves illusory.

Toller's plays exhibit a stylistic development away from abstraction and toward increasing realism, the ''new sobriety.'' But they also evolve in a political sense, away from the optimism and concern with the longing for the spiritual of *Die Wandlung*, quite in the tradition of the German anarchists, Buber and Landauer, toward an anguished wrestling in *Masse Mensch* with the question of whether ethical considerations have any place in an economically determined society. In *Die Maschinenstürmer*, the focus shifts again from the ethical sphere to the economic, and we have seen that Toller states the problem in terms of the struggle between Social Darwinism and Kropotkin's reply to it, his theory of mutual aid. On both ideological and textual grounds one can argue for the direct influence of the two anarchists, Kropotkin, and through his translation of Kropotkin, Landauer, on Toller. We have noted that the same notion of mutual aid that Jimmy preaches and that looms so large in *Die Maschinenstürmer* also appears in metaphorical form in the lyric cycles, particularly in *Das Schwalbenbuch*. Finally, in *Hoppla, wir leben!* and *Hinkemann* we have seen that Toller moves even further from his spiritual origins and towards the sphere of "practical politics," only to conclude that like the pragmatism of the extreme left that of the center has no chance of success. It cannot give man the society for which he strives, and even if it could, his deeper needs and longings would remain unfulfilled.

But this descent from the rarified spheres of theory to the dirty business of Europe in the nineteen-thirties was not on that account marked by the embrace of compromise. For Toller recognized that if the optimistic idealism of *Die Wandlung* was anachronistic, the ruthless pragmatism of the Nameless One was odious and demeaning, and ultimately just as ineffectual.

We have seen that in his political plays Toller confronts all of the problems that have troubled leftists since Marx. In doing so, he decides in nearly every case in favor of solutions which assert the sanctity of the individual over all collectivist demands on him and which, taken together, add up to more than simply "unorthodox Marxism" or "humanism"; they form a consistent and detailed, non-trivial anarchistic philosophy in the tradition of Kropotkin. That this philosophy would never be realized in the Europe of the 1930's Toller knew full well. But he also knew that this fact did not invalidate his ideals. He perceived plainly that an exploitative society could not be changed through *Wandlung*, inner transformation, but he saw that, although it could be changed through the methods of the KPD, what would emerge would not be the society he wished. Werner Hirsch complains in *Die rote Fahne* of *Hoppla, wir leben!*: "So Toller comes out against the prevailing system and *against* social-democratic coalition politics ...[but] not *for* the proletarian mass."[10]

Toller did not want *Masse*, he wanted *Mensch*.

Guthke,[11] in the passage quoted in Chapter 3, accuses the Expressionists of naiveté, of diffuseness, of platitudes, of lack of a really convincing blueprint for the solution of the ills they recognized and portrayed. Many of these accusations are correct, given certain assumptions about the functions of a work of art. But whether it need be the task of art at all to describe in detail plans for ameliorating social ills is of course a controversial question. Yet, one might object, the Expressionists expose themselves to such criticism by moving in these regions in the first place. But even if one concedes that the theater is a moral institution (and not solely a propagator of pure aestheticism), that poets are the "unacknowledged legislators of the world," surely it is not the place to plan the new world in detail. T. S. Eliot wrote that "neither Shakespeare nor Dante did any thinking on his own,"[12] apparently considering their ideas either obvious or trivial. There is some truth in this, for the objective, the *Allgemeinmenschliche* which is one component of any enduring work of art is "obvious" in the resonant chord it excites in every perceiver; and the subjective, the idiosyncratic, in its grotesqueness, which is another component, is often "trivial" in the sense that its very uniqueness militates against its having consequences for mankind in general. The important ideas are no secrets (and are, in that sense, clichés) and neither are the important phenomena of this world. When Georg Kaiser employs a metaphor involving a community of men in a state of grace and brotherhood to evoke associations of the ideal realization of the highest human potentialities of creativity, or when Toller demands that each man create and live and die by moral standards as demanding as the Woman's, then it is pedantry or worse to castigate these poets for the nebulousness of their visions. For visions are frequently "visionary"—they are delicate blossoms. When critics tell us that Toller's prescription is useless because he has not shown us how it is workable, that he and his ilk are fuzzy-minded idealists, then one must reply that one of Toller's merits, in fact the nucleus of his *Weltanschauung* altogether, is that he showed us once again the choice which confronts man (and that it confronts *each* man) in its most extreme form. That it may not be humanly possible for each of us to choose correctly does not alter the essential reality of Toller's idealism, for if we do not, it is as good as objectively certain that the new world will remain a dream and the old world will disappear altogether. Toller was of course not the first to preach a vague and foggy cliché that is older than Jesus nor was he the first to experience the alternatives as hopeless—yet his life provided both cause for the extremity of his despair in this hopelessness and cause for the sincerity of his vision. He had experienced a war which Büchner had not and one can well imagine the effects of a life of practically unrelieved poignancy, of the intensity of the episode which led to *Das Schwalbenbuch*. These are perhaps the reasons why Toller felt it necessary to cry out in unabashed terms and in such an elementary, tactless and "childish" way. Yet, it is just this consciousness of the *extremity* of the human situation which is the origin of Toller's sense of the tragicomic. The world will not be made livable by committees which abolish superhighways and cigarette advertising or which provide enlightened sexual education for adolescents or other such pleasantly concrete measures. The recognition of this desperate fact, that all human ingenuity is irrelevant to making the world any better than it ever was (and that in fact even the efficacy of the idea of progress in an external and superficial sense is suspect) was Toller's theme.

Notes to Chapter 1
I was a German

[1] Romain Rolland, *Jean-Christophe in Paris: The Market-Place. Antoinette. The House*, trans. Gilbert Cannan (New York: Henry Holt, 1915).

[2] John M Spalek, *Ernst Toller and his Critics. A Bibliography* (Charlottesville: Univ. Press of Virginia, 1968), p. vii.

[3] Hermann Kesten, *Meine Freunde die Poeten* (Vienna: Donau Verlag, 1953), p. 160.

[4] Ernst Toller, *Eine Jugend in Deutschland* in *Prosa Briefe Dramen Gedichte. Mit einem Vorwort von Kurt Hiller* (Reinbek bei Hamburg: Rowohlt, 1961), p. 32. Henceforth cited as *PBDG*. Subsequent references to Toller's works will give the original edition cited as well as volume and page number in the new Toller edition by Wolfgang Frühwald and John M. Spalek, *Gesammelte Werke*, Reihe Hanser 250-255 (Munich: Hanser, 1978), in this case IV, 14.

[5] Ernst Toller, *Eine Jugend*, *PBDG*, p. 44; IV, 30-31. In an issue of the popular Hamburg magazine *Junge Menschen* dedicated to him, Toller refers to a childhood experience that predisposed him emotionally towards socialism. See Carel ter Haar, *Ernst Toller: Appell oder Resignation?* (Munich: tuduv Verlag, 1977) p. 152.

[6] Ernst Toller, *Eine Jugend*, *PBDG*, p. 52; IV, 43.

[7] Ernst Toller, *Eine Jugend*, *PBDG*, p. 52; IV, 69.

[8] Ernst Toller, *Eine Jugend*, *PBDG*, p. 88; IV, 95.

[9] Ernst Toller, *Eine Jugend*, *PBDG*, pp. 107-108; IV, 124. This is a misrepresentation on Toller's part. In fact, it was Toller himself who had proposed Lipp, according to Ernst Niekisch in *Revolution und Räterepublik in München 1918/19 in Augenzeugenberichten*, ed. Gerhard Schmolze (Düsseldorf: Rauch Verlag, 1969) p. 268.

[10] Ernst Toller, *Eine Jugend*, *PBDG*, p. 124; IV, 147.

[11] Ernst Toller, *Briefe*, p. 207; V, 154.

[12] E. J. Gumbel, *Vier Jahre politischer Mord. Statistik und Darstellung der politischen Morde in Deutschland von 1919 bis 1922* (Berlin: Verlag der neuen Gesellschaft, 1922).

[13] Ernst Toller, "Rede auf dem Penklub-Kongress," in Frühwald-Spalek, I, 172.

[14] Hermann Kesten, *Meine Freunde*, pp. 160-161.

[15] Hermann Kesten, *Meine Freunde*, p. 164.

Notes to Chapter 2
Toller and His Critics

[1] Ishikawa Takoboku, *Romanji Diary*, quoted in Donald Keene, *Modern Japanese Literature* (New York: Grove Press, 1956), p. 218.

[2] John Spalek, "Ernest Toller: The Need for a New Estimate," *German Quarterly*, 39, No. 4 (1966), 588.

[3] Karl S. Guthke, *Geschichte und Poetik der deutschen Tragikomödie* (Göttingen: Vandenhoeck und Ruprecht, 1961), p. 323.

[4] Ernst Toller, *Briefe aus dem Gefängnis* (Amsterdam: Querido Verlag, 1935), p. 42. In the new Toller edition by Wolfgang Frühwald and John M. Spalek, *Gesammelte Werke* (Munich: Hanser, 1978) the quotation is in Vol. V, p. 35. In subsequent citations to Toller's works, the first reference will indicate the original edition; the second will be to volume and page number of the Frühwald-Spalek edition.

* "Tessa" was Nanette Katzenstein, the wife of Dr. Erich Katzenstein. Their apartment in Munich

Notes

served as a meeting-place for Toller and his friends during the period of the revolution.

[5]Jean Paul Marat, quoted by Maxime Leroy in: *Histoire des idées sociales en France*, Vol. I: *De Montesquieu à Robespierre* (Paris: Gallimard, 1946), p. 282.

[6]Karl Marx, quoted by Peter Gay in: *The Dilemma of Democratic Socialism: Eduard Bernstein's Challenge to Marx* (New York: Collier Books, 1962), p. 85.

[7]Ernst Toller, *Briefe*, p. 166; V, 126.

[8]Ernst Toller, *Briefe*, p. 260; V, 192.

[9]John Spalek, "Ernst Toller: The Need for a New Estimate," 584.

[10]Jost Hermand, *Unbequeme Literatur: Eine Beispielreihe* (Heidelberg: Lothar Stiehm, 1971).

[11]Jost Hermand, *Unbequeme Literatur*, pp. 146-147.

[12]Jost Hermand, *Unbequeme Literatur*, pp. 147-148.

[13]Jost Hermand, *Unbequeme Literatur*, p. 149.

[14]Friedrich Nietzsche, *The Will to Power*, trans. Walter Kaufmann and R. J. Hollingdale (New York: Random House, 1967), p. 451.

[15]Ernst Toller, *Eine Jugend in Deutschland* in *Prosa Briefe Dramen Gedichte*, Foreward by Kurt Hiller (Reinbek bei Hamburg: Rowohlt, 1961), p. 88; in Frühwald-Spalek, IV, 95-96.

[16]Ernst Toller, *Die Wandlung: Das Ringen eines Menschen* (Potsdam: Gustav Kiepenheuer Verlag, 1920), pp. 82-83; II, 54.

[17]Ernst Toller, *Eine Jugend in Deutschland*, PBDG, pp. 169-170. The phrase "inertia of the heart" had been used by the novelist Jakob Wassermann in the novel *Caspar Hauser or Inertia of the Heart* (1908), the story of a pure man caught in a brutal world. Interestingly, Wassermann's own autobiography, *Mein Weg als Deutscher und Jude* (*My Path as a German and a Jew*, 1921) has often been compared with Toller's.

[18]Ernst Toller, *Briefe*, pp. 245-246; V, 181-182.

[19]One thinks of Shelly and his wife Harriet setting out to free the Irish. Ellsworth Barnard writes in his *Shelley* (New York: The Odyssey Press, XIV, 1944): "The project was fantastic enough, but...not quite so naive as one might be led to think by the familiar story of his dropping revolutionary pamphlets from his hotel window upon the heads of those passers-by who promised by their appearance to furnish good soil for the Shelleyan gospel; a gospel of passive resistance and peaceful reform through education and the efforts of an 'Association of Philanthropists.' Still his plea (in capital letters) 'O IRISHMEN, REFORM YOURSELVES!' was not likely to make him popular. Moreover, as he wrote to a friend, 'More hate me as a freethinker than love me as a votary of freedom.'"

[20]William Anthony Willibrand, *Ernst Toller and His Ideology*, Iowa Humanistic Series, Vol. 7 (Iowa City: Univ. of Iowa Press, 1945), pp. 118-119.

[21]Martin Reso, "Der gesellschaftlich-ethische Protest im dichterischen Werk Ernst Tollers," Diss. Jena 1957, pp. 236-303.

[22]Carl von Ossietsky, "Gibt es nicht eine Opposition?." *Die Weltbühne* 26 (1930), p. 40. Alfred Hugenberg was a reactionary press magnate, who controlled the Scherl group of publications, newsreel companies, and the UFA film studios. In 1932, in a famous speech to the Düsseldorf *Industrieklub*, Hitler gained the support of leading German industrialists.

[23]Ernst Toller, "Reichskanzler Hitler," *Die Weltbühne*, 26 (1930), pp. 537-539; I, 69-72.

[24]Ernst Niekisch, *Gewagtes Leben: Begegnungen und Begebnisse* (Cologne: Kiepenheuer und Witsch, 1958), p. 101.

[25]Martin Reso, "Protest," p. 277.

[26]Martin Reso, "Protest," p. 269.

[27]Martin Reso, "Protest," p. 249.

[28]Martin Reso, "Protest," pp. 239-240.

[29]Ernst Toller, "Man and the Masses: The Problem of Peace," typescript in the Yale Toller Collection, Trans. Alexander Henderson; probably written before 1937. I, 82.

[30]Jacqueline Rodgers, "Ernst Toller's Prose Writings," Diss. Yale Univ. 1972.

Notes to Chapter 3
Anarchism

[1]Friedrich Engels, "Herrn Eugen Dührings Umwälzung der Wissenschaft," in *Marx-Engels: Werke*, Vol. XX (Berlin: Dietz, 1973), 264.

[2]I am indebted in the following outline of the various anarchist systems to the presentations and analysis in James Joll, *The Anarchists* (New York: Grosset and Dunlap, 1964); James W. Hulse, *Revolutionists in London: A Study of Five Unorthodox Socialists* (Oxford: Clarendon Press, 1950); George Woodcock, *Anarchism* (New York: World, 1962). The following were also found useful: Hans Manfred Bock, *Syndikalismus und Linkskommunismus von 1919-1923* (Meisenheim/Glan: Hain, 1969); April Carter, *The Political Theory of Anarchism* (London: Routledge and Kegan Paul, 1971); G.D.H. Cole, *Socialist Thought: Marxism and Anarchism*, Vol. II of *A History of Socialist Thought* (London: Macmillan, 1957); Karl Diehl, *Über Sozialismus, Kommunismus und Anarchismus: 25 Vorlesungen*, 4th expanded ed. (Jena: Gustav Fischer, 1922); Paul Eltzbacher, *Anarchism: Exponents of the Anarchist Philosophy*, trans. Steven T. Byington (New York: Libertarian Book Club, 1960); Daniel Guérin, *Anarchism*, trans. Mary Klopper with introduction by Noam Chomsky (New York: Monthly Review Press, 1970); Irving L. Horowitz, *The Anarchists* (New York: Dell, 1964); Oscar Jászi, "Anarchism," in *The Encyclopedia of the Social Sciences* (New York: Macmillan, 1930); Leonard I. Krimerman and Lewis Perry, eds., *Patterns of Anarchy: A Collection of Writings on the Anarchist Tradition* (Garden City, New York: Anchor Books, 1966); George Lichtheim, *Marxism: An Historical and Critical Study*, 2nd rev. ed. (New York: Praeger, 1965); Ulrich Linse, *Organisierter Anarchismus im Deutschen Kaiserreich von 1871* (Berlin: Dunker and Humblot, 1969); Karl Marx et al., *Marx, Engels, Lenin. Anarchism and Anarchosyndicalism* (New York: International Publishers, 1972); Erich Mühsam, *Die Befreiung der Gesellschaft vom Staat. Was ist kommunistischer Anarchismus?* Fanal Sonderheft (Berlin: Fanal Verlag, 1933); George Plechanoff, *Anarchism and Socialism* (Chicago: Charles Kerr, 1912); Gerald Runkle, *Anarchism: Old and New* (New York: Delta, 1972); Bertrand Russell, *Proposed Roads to Freedom: Socialism, Anarchism and Syndicalism* (New York: Henry Holt, 1919); Bertrand Russell, *Theory and Practice of Bolshevism* (New York: Simon and Schuster, 1964); Marshall Schatz, ed., *The Essential Works of Anarchism* (New York: Bantam, 1971).

[3]Oscar Jászi, "Anarchism" in *The Encyclopedia of the Social Sciences*, Vol. II (New York: Macmillan, 1937), p. 52.

[4]Alan Ritter, "Anarchism and Liberal Theory in the Nineteenth Century," *Bucknell Review*, 19 (Fall, 1971), pp. 37-66.

[5]James Joll, *The Anarchists* (New York: Grosset and Dunlap, Universal Library UL 191, 1964), p. 12.

[6]Leo Tolstoy, *Das Reich Gottes ist in euch* (Stuttgart: 1894), pp. 302-303.

[7]Leo Tolstoy, *Das Reich Gottes*, pp. 303-304.

[8]quoted in George Woodcock, *Anarchism: A History of Libertarian Ideas and Movements* (New York: World Publishing Co., 1962), p. 83.

[9]Georg Adler, *Handwörterbuch der Staatswissenschaften*, 2nd edition, ed. by J. Conrad et al. (Jena: G. Fischer, 1902), p. 319.

[10]Ulrich Linse, "Die Transformation der Gesellschaft durch die anarchistische Weltanschauung," *Archiv für Sozialgeschichte*, 11 (1971), pp. 343-344.

[11]Bertolt Brecht, *Die Maßnahame*, in *Gesammelte Werke in 8 Bänden*, edited by Suhrkamp Verlag in collaboration with Elisabeth Hauptmann (Frankfurt/M.: Suhrkamp, 1967), Vol. I, p. 652.

[12]Bertolt Brecht, "An die Nachgeborenen," in *Gesammelte Werke in 8 Bänden*, Vol. IV, p. 725.

[13]James Joll, *The Anarchists*, p. 12.

[14]quoted by George Woodcock, *Anarchism*, p. 34.

[15]quoted by George Woodcock, *Anarchism*, p. 34.

[16]quoted by George Woodcock, *Anarchism*, p. 34. In a similar sense we note Diderot's famous

phrase: "I wish neither to give nor to receive laws," Tolstoy's remarks: "I only know that on the one hand the State is no longer necessary for me, and that on the other I can no longer do the things that are necessary for the existence of the State," (*Das Reich Gottes*, pp. 335-336) and, "All governments, the despotic and the liberal alike, have in our time become what Herzen so aptly called a Genghis Khan with telegraphs." (*Das Reich Gottes*, p. 274).

[17]Max Stirner, *The Ego and His Own*, trans. Steven Byington (New York: Libertarian Book Club, 1963), p. 179.

[18]William Godwin, *An Enquiry Concerning the Principles of Political Justice and Its Influence on General Virtue and Happiness*, facsimile of the 3rd edition with notes and introduction by F.E.L. Priestly, in 3 volumes (Toronto: Univ. of Toronto Press, 1946), Vol. I, p. 11.

[19]William Godwin, *Political Justice*, Vol. I, p. 31.

[20]William Godwin, *Political Justice*, Vol. II, p. 858.

[21]William Godwin, *Political Justice*, Vol. II, p. 851.

[22]William Godwin, *Political Justice*, Vol. I, p. 269.

[23]William Godwin, *Political Justice*, Vol. II, p. 564.

[24]George Orwell, "Politics vs. Literature," in *Shooting an Elephant* (New York: Harcourt Brace and Company, 1945), p. 65.

[25]George Woodcock, *Anarchism*, p. 123.

[26]quoted by George Woodcock, *Anarchism*, p. 125. Hermann Kesten *Meine Freunde die Poeten* (Vienna: Donau Verlag, 1953), p. 158.

[27]George Woodcock, *Anarchism*, p. 118.

[28]quoted by George Woodcock, *Anarchism*, p. 120.

[29]Ernst Toller, *Briefe aus dem Gefängnis* (Amsterdam: Querido Verlag, 1935), p. 260; V, 192.

[30]quoted by George Woodcock, *Anarchism*, p. 122.

[31]Ernst Toller, *Masse Mensch* (Potsdam: Gustav Kiepenheuer Verlag, 1922), p. 66; II, 103.

[32]Ernst Toller, *Masse Mensch*, p. 77; II, 110.

[33]Ernst Toller, *Eine Jugend* in *PBDG*, p. 35; IV, 18.

[34]Here I follow the analyses in Joll, Woodcock, Alan Ritter, *The Political Thought of Pierre-Joseph Proudhon* (Princeton: Princeton Univ. Press, 1969), and J. Hampden Jackson, *Marx, Proudhon and European Socialism* (New York: Collier Books, 1962).

[35]Pierre-Joseph Proudhon, *Système des Contradictions*, Vol. II, p. 361.

[36]Pierre-Joseph Proudhon, *Système des Contradictions*, Vol. I, p. 372.

[37]E.H. Carr, *Michael Bakunin* (London: Macmillan, 1937), p. 130.

[38]Pierre-Joseph Proudhon, *La Révolution sociale démontrée par le coup d'état du deux décembre* (Paris: Marcel Rivière, 1938), p. 290.

[39]George Woodcock, *Anarchism*, p. 111.

[40]Pierre-Joseph Proudhon, *L'Idée générale de la Révolution au 19e siècle* (Paris: Marcel Rivière, 1929), p. 344.

[41]G.D.H. Cole, *History of Socialist Thought*, p. 236.

[42]R.W.K. Paterson denies that Stirner is an anarchist at all. See his *The Nihilistic Egoist Max Stirner* (London: Oxford Univ. Press, 1971), pp. 126-144.

[43]quoted from *Paroles d'un révolté* in: William H. Hurlbert, "State Christianity and the French Revolution," *The Nineteenth Century*, 18, 750.

[44]Peter Kropotkin, *The Conquest of Bread* (London: Chapman and Hall, 1906), pp. 132-133.

[45]Peter Kropotkin, *Conquest*, p. 112.

[46]Karl S. Guthke, *Geschichte und Poetik der deutschen Tragikomödie* (Göttingen: Vandenhoeck und Ruprecht, 1961), p. 323.

[47]G.D.H. Cole, *History of Socialist Thought*, Vol. II, p. 359f.

[48]Ernst Toller, *Briefe aus dem Gefängnis*, p. 229; V, 170-171.

[49]G.D.H. Cole, *History of Socialist Thought*, Vol. II, p. 351f.

[50]George Woodcock and Ivan Avakumović, *The Anarchist Prince: A Biographical Study of Peter Kropotkin* (London: T.V. Boardman, 1970), p. 225.

[51]Ernst Toller, *Briefe aus dem Gefängnis*, p. 143; V, 109.

[52]Peter Kropotkin, *Mutual Aid: A Factor in Evolution* (Boston: Expanding Horizons Books, 1955), p. 9f.
[53]Bertrand Russell, *Proposed Roads to Freedom* (New York: Henry Holt, 1919), p. 53.
[54]Peter Kropotkin, "Anarchism," in *The Encyclopedia Britannica*, 11th ed. (1910-1911), Vol. I, pp. 914-919.
[55]Peter Kropotkin, *The Terror in Russia: An Appeal to the British Nation* (London: Methuen, 1909).
[56]Peter Kropotkin, *The Great French Revolution*, trans. N.F. Dryhurst (London: Heinemann, 1909).
[57]James Hulse, *Revolutionists*, p. 179.
[58]*Freedom*, 13 (December, 1899), pp. 81-82.
[59]Peter Kropotkin, *Les Temps nouveaux*, V (Jan. 27-Feb. 2, 1900), p. 2.
[60]Ernst Toller, *Briefe aus dem Gefängnis*, p. 87; V, 67.
[61]quoted by Woodcock and Avakumović, *The Anarchist Prince*, p. 351.
[62]quoted by James Joll, *The Anarchists*, p. 161.
[63]quoted by James Joll, *The Anarchists*, p. 161.
[64]Oscar Wilde, *De Profundis* (London: Methuen, 1950), p. 112.

Notes to Chapter 4
German Heirs to European Anarchism

[1]J.W. von Goethe, *Faust: The Original German and a New Translation* by Walter Kaufmann (Garden City, New York: Doubleday, 1961), lines 1972-1977, p. 203.
[2]Peter Lösche, *Anarchismus*, Erträge der Forschung 66 (Darmstadt: Wissenschaftliche Buchgesellschaft, 1977), p. 8.
[3]George Woodcock, *Anarchism: A History of Libertarian Ideas and Movements* (New York: World, 1962), p. 425.
[4]Richard N. Hunt, *German Social Democracy* (New Haven: Yale Univ. Press, 1964), p. 21.
[5]cf. the standard treatments in Hunt, *German Social Democracy*; Carl Schorske, *German Social Democracy 1905-1917* (Cambridge, Mass.: Harvard Univ. Press, 1955); Franz Mehring, *Geschichte der deutschen Sozialdemokratie*, 4 vols., 12th ed. (Stuttgart: J.H.W. Dietz Nachf., 1922); Richard Lipinski, *Die Sozialdemokratie von ihren Anfängen bis zur Gegenwart*, 2 vols. (Berlin: J.H.W. Dietz Nachf., 1927-28); A. Joseph Berlau, *The German Social Democratic Party 1914-1921* (New York: Columbia Univ. Press, 1949); James Joll, *The Second International 1889-1914* (New York: Harper and Row, 1966).
[6]Rosa Luxemburg, "Leninism or Marxism," in *The Russian Revolution and Leninism or Marxism* (Ann Arbor: Univ. of Michigan Press, 1961), pp. 88-89.
[7]Rosa Luxemburg, "Leninism or Marxism," p. 94.
[8]Pierre-Joseph Proudhon quoted by Martin Buber in *Pfade in Utopia* (Heidelberg: Lambert Schneider, 1950), pp. 57-58.
[9]Ernst Toller, *Quer Durch* (Berlin: Kiepenheuer Verlag, 1930), p. 136.
[10]Ernst Toller, *Quer Durch*, p. 130.
[11]Peter Kropotkin, "Law and Authority, an Anarchist Essay" (London: William Reeves, n.d.), p. 23. See also his *In Russian and French Prisons*.
[12]Ernst Toller, *Quer Durch*, p. 136.
[13]Ernst Toller, *Quer Durch*, pp. 121-124.
[14]Ernst Toller, *Quer Durch*, pp. 20-27.
[15]Ernst Toller, *Quer Durch*, p. 123.
[16]quoted in Manfred Brauneck, *Die rote Fahne: Kritik, Theorie, Feuilleton 1918-1933* (Munich: Fink Verlag, 1973), p. 56.
[17]Ernst Toller, *Quer Durch*, pp. 123-124.
[18]Peter Kropotkin, *The Conquest of Bread* (London: Chapman and Hall, 1913), pp. 1-2.
[19]Ernst Toller, *Eine Jugend in Deutschland* in *Prosa Briefe Dramen Gedichte* (Reinbek bei Ham-

Notes

burg: Rowohlt, 1961), p. 80f.; IV, 84.

[20]Martin Reso, "Die Novemberrevolution und Ernst Toller," *Weimarer Beiträge*, III (1959), 390.
[21]Martin Reso, "Die Novemberrevolution," 390.
[22]Martin Reso, "Die Novemberrevolution," 398.
[23]Martin Reso, "Die Novemberrevolution," 405-406.
[24]Gustav Landauer, *Aufruf zum Sozialismus*, 2nd ed. (Cologne: F.J. Marcan Verlag, 1925).
[25]Kurt Hiller in the *Vorwort* to Ernst Toller, *PBDG*, p. 20.
[26]Hans Marnette, "Untersuchungen zum Inhalt-Form Problem in Ernst Tollers Dramen," Diss. Pädagogische Hochschule Potsdam 1963, pp. 186-188.
[27]cf. *Dresdner Montagsblatt*, No. 26 (June 16, 1919), p. 3; see also Marianne Weber, *Max Weber: Ein Lebensbild* (Tübingen: J.C.B. Mohr, 1926), pp. 608-673 and 677ff.
[28]Kurt Hiller, *Vorwort* to *PBDG*, p. 20.
[29]*Der Freihafen*, Vol. III (Hamburg: Verlag der Hamburger Kammerspiele, 1920), pp. 5-7.
[30]Ernst Toller, *Quer Durch*, pp. 189-191.
[31]*Vorwärts*, No. 11, Morgen-Ausgabe (Jan. 8, 1926), p. 2.
[32]Ernst Toller, *Eine Jugend* in *PBDG*, p. 94; IV, 104.
[33]quoted in *Eine Jugend* in *PBDG*, pp. 126-127; IV, 150-151. From April 4 until April 13 Landauer had served as Provisional Commissioner for Education. He resigned with the advent of the Communist Council Republic.
[34]Ernst Toller, *Eine Jugend* in *PBDG*, p. 118; IV, 138.
[35]Ernst Toller, *Eine Jugend* in *PBDG*, p. 159; IV, 199.
[36]Ernst Toller, *Briefe aus dem Gefängnis* (Amsterdam: Querido Verlag, 1935), pp. 39-41; V, 33-34.
[37]Ernst Toller, *Tag des Proletariats: Requiem den gemordeten Brüdern* (Potsdam: Kiepenheuer Verlag, 1925), p. 22.
[38]Gustav Landauer, *Der werdende Mensch: Aufsätze über Leben und Schrifttum*, ed. Martin Buber (Potsdam: Kiepenheuer, 1921).
[39]Ernst Toller, *Briefe aus dem Gefängnis*, p. 133; V, 86.
[40]Gustav Landauer, in *Beginnen: Aufsätze über Sozialismus*, ed. Martin Buber (Cologne: F.J. Marcan, 1924).
[41]cf. Charles Maurer, *The Call to Revolution: The Mystical Anarchism of Gustav Landauer* (Detroit: Wayne State University Press, 1971); Thomas Esper, "The Anarchism of Gustav Landauer," Masters thesis, Univ. of Chicago, Dept. of History, 1961; Wolf Kalz, *Gustav Landauer: Kultursozialist und Anarchist* (Meisenheim/Glan: Hain, 1967); Martin Buber, *Pfade in Utopia* (Heidelberg: Verlag Lambert Schneider, 1950); Eugene Lunn, *Prophet of Community* (Berkeley: University of California Press, 1973).
[42]Gustav Landauer, *Aufruf*, p. 34.
[43]cf. Carl Schorske, *German Social Democracy* (Cambridge: Harvard Univ. Press, 1955), passim.
[44]Gustav Landauer, *Aufruf zum Sozialismus*, p. 33.
[45]Gustav Landauer, *Aufruf*, p. 31.
[46]Ernst Toller, *Die Maschinenstürmer* (Leipzig: E.P. Tal, 1922), p. 119; II, 190.
[47]Ernst Toller, *Masse Mensch* (Potsdam: Gustav Kiepenheuer Verlag, 1922), p. 54; II, 95.
[48]Ernst Toller, *Die Wandlung* (Potsdam: Gustav Kiepenheuer Verlag, 1920), p. 55; II, 39.
[49]Charles Maurer, *Call to Revolution*, p. 83.
[50]Gustav Landauer, *Beginnen: Aufsätze über Sozialismus*, ed. Martin Buber (Cologne: F.J. Marcan Verlag, 1924), p. 7, quoted by Maurer, p. 84.
[51]quoted by Maurer, *Call to Revolution*, p. 89.
[52]Ernst Toller, *Quer Durch*, p. 233.
[53]Ernst Toller, *Die Maschinenstürmer*, p. 43; II, 142.
[54]Ernst Toller, *Die Maschinenstürmer*, p. 72; II, 160.
[55]Ernst Toller, *Die Wandlung*, p. 24; II, 21.
[56]Ernst Toller, *Die Wandlung*, p. 77; II, 51.
[57]Gustav Landauer, *Aufruf*, p. 25.

[58]Gustav Landauer, *Aufruf*, p. 48.
[59]Gustav Landauer, *Aufruf*, p. 112.
[60]Charles Maurer, *Call to Revolution*, p. 149.
[61]Charles Maurer, *Call to Revolution*, p. 169.
[62]Charles Maurer, *Call to Revolution*, p. 174.
[63]Charles Maurer, *Call to Revolution*, p. 174.
[64]Charles Maurer, *Call to Revolution*, p. 176.
[65]Fritz Mauthner, *Beiträge zu einer Kritik der Sprache*, 3 vols., 1st ed. (Stuttgart: J. Cotta Nachf., 1901-1902).
[66]Charles Maurer, *Call to Revolution*, p. 179.
[67]Ernst Toller, *Eine Jugend* in PBDG, p. 118, IV, 138-139.
[68]Gustav Landauer, *Aufruf*, p. 106.
[69]Gustav Landauer, *Shakespeare: dargestellt in Vorträgen*, ed. Martin Buber, 2 vols. (Frankfurt/M.: Rütten und Loening, 1920), quoted by Maurer, p. 197.

Notes to Chapter 5
Die Wandlung: Anarchism and the New Man

[1]Gustav Landauer, *Beginnen: Aufsätze über Sozialismus*, ed. Martin Buber (Cologne: F. J. Marcan, 1924), pp. 45-46.
[2]Martin Buber, *Ich und Du* (Leipzig: Insel, 1923).
[3]Katharina Maloof, "Mensch und Masse: Gedanken zur Problematik des Humanen in Ernst Tollers Werk," Diss. Univ. of Washington 1965, p. 70.
[4]Ernest Toller, *Quer Durch* (Berlin: Kiepenheuer Verlag, 1930), p. 284.
[5]Martin Buber, *Pfade in Utopia* (Heidelberg: Lambert Schneider, 1950).
[6]Paul E. Wyler, "Der 'neue Mensch' im Drama des Expressionismus," Diss. Stanford 1943, Chapter I,C.
[7]Martin Buber, *Hinweise* (Zurich: Manesse Verlag, 1953), p. 259; cf. *Pointing the Way: Collected Essays*, trans. Maurice S. Friedman, New York: Harper, 1957.
[8]Martin Buber, *Pfade*, p. 95.
[9]Maurice S. Friedman, *Martin Buber: The Life of Dialogue* (Chicago: Univ. of Chicago Press, 1955), p. 43.
[10]Maurice S. Friedman, *Martin Buber*, p. 43.
[11]Ernst Toller, *Die Wandlung* (Potsdam: Kiepenheuer Verlag, 1920), p. 88; II 58. Subsequent citations in the text. Carel ter Haar points out that the final words of this scene are based on Franz Werfel's well-known poem, "Lächeln Atmen Schreiten." See *Ernst Toller: Appell oder Resignation?*(Munich: tuduv Verlag, 1977). p. 94.
[12]Martin Buber, *Hinweise*, pp. 290-293.
[13]Martin Buber, *Hinweise*, p. 290f.
[14]Martin Buber, *Hinweise*, p. 291.
[15]Martin Buber, *Hinweise*, p. 291.
[16]Maurice Friedman, *Martin Buber*, p. 44. In a similar sense, Shelley wrote:

Man is of soul and body, formed for deeds
Of high resolve, on fancy's boldest wing
To soar unwearied, fearlessly to turn
The keenest pangs to peacefulness, and taste
The joys which mingled sense and spirit yield.
Or he is formed for abjectness and woe,
To grovel on the dunghill of his fears,
To shrink at every sound, to quench the flame
Of natural love in sensualism, to know
That hour as blest when on his worthless days

The frozen hand of death shall set its seal,
Yet fear the cure, though hating the disease.
The one is man that shall hereafter be;
The other, man as vice has made him now.

[Percy Bysshe Shelley: *Queen Mab*, IV, 154-167]

[17]Daniel Guérin, *Anarchism* (New York: Monthly Review Press, 1970), pp. 41-42.

[18]Michael Georg Conrad, *Die clerikale Schilderhebung. Aus italienisch-deutschen Gesichtspunkten*, 2nd ed. (Breslau: Schottländer, 1878), p. 7.

[19]Maurice Friedman, *Martin Buber*, p. 44.

[20]Martin Buber, *Pointing the Way*, trans. and ed. by Maurice Friedman (New York: Harper & Brothers, 1957), p. 145. Omitted in the German edition.

[21]Ernst Toller, *Eine Jugend in Deutschland* in *Prosa Briefe Dramen Gedichte*, mit einem Vorwort von Kurt Hiller (Reinbek bei Hamburg: Rowohlt, 1961), p. 152; IV 189.

[22]Maurice Friedman, *Martin Buber*, p. 45.

[23]Maurice Friedman, *Martin Buber*, p. 46.

[24]Maurice Friedman, *Martin Buber*, p. 46.

[25]quoted in the introduction to the English edition, *Paths in Utopia*, trans. R.F.C. Hull, introd. Ephraim Fischoff (Boston: Beacon Press, 1971), p. xv.

[26]cf. Ephraim Fischoff's introduction to *Paths in Utopia* and also Buber's essay, "Die Forderung des Geistes und die geschichtliche Wirklichkeit," in *Hinweise*.

[27]Ernst Toller *Eine Jugend* in PBDG, p. 177; IV, 226. Hinkemann's emasculation is not a unique instance of the theme; it also appears for example in *Lady Chatterley's Lover* and *The Sun Also Rises*.

[28]Ernst Toller, *Briefe aus dem Gefängnis* (Amsterdam: Querido Verlag, 1935), pp. 204-205; V 152f. Toller's notion of continuing the struggle "although one knows" is examined in detail by ter Haar. He traces it back to Ferdinand Freiligrath, Ferdinand Lassalle, and especially Rosa Lusemburg. With the suppression of the Spartakus-uprising in Berlin in January of 1919, an article by Karl Liebknecht appeared in *Die rote Fahne* with the title "*Trotz alledem!*" (in spite of all). The article, which appeared on the day of Liebknecht's murder, provided the KPD with a slogan that was popular throughout the Weimar Republic. (Ter Haar, p. 49).

(ter Haar, p. 49). [29]Martin Buber, *Pfade*, pp. 217-248. See also the English translation, *Paths in Utopia*.

[30]Martin Buber, *Pfade*, p. 11f.

[31]Martin Buber, *Pfade*, p. 13.

[32]Martin Buber, *Pfade*, p. 14.

[33]Martin Buber, *Pfade*, p. 19f.

[34]Martin Buber, *Pfade*, p. 20f.

[35]Ernst Toller, *Die Wandlung*, p. 9; II, 12.

[36]Martin Buber, *Pfade*, p. 21.

[37]Martin Buber, *Pfade*, p. 23f.

[38]Martin Buber, *Pfade*, p. 25.

[39]Martin Buber, *Pfade*, p. 25.

[40]Martin Buber, *Pfade*, p. 26f.

[41]Martin Buber, (*Paths*, 13); *Pfade*, p. 28.

[42]Martin Buber, paraphrasing Landauer, *Pfade*, p. 87.

[43]quoted by Martin Buber, *Pfade*, pp. 46-47.

[44]Eberhard Lämmert, "Das expressionistische Verkündigungsdrama," in *Der deutsche Expressionismus: Formen und Gestalten*, ed. Hans Steffen (Göttingen: Vandenhoeck und Ruprecht, 1965), p. 139f.

[45]Rosemarie Altenhofer, "Ernst Tollers politische Dramatik," Diss. Washington Univ. 1976, pp. 38-39.

[46]Gustav Landauer, "Manchesterfreiheit-Staatshülfe-Anarchie," *Der Sozialist*, June 24, 1893.

[47]Martin Buber, *Pfade*, p. 30.

[48]Martin Buber, *Pfade*, p. 31.

[49]Gustav Landauer, *Skepsis und Mystik: Versuch im Anschluss an Mauthners Sprachkritik*, 2nd ed. (Cologne: Marcan, 1923), pp. 7-8.

[50]Gustav Landauer, *Der werdende Mensch: Aufsätze über Leben und Schrifttum*, ed. Martin Buber (Potsdam: Kiepenheuer, 1921), p. 26.

[51]Martin Buber, *Hinweise*, p. 135.

[52]Martin Buber, *Hinweise*, pp. 308-309.

[53]Martin Buber, *Hinweise*, p. 295.

Notes to Chapter 6
Masse Mensch: Anarchism and Communism

[1]Walter Sokel, "Ernst Toller," in *Gestalten*, Vol. II of *Deutsche Literatur im 20. Jahrhundert: Strukturen und Gestalten*, eds. Otto Mann and Wolfgang Rothe, 5th ed. (Bern: Francke, 1967), p. 304.

[2]Julius Bab, *Die Chronik des deutschen Dramas. IV. Teil, 1919-1926* (1926; rpt. Darmstadt: Wissenschaftliche Buchgesellschaft, 1972), p. 43. Similar sentiments were voiced by Herbert Ihering, writing in the *Berliner Börsen-Courier* of Oct. 1, 1921, and by Artur Michel in the *Deutsche Allgemeine Zeitung*, No. 459, Sept. 30, 1921.

[3]*Der Spiegel* "Schöne Tangos," March 26, 1973, p. 160.

[4]Walter Sokel, "Ernst Toller," p. 304.

[5]Ernst Toller, *Masse Mensch* (Potsdam: Gustav Kiepenheuer Verlag, 1922), p. 77; II, 109. Subsequent citations will be given in the text and denoted "MM."In the first edition, the title *Masse Mensch* appeared without a hyphen. Toller commented on its interpretation in a debate with the Nazi, Alfred Mühr: "'Mass man' is a concept that I do not understand. It arose through the misinterpretation of the title of my play, which was intended to convey an antinomy." Accordingly, Toller added the hyphen in subsequent editions to express this antithesis.

[6]Ernst Toller, *Masse Mensch*, p. 77.

[7]Ernst Toller, *Eine Jugend in Deutschland in Prosa Briefe Dramen Gedichte*, mit einem Vorwort von Kurt Hiller (Reinbek bei Hamburg: Rowohlt, 1961), p. 175; IV, 222f. The problem that Toller is wrestling with here can be analysed as an example of the distinction that Max Weber draws between the *Gesinnungsethiker*, motivated solely by fidelity to his ideals, and the *Verantwortungsethiker*, who sees the necessity for putting his ideals into practice. Cf. Max Weber, "Polirik als Beruf" in *Gesammelte politische Schriften*, ed. by Johannes von Winckelmann, 3rd expanded edition (Tübingen: Mohr, 1971), pp. 505-560. This was first noticed by Dorothea Klein, and has been convincingly demonstrated in some detail by Thomas Bütow in his *Der Konflikt zwischen Revolution und Pazitismus im Werk Ernst Tollers* (Hamburg: Lüdke, 1975).

[8]Paul Frölich, "Pravda ob Ernste Tollere," *Pravda*, No. 64, March 20, 1926, 4:3-4.

[9]Martin Reso, "Die Novemberrevolution und Ernst Toller," *Weimarer Beiträge*, 5, No. 3 (1959), 387-409.

[10]Ernst Toller, *Briefe aus dem Gefängnis* (Amsterdam: Querido Verlag, 1935), p. 89; V, 69. Henceforth cited as *Briefe*.

[11]Georg Kaiser, *Die Koralle* (Potsdam: Kiepenheuer, 1928), p. 140.

[12]quoted in A.J. Ryder, *The German Revolution of 1918* (Cambridge: Cambridge Univ. Press, 1967), p. 8.

[13]Ferdinand Tönnies, *Gemeinschaft und Gesellschaft*, 2nd ed. (Berlin: K. Curtius, 1912), passim.

[14]Ernst Toller, *Quer Durch: Reisebilder und Reden* (Berlin: Gustav Kiepenheuer Verlag, 1930), p. 284; I, 140.

[15]Ernst Toller, *Masse Mensch*, p. 36; II, 84.

[16]Ernst Toller, *Quer Durch*, p. 98f.

[17]Ernst Toller, *Quer Durch*, p. 100.

Notes

[18]Ernst Toller, *Die Maschinenstürmer*, p. 53.

[19]Ernst Toller, *Quer Durch*, p. 103.

[20]Ernst Toller, *Briefe aus dem Gefängnis*, p. 197; V, 147.

[21]Martin Reso, "Die Novemberrevolution," 394.

[22]V.I. Lenin, *Ausgewählte Werke* (Berlin: Dietz, 1959), II, 571.

[23]V.I. Lenin, *Sonderheft zum XXXV.Jahrestag der Großen Sozialistischen Oktoberrevolution* in: *Neue Deutsche Literatur* (Berlin: Volk und Welt, 1952), p. 8.

[24]Ernst Toller, *Quer Durch*, p. 288; I, 143.

[25]Martin Reso, "Die Novemberrevolution," 399.

[26]Martin Reso, "Die Novemberrevolution," 399; *Briefe*, p. 153; V, 116.

[27]Martin Reso, "Die Novemberrevolution," 390. Cf. *Eine Jugend in Deutschland* in *PBDG*, p. 80f.; IV, 84: "On the evening before I leave Heidelberg I receive a letter Gustav Landauer, whose *Aufruf zum Sozialismus* has moved me and had a decisive influence on me." See also the description on Landauer's death in *Briefe*, V, 33f.

[28]Ernst Toller, *Quer Durch*, p. 189f.; I, 34-36; IV, 84f.

[29]Martin Reso, "Die Novemberrevolution," 390.

[30]Franz Werfel, *Schlußwort von der christlichen Sendlung* in *Tätiger Geist*, Vol. III of *Ziel-Jahrbücher* (Munich: 1917-1918), p. 202f. quoted by Adolf Klarmann in his essay, "Der expressionistische Dichter und die politische Sendung," in *Der Dichter und seine Zeit: Politik im Spiegel der Literatur*, ed. Wolfgang Paulsen (Heidelberg: Lothar Stiehm, 1970), pp. 167-168. Kurt Hiller propounded an elitist, left-wing political philosophy called activism. He wrote the polemical foreword to the Rowohlt anthology of Toller's works, *Prosa Briefe Dramen Gedichte* (Reinbek bei Hamburg: Rowohlt, 1961).

[31]Ernst Toller, *Quer Durch*, p. 191; I, 36.

[32]Martin Reso, "Die Novemberrevolution," 393.

[33]Martin Reso, "Die Novemberrevolution," 395.

[34]Martin Reso, "Die Novemberrevolution," 396f.

[35]Alfred Klein, "Zwei Dramatiker in der Entscheidung," in *Die Dichter des sozialen Humanismus*, ed. Helmut Kaiser, Wissen der Gegenwart, Vol. 7 (Munich: Dobbeck Verlag, 1960), p. 24.

[36]Martin Reso, "Der gesellschaftlich-ethische Protest im dichterischen Werk Ernst Tollers," Diss. Jena 1957, p. 89.

[37]Martin Reso, "Protest," p. 86.

[38]Andor Gábor, "Drei Berichtigungen, die berichtigt werden," *Die Linkskurve*, February, 1939. *Linkskurve* was the organ of the *BPRS*, the Proletarian Revolutionary Writers' League. See the fine study by Helga Gallas, *Marxistische Literaturtheorie* (Neuwied & Berlin: Luchterhand, 1971).

[39]Walter Sokel, "Ernst Toller," pp. 299-315.

[40]Walter Sokel, "Ernst Toller," p. 307.

[41]Katharina Maloof, "Mensch und Masse: Gedanken zur Problematik des Humanen in Ernst Tollers Werk," Diss. Univ. of Washington 1965.

[42]Katharina Maloof, "Mensch und Masse," p. 94.

[43]Katharina Maloof, "Mensch und Masse," p. 94.

[44]Ernst Toller, *Eine Jugend* in *PBDG*, p. 175; IV, 223.

[45]Katharina Maloof, "Mensch und Masse," p. 95.

[46]Ernst Toller, *Quer Durch*, p. 282; I, 139.

[47]Ernst Toller, *Briefe*, p. 63; V, 50.

Notes to Chapter 7
Die Maschinenstürmer: Anarchism and Social Darwinism

[1]cf. Dorothea Klein, "Der Wandel der dramatischen Darstellungsform im Werk Ernst Tollers," Diss. Bochum 1968, p. 77: "Toller views the events of the period of the Luddite movement as he

does those of the present....This allows us to see that *Die Maschinenstürmer*, only slightly veiled by [its] historical dress, deals with the problem of *Masse Mensch.*''

²Ernst Toller, Die Maschinenstürmer (Leipzig: E.P. Tal, 1922), p. 113ff.; II, 187f. Subsequent references given in text as "MS."

³cf. Hans Marnette, "Untersuchungen zum Inhalt-Form Problem in Ernst Tollers Dramen," Diss. Pädagogische Hochschule, Potsdam, 1963, pp. 22 and 230-231.

⁴Walter Sokel, "Ernst Toller," in *Gestalten*, Vol. II of *Deutsche Literatur im 20. Jahrhundert: Strukturen und Gestalten*, eds. Otto Mann and Wolfgang Rothe, 5th ed. (Bern: Francke, 1967), p. 307.

⁵Klein, "Der Wandel," p. 75.

⁶Toller, *Briefe aus dem Gefängnis* (Amsterdam: Querido Verlag, 1935), p. 77; V, 60. Henceforth cited as *Briefe*.

⁷Marnette, "Untersuchungen," pp. 228 and 225-228.

⁸cf. Klein, "Der Wandel," p. 76. See also N.S. Furness, "Toller and the Luddites: Fact and Symbol in 'Die Maschinenstürmer," *Modern Language Review*, No. 4 (October 1978).Bütow demonstrates the importance of *Das kommunistische Manifest* in his *Der Konflickt zwischen Revolution und Pazifismus im Werk Ernst Tollers* (Hamburg: Lüdke, 1975).

⁹Toller, *Briefe*, p. 76f.; V. 59.

¹⁰Paul Nikolaus, "Manifest gegen den Bürger," in :Friedrich Albrecht, *Deutsche Schriftsteller in der Entscheidung* (Berlin: Aufbau, 1970), p. 502.

¹¹Ernst Toller, *Eine Jugend in Deutschland* in *Prosa Briefe Dramen Gedichte* mit einem Vorwort von Kurt Hiller (Reinbek bei Hamburg: Rowohlt, 1961), p. 128; IV, 153.

¹²Ernst Toller, *Eine Jugend*, p. 128; IV, 153.

¹³Percy Bysshe Shelley, "The Mask of Anarchy," in *Selected Poems, Essays, and Letters*, selected and edited by Ellsworth Barnard (New York: The Odyssey Press, 1944), p. 273.

¹⁴Shelley, *Selected Poems*, p. 272. We know that Toller had been reading Shelley, since he notes in a letter to Adolf von Hatzfeld of January 27, 1922 (*Briefe*, p. 118): "Great men shower me with gifts—Aeschylus, Sophokles, Eckehart, Shelley, Milton, Goethe, Kleist, Hölderlin," In the introduction to the English translation, *Seven Plays*, Toller refers to England as "the land of Shakespeare and Shelley."

¹⁵This represents a decisive point of difference between him and Marx and Engels and a point in common with Buber and the anarchists. See Buber, *Pfade in Utopia* (Heidelberg: Verlag Lambert Schneider, 1950), p. 152.

¹⁶Shelley, *Selected Poems*, p. xxx.

¹⁷Shelley, *Selected Poems*, p. xxxiv.

¹⁸Shelley, *Selected Poems*, p. xvi.

¹⁹Toller, *Das Schwalbenbuch* (Potsdam: Kiepenheuer, 1924), p. 11:

> You resemble the poets, my swallows,
> Suffering for man's sake, you love him with
>   inexhaustible ardor,
> You who are more profoundly tied to the stones, to the storms
>   than to mankind.

²⁰Gustav Landauer, *Ein Weg deutschen Geistes* (Munich: Forum Verlag, 1916), p. 15.

²¹Georg Lukács, *Essays über Realismus* (Berlin: Aufbau, 1949), p. 159.

²²Charles Darwin, *The Descent of Man* (London: J. Murray, 1888), pp. 133-134.

²³Herbert Spencer, *Principles of Sociology* (New York: D. Appleton, 1897), II, 240.

²⁴Herbert Spencer, *The Study of Sociology* (New York: Appleton, 1882), p. 401.

²⁵quoted by Richard Hofstadter, *Social Darwinism in American Thought*, revised ed. (New York: Braziller, 1955), p. 45.

²⁶Lukács, *Die Zerstörung der Vernunft*, *Werke* (Neuwied: Luchterhand, 1962), IX, 577-662.

²⁷Lukács, *Die Zerstörung*, p. 593.

²⁸Ludwig Gumplowicz, *Grundriß der Soziologie* (Innsbruck: Universitätsverlag Wagner, 1926).

²⁹Ferdinand Tönnies, *Soziologische Studien und Kritiken* (Jena: G. Fischer, 1925), I, 204.

[30]Toller, *Briefe*, p. 36; V, 31.

[31]quoted by Hofstadter, *Social Darwinism*, p. 84.

[32]Peter Kropotkin, *Mutual Aid: A Factor in Evolution*, ed. Paul Avrich (New York: New York Univ. Press, 1972), p. 71.

[33]Kropotkin, *Mutual Aid*, p. 30.

[34]Peter Kropotkin, *Ethics: Origin and Development* (New York: McVeagh, 1924), p. 22.

[35]Toller, *Gedichte der Gefangenen: Ein Sonettenkreis* (Munich: Kurt Wolff, 1921), p. 5; II, 305. Altenhofer does not agree that Jimmy's philosophical and tactical position represents an extention of the anarchism of *Die Wandlung*. She writes, "The choice of the historical subject...is a logical consequence of Toller's more discerning political point of view which has substantially rid itself of anarchist concept(s)." ["Ernst Tollers politische Dramatik," Diss. Washington Univ. 1976, p. 104.] Elsewhere she remarks: "Jimmy's political stance differs considerably from the ethical and anarchist position of Sonja Irene L." We shall see that this is not so; Altenhofer's otherwise very level-headed and reliable study ignores both the syndicalist connection with anarchism and the very substantial philosophical influence of Kropotkin. As I shall demonstrate, it is likely that Kropotkin's works (in Landauer's translation) were used as sources by Toller.

[36]Rosa Luxemburg, "Leninism or Marxism," in *The Russian Revolution and Leninism or Marxism* (Ann Arbor: Univ. of Michigan Press, 1961), p. 90.

[37]Katharina Maloof, "Masse und Mensch: Gedanken zur Problematik des Humanen in Ernst Tollers Werk," Diss. Univ. of Washington 1965, p. 108.

[38]Toller, *Eine Jugend* in PBDG, p. 177; IV, 225.

[39]quoted in J.H. Jackson, *Marx, Proudhon and European Socialism* (New York: Collier Books, 1962), p. 83.

[40]Hofstadter, *Social Darwinism*, p. 40.

[41]quoted by Hofstadter, *Social Darwinism*, p. 51.

[42]"Any comparison with *Die Weber* is a lame one." Toller, *Briefe*, p. 214.

[43]Kropotkin, *Mutual Aid*, pp. 61-62.

[44]Kropotkin, *Mutual Aid*, p. 41.

[45]Kropotkin, *Mutual Aid*, p. 91.

[46]Ernst Toller, *Das Schwalbenbuch* (Potsdam: Kiepenheuer, 1924), p. 31; II, 338f.

[47]Toller, *Das Schwalbenbuch*, p. 16; II, 331.

[48]Ernst Toller, *Gedichte der Gefangenen: Ein Sonettenkreis, Der jüngste Tag*, 84 (Munich: Kurt Wolff, 1921), p. 3; II, 304.

[49]Toller, *Gedichte*, p. 3f.

[50]Toller, *Gedichte*, p. 26; II, 320.

[51]Toller, *Gedichte*, p. 27; II, 320.

[52]Toller, *Gedichte*, p. 28; II, 321.

[53]Toller, *Das Schwalbenbuch*, p. 17; II, 331.

[54]Toller, *Das Schwalbenbuch*, p. 12; II, 329.

[55]Toller, *Das Schwalbenbuch*, p. 25; II, 335.

[56]Martin Reso, "Gefängniserlebnis und dichterische Widerspiegelung in der Lyrik Ernst Toller," *Weimarer Beiträge*, 7, No. 3 (1961), 549.

[57]Reso, "Gefängniserlebnis," 551.

[58]Reso, "Gefängniserlebnis," 543.

[59]Toller, *Das Schwalbenbuch*, pp. 54-55; II, 349f.

[60]Toller, *Das Schwalbenbuch*, p. 32; II, 339.

[61]Toller, *Briefe*, p. 193; V, 144.

[62]Toller, *Briefe*, p. 122; V, 93.

[63]T. S. Eliot, "The Hollow Men," in *The Complete Poems and Plays 1909-1950* (New York: Harcourt Brace, 1952), p. 59.

Notes to Chapter 8
Hinkemann: Anarchism and Psychology

[1]Ernst Toller, *Hinkemann* (Potsdam: Kiepenheuer Verlag, 1924). Cited in text as "H."

[2]John Spalek, *Ernst Toller and His Critics*: A Bibliography (Charlottesville: Univ. of Virginia Press, 1968), pp. 562-609.

[3]cf. Toller's own remarks in *Briefe aus dem Gefängnis* (Amsterdam: Querido Verlag, 1935), pp. 148-150, 203-205, 239-249 and 258. Henceforth cited as *Briefe*.

[4]cf. Alfred Kerr, "Toller und Brecht in Leipzig," *Berliner Tageblatt*, No. 571, Abend-Ausgabe (December 11, 1923), p. 2.

[5]Max Freyhan, "Tollers 'Hinkemann.' Residenz-Theater," *Deutsche Allgemeine Zeitung*, No. 336-337, Reichs-Ausgabe (July 20, 1924), p. 2.

[6]Friedrich Hussong, "Der deutsche Hinkemann," *Berliner Lokal-Anzeiger*, No. 181 (April 15, 1924).

[7]Werner Gilles, "Eine expressionistische Moritat. Zu Hansgünther Heymes Heidelberger Ausgrabung der Tragödie 'Hinkemann' von Ernst Toller," *Mannheimer Morgen* (Feb. 17, 1959), quoted by John Spalek, pp. 588-589.

[8]John Spalek, "Ernst Toller: The Need for a New Estimate," *German Quarterly*, 39, No. 4 (November 1966), 581-598.

[9]Dorothea Klein, "Der Wandel der dramatischen Darstellungsform im Werk Ernst Tollers," Diss. Bochum 1968.

[10]Katharina Maloof, "Mensch und Masse: Gedanken zur Problematik des Humanen in Tollers Werk," Diss. Univ. of Washington 1965.

[11]William Anthony Willibrand, *Ernst Toller and His Ideology*, Iowa Humanistic Series, 7 (Iowa City: Univ. of Iowa Press, 1945), pp. 63-68.

[12]Walter Sokel, "Ernst Toller," in *Gestalten*, Vol. II of *Deutsche Literatur im 20. Jahrhundert: Strukturen und Gestalten*, eds. Otto Mann and Wolfgang Rothe, 5th ed. (Bern: Francke, 1967), pp. 308-309. Altenhofer, on the other hand, regards *Hinkemann* as Toller's weakest play, in spite of its successful plot, three-dimensional characters and classical structure. Cf. "Ernst Tollers politische Dramatik," Diss. Washington Univ. 1976, p. 125.

[13]cp. for example Toller's Großhahn with Hauptmann's Streckmann.

[14]Georg Büchner, *Dichtungen und Übersetzungen*, Vol. I of *Sämtliche Werke und Briefe*, ed. Werner R. Lehmann (Hamburg: Wegner, 1967), p. 442.

[15]Ernst Toller, *Hinkemann*, p. 46; II, 234.

[16]Dorothea Klein, "Der Wandel," pp. 211-212. See also Helen Cafferty's dissertation, "Georg Büchner's Influence on Ernst Toller: Irony and Pathos in Revolutionary Drama," Diss. Univ. of Michigan 1976, for a detailed discussion of this point.

[17]Ernst Toller, "An den Regisseur des Dresdner Staatstheaters," *Briefe aus dem Gefängnis* (Amsterdam: Querido Verlag, 1935), letter of Feb. 1, 1924, p. 239; V, 177.

[18]Sergei Gorodetskii, "T. Komediia 'Eugen Neschastnyi,'" *Iskusstvo trudiaschahimia* (Moscow, 1925), No. 2, p. 10.

[19]cf. P. Markov, "Eugen Neschastnyi," *Pravda*, No. 21 (Jan. 27, 1925), 7:5-6.

[20]Hans Marnette, "Untersuchungen zum Inhalt-Form-Problem in Ernst Tollers Dramen," Diss. Pädagogische Hochschule Potsdam 1963, p. 280.

[21]Martin Reso, "Der gesellschaftlich-ethische Protest im dichterischen Werk Ernst Tollers," Diss. Jena 1957, p. 109.

[22]Arnfried Astel in *Aussichten*: *Junge Lyriker des deutschen Sprachraumes*, ed. Peter Hamm (Munich: Biederstein Verlag, 1966), p. 82.

[23]Dorothea Klein points this out in "Der Wandel," p. 115.

[24]Ernst Toller, *Briefe*, pp. 204-206; V, 152-153. Christopher Isherwood, in his essay "The Head of a Leader," gives a quite moving portrait of a man who has lost the strength to dream. He describes a number of encounters with Toller, the first in London:

"Comme il est beau!" someone murmured in my ear, at the moment of our first meeting—and I agreed without hesitation. He *was* beautiful, with the immediately striking, undeniable beauty of a peacock, or a great lady of the theatre. But, as he advanced to greet us from the hotel doorway—the smallest central figure of a little group—I could not help noticing that the square vigorous body was a trifle too short for his splendid silver head—the head which a dictator had valued at five thousand dollars.

A girl introduced us, and I found myself looking into those famous, burning dark eyes, which every photograph had failed to reproduce: "Ah ...Mr. Isherwood. This is a great pleasure."

Later on, Isherwood met Toller again shortly before his death:

It was in New York that we met again—for the fourth and last time. Six months had passed. The Spanish Civil war was over. The dictators, in the hour of their triumph, were uttering new threats. On a beautiful cold spring afternoon I crossed Central Park to the hotel at which he was staying.

He opened the door to me himself. To my surprise, I found him quite alone:

"You must please excuse all this untidiness," he told me.... Even as we sat down, I was struck by the change in his appearance, and in his manner. He looked older, yellower, thinner. The black eyes were sombre, and almost gentle. And his pleasure at my visit was quite touching.

"How are you my friend? What have you been doing? Please tell me some news of England." I told him everything I could think of....At length I asked:

"But what about your work?"

The eyes did not brighten, as I had expected. Instead, he shrugged his shoulders slightly:

"It is accomplished.... There were difficulties, of course.... When I landed in New York I had hoped to make great publicity for the scheme, to give interviews to the Press.... But I was unlucky. Not one single journalist came to my cabin. Not one. And do you know why? They were all crowding around a foreign film actress, and a dwarf!"

"A dwarf?"

"Yes. This dwarf, it seems, was particularly important, because of his extremely small size. He was more interesting to the reporters than all the thousands of my unhappy countrymen."

"And what are you doing now?" I asked him.

Once more, he shrugged his shoulders.

"I am here. as you see."

[in *Exhumations: Stories. Articles. Verses* (New York: Simon and Schuster, 1966), pp. 125-132.]

[25]Ernst Toller, *Hinkemann*, p. 61; II, 246.

[26]Walter Sokel, "Ernst Toller," p. 308.

[27]Ernst Toller, *Briefe*, p. 239; V, 177.

[28]Ernst Toller, *Briefe*, p. 210; V, 156.

[29]Ernst Toller, *Briefe*, p. 154; V, 116-117.

[30]Rosemarie Altenhofer, "Ernst Tollers politische Dramatik," p. 118.

[31]Altenhofer, "E.T.'s politische Dramatik," p. 119f.

[32]*New German Critique*, No. 10 (Winter 1977), p. 106. See the discussion of the connections between Gross and various Expressionists in the article by Arthur Mitzman," Anarchism, Expressionism and Psychoanalysis," *New German Critique*, No. 10 (Winter 1977), pp. 77-104.

[33]Ernst Toller, *Quer Durch: Reisebilder und Reden* (Berlin: Gustav Kiepenheuer, 1930) p. 255; I, 167.

[34]Ernst Toller, *Hinkemann*, p. 25; II, 217.

Notes to Chapter 9
Hoppla, Wir leben!: Anarchism and Revisionism

[1]Jost Hermand, in *Unbequeme Literatur: Eine Beispielreihe, Literatur und Geschichte*, Vol. 3 (Heidelberg: Lothar Stiehm Verlag, 1971), pp. 128-149.

[2]Julius Bab, *Chronik des deutschen Dramas: Teil V: Deutschlands dramatische Produktion: 1919-1926* (Berlin, 1926; rpt. Darmstadt: Wissenschaftliche Buchgesellschaft, 1972), pp. 40-41.

[3]Ernst Toller, *Briefe aus dem Gefängnis* (Amsterdam: Querido Verlag, 1935), p. 149; V, 113.

[4]Ernst Toller, *Prosa Briefe Dramen Gedichte* mit einem Vorwort von Kurt Hiller (Reinbek bei Hamburg: Rowohlt, 1961). Cited as *PBDG*.

[5]Ernst Toller, *Ausgewählte Schriften*, eds. Bodo Uhse and Bruno Kaiser (Berlin: Volk und Welt, 1961).

[6]John Spalek, *Ernst Toller and His Critics: A Bibliography* (Charlottesville: Univ. of Virginia Press, 1968), p. 879ff.

[7]Erwin Piscator, *Das politische Theater* (Reinbek bei Hamburg: Rowohlt, 1963), p. 154.

[8]Ernst Toller, *Hoppla, sir leben!: Ein Vorspiel und fünf Akte* (Potsdam: Gustav Kiepenheuer, 1927). Cited in text as "HL."

[9]Felix Hollaender, "Ernst Toller: 'Hoppla—wir leben!' Eröffnung der Piscator-Bühne," *8 Uhr Abendblatt*, Sept. 4, 1927. cf. also Felix Hollaender, *Lebendes Theater: Eine Berliner Dramaturgie* (Berlin: S. Fischer, 1932), pp. 155-160.

[10]John Spalek, *Ernst Toller and His Critics*, pp. 609-673.

[11]Frank Wedekind, *Die Büchse der Pandora*, in *Stücke* (Munich: Langen-Müller, 1970), p. 217.

[12]Jost Hermand, *Unbequeme Literatur*, p. 141. One thinks of the picture of America in the early work of Bertolt Brecht: *Im Dickicht der Städte* (1924), *Aufstieg und Fall der Stadt Mahagonny* (1929), and *Die heilige Johanna der Schlachthöfe* (1929–1930), all written about the same time as *Hoppla, wir leben!* and before Brecht found it desirable to travel through Russia on his flight to Santa Monica.

[13]Jost Hermand, *Unbequeme Literatur*, p. 133.

[14]Ernst Toller, *Ausgewählte Schriften*, p. 353.

[15]Alexander Abusch, "Einige Bemerkungen zu Piscator und Toller," *Die rote Fahne*, No. 2 (Sept. 7, 1927), Beilage.

[16]Frida Rubiner, "Zur Toller-Aufführung bei Piscator: Großes Können am untauglichen Objekt," *Die rote Fahne*, No. 210 (Sept. 7, 1927), Beilage.

[17]Fritz Hampel, "Eröffnung der Piscator-Bühne: Mit Ernst Tollers 'Hoppla, wir leben!,'" *Die rote Fahne*, No. 209 (Sept. 6, 1927), Beilage.

[18]Ernst Stekel, "Zur Diskussion über die Piscator-Bühne," *Die rote Fahne*, No. 212 (Sept. 9, 1927), Beilage.

[19]cf. Ernst Toller, *Eine Jugend in Deutschland* in *PBDG*, pp. 94-96; IV, 104-107.

[20]Ernst Toller, *Eine Jugend* in *PBDG*, pp. 70-71; IV, 69-70.

[21]Fritz Hampel, "Eröffnung der Piscator-Bühne," *Die rote Fahne*, No. 209 (Sept. 6, 1927), Beilage.

[22]Dorothea Klein, "Der Wandel der dramatischen Form im Werk Ernst Tollers," Diss. Bochum 1968, p. 228.

[23]Dorothea Klein, "Der Wandel," p. 136.

[24]Jost Hermand, *Unbequeme Literatur*, p. 134.

[25]Martin Reso, "Der gesellschaftlich-ethische Protest im dichterischen Werk Ernst Tollers," Diss. Jena 1957, pp. 172-173.

[26]Werner Malzacher, "Ernst Toller—ein Beitrag zur Dramaturgie der zwanziger Jahre," Diss. Vienna 1961, p. 83.

[27]Dorothea Klein, "Der Wandel," p. 132.

[28]Katharine Maloof, "Mensch und Masse: Gedanken zur Problematik des Humanen in Ernst Tollers Werk," Diss. Univ. of Washington 1965, p. 157.

[29]Ernst Toller, *Quer Durch: Reisebilder und Reden* (Berlin: Gustav Kiepenheuer Verlag, 1930),

Notes

pp. 293-294; I, 147.

[30]Ernst Toller, *Briefe*, p. 30; V, 26.

[31]Ernst Toller, *Briefe*, p. 209; V, 156.

[32]Ernst Toller, *Quer Durch*, p. 287; I, 142.

[33]Ernst Toller, *Briefe*, p. 89; V, 69.

[34]Ernst Toller, *Briefe*, p. 181; V, 135.

[35]Dorothea Klein, "Der Wandel," pp. 135-143.

[36]Eduard Bernstein, quoted in Peter Gay, *The Dilemma of Demoncratic Socialism: Eduard Bernstein's Challenge to Marx* (New York: Collier Books, 1970), p. 74.

[37]Ernst Toller, *Briefe*, p. 213; V, 158.

[38]Ernst Toller, *Briefe*, pp. 89-90; V, 69-70.

[39]Ernst Toller, *Die Wandlung: Das Ringen eines Menschen* (Potsdam: Gustav Kiepenheuer Verlag, 1920), p. 8.

[40]Ernst Toller, *Quer Durch*, p. 193.

[41]Rosa Luxemburg, quoted in Peter Gay, *The Dilemma of Democratic Socialism*, p. 265. Kurt Tucholsky once commented in a similarly sardonic vein: "Because of unfavorable weather conditions, the German Revolution took place in [the realm of] music." See Tucholsky, *Gesammelte Werke*, ed. Mary Gerold-Tucholsky and Fritz Raddatz (Hamburg: Rowohlt, 1960). III. 656.

[42]Ernst Toller, *Hoppla*, p. 48; III, 43; cf. Dorothea Klein, "Der Wandel," pp. 143-146.

[43]Dorothea Klein, "Der Wandel," p. 142.

[44]Erwin Piscator, *Das politische Theater*, p. 148.

[45]Ernst Toller, *Briefe*, p. 146; V, 111.

[46]Peter Gay, *The Dilemma of Democratic Socialism*, p. 137.

[47]Martin Reso, "Der gesellschaftlich-ethische Protest," p. 176.

[48]Ernst Toller, *Briefe*, p. 151; V, 115.

[49]Eduard Bernstein, *Die Voraussetzungen des Sozialismus und die Aufgaben der Sozialdemokratie*, Günther Hilmann, ed. (Reinbek bei Hamburg: Rowohlt, 1969).

[50]quoted by Peter Gay, *The Dilemma of Democratic Socialism*, p. 76.

[51]quoted by Peter Gay, *The Dilemma of Democratic Socialism*, p. 77.

[52]Walter Sokel, "Ernst Toller," in *Gestalten*, Vol. II of *Deutsche Literatur im 20. Jahrhundert: Strukturen und Gestalten*, eds. Otto Mann and Wolfgang Rothe, 5th ed. (Bern: Francke, 1967), p. 314.

[53]Erwin Piscator, *Das politische Theater*, p. 154.

Notes to Chapter 10
Conclusion

[1]Matthew Arnold, *The Poems of Matthew Arnold*, ed. Kenneth Allott (New York: Norton, 1965), p. 285.

[2]Rosemarie Altenhofer, "Ernst Tollers politische Dramatik," Diss. Washington Univ. 1976.

[3]Ernst Toller, *Feuer aus den Kesseln: Historiches Schauspiel. Anhang: Historisch Dokumente* (Berlin: Oesterheld & Co., 1930), p. 40.

[4]Ernst Toller, *Feuer aus den Kesseln*, p. 40.

[5]Ernst Toller, *Feuer aus den Kesseln*, p. 82.

[6]Rosemarie Altenhofer, "Ernst Tollers politische Dramatik," pp. 207-208.

[7]Ernst Toller, *Pastor Hall* (Berlin-Charlottenburg: Bühnenvertrieb-B. Henschel, 1946), p. 41.

[8]Ernst Toller, *Briefe aus dem Gefängnis* (Amsterdam: Querido Verlag, 1935), p. 203; V, 151.

[9]Ernst Toller, *Briefe*, pp. 177-178; V, 134.

[10]Werner Hirsch in *Die rote Fahne: Kritik, Theorie, Feuilleton 1918-1933*, ed. Manfred Brauneck, Uni-Taschenbücher 127 (Munich: Wilhelm Fink, 1973), p. 290.

[11]Karl S. Guthke, *Geschichte und Poetik der deutschen Tragikomödie* (Göttingen: Vandenhoeck und Ruprecht, 1961), p. 323.

[12]T.S. Eliot, *Selected Essays* (New York: Harcourt Brace and World, 1964), p. 116.

Bibliography

The bibliography contains works cited in the text as well as the most important theoretical works on anarchism and material on Toller that has appeared since the publication of John M. Spalek's Toller bibliography in 1968. For the sake of convenience, the list of Toller's works includes all works published in book form. I have indicated abbreviated translations of titles that appear in the text. For a definitive bibliography of Toller's letters, essays, poems, speeches and unpublished material as well as secondary literature, the reader is referred to the annotated bibliography: John Spalek, *Ernst Toller and His Critics: A Bibliography* (Charlottesville: Univ. of Virginia Press, 1968). Toller's works are cited in the text according to the editions listed, with a second citation to the volume and page number of the new Toller edition: Wolfgang Frühwald and John M. Spalek: *Ernst Toller: Gesammelte Werke*, 6 vols., Reihe Hanser 250-255 (Munich: Hanser, 1978). The edition is arranged as follows:

Vol. I—*Kritische Schriften und Reportagen*
Vol. II—*Dramen und Gedichte aus dem Gefängnis 1918-1924*
Vol. III—*Politisches Theater und Dramen im Exil 1927-1939*
Vol. IV—*Eine Jugend in Deutschland*
Vol. V—*Briefe aus dem Gefängnis*
Vol. VI—*Kommentar und Materialien* has not yet appeared as of this writing.

Works by Ernst Toller

Toller, Ernst. *Ausgewählte Schriften (Selected Writings)*. Edited by Bodo Uhse and Bruno Kaiser. Berlin: Volk und Welt, 1961.

_____. *Berlin, letzte Ausgabe! Hörspiel (Berlin, Last Edition)*. "Als unverkäufliches Manuskript vervielfältigt." Sole copy at Harvard Univ. Approximate date 1928.

_____. *Die blinde Göttin: Schauspiel in fünf Akten (The Blind Goddess)*. Potsdam: Gustav Kiepenheuer Verlag, 1933.

_____. *Briefe aus dem Gefängnis (Letters from Prison; published also as Look Through the Bars: Including Poems and a New Version of "The Swallow Book."* Trans. R. Ellis Roberts. London: John Lane The Bodley Head, 1936). Amsterdam: Querido Verlag, 1935.

_____. *Deutsche Revolution: Rede, gehalten vor Berliner Arbeitern am 8. November 1925 im Großen Schauspielhause zu Berlin (German Revolution. Speech Given to Berlin Workers on November 8, 1925 in the Großen Schauspielhaus in Berlin)*. Berlin E. Laub'sche Verlagsbuchhandlung, 1925.

_____. *Eine Jugend in Deutschland (Growing up in Germany; published as I was a German)*. In *Prosa Briefe Dramen Gedichte*. With foreward by Kurt Hiller. Reinbek bei Hamburg: Rowohlt, 1961.

_____. *Der entfesselte Wotan: Eine Komödie (Wotan Unbound)*. Potsdam: Gustav Kiepenheuer Verlag, 1923.

Bibliography

_____. *Feuer aus den Kesseln: Historisches Schauspiel (Draw the Fires)*. *Anhang: Historische Dokumente*. Berlin: Gustav Kiepenheuer Verlag, 1930.

_____. *Gedichte der Gefangenen: Ein Sonettenkreis (Poems of Prisoners. A Sonnet Cycle)*. *Der jüngste Tag*, Vol. 84. Munich: Kurt Wolff, 1921.

_____. *Hinkemann: Eine Tragodie (Hinkemann*; translated as *Brokenbow)*. Potsdam: Gustav Kiepenheuer Verlag, 1924.

_____. *Hoppla, wir leben!: Ein Vorspiel und fünf Akte (Hoppla, we're alive!*; trans. as *Hoppla, Such is Life* in *Seven Plays)*. Potsdam: Gustav Kiepenheuer Verlag, 1927.

_____. *I Was a German. The Autobiography of Ernst Toller*. Trans. Edward Crankshaw. New York: William Morrow, 1934.

_____. *Justiz. Erlebnisse (Justice. Experiences)*. Berlin E. Laubsche Verlagsbuchhandlung, 1927.

_____. "Leitsätze für einen kulturpolitischen Bund der Jugend in Deutschland" ("Guidelines for a Cultural-political Association of Youth in Germany". *Dresdner Montagsblatt — früher — Menschen*. No. 26 (June 16, 1919), p. 3.

_____. *Die Maschinenstürmer: Drama (The Machine-Wreckers)*. Ausgabe für das Große Schauspielhaus, Berlin. Leipzig: E.P. Tal, 1922.

_____. *Masse Mensch: Ein Stück aus der sozialen Revolution des 20. Jahrhunderts (Masses and Man)*. Potsdam: Gustav Kiepenheuer Verlag, 1922.

_____. *Nationalsozialismus: Eine Diskussion über den Kulturbankrott des Bürgertums zwischen Ernst Toller und Alfred Mühr, Redakteur der Deutschen Zeitung (National Socialism. Discussion on the Cultural Bankruptcy of the Bourgeoisie between Ernst Toller and Alfred Mühr, Editor of the Deutsche Zeitung)*. Berlin: Gustav Kiepenheuer Verlag, 1930.

_____. *Nie wieder Friede!: Komödie (No More Peace. Comedy)*. Sole German copy at the Toller collection, Yale Univ. Library. First produced on June 11, 1936.

_____. *No More Peace: Comedy in Three Acts*. Trans. Stephen Spender. New York: Random House, 1939.

_____. *Pastor Hall*. Berlin-Charlottenburg: Bühnenvertrieb und Verlag Bruno Henschel, 1946.

_____. *Prosa Briefe Dramen Gedichte (Prose Letters Plays Poems*; referred to in notes as *PBDG)*. With foreword by Kurt Hiller. Reinbek bei Hamburg: Rowohlt, 1961.

_____. *Quer Durch: Reisebilder und Reden (Right Across. Travel Impressions and Speeches*; translated in part as *Which World—Which Way? Travel Pictures from America and Russia)*. Berlin: Gustav Kiepenheuer Verlag, 1930.

_____. *Die Rache des verhöhnten Liebhabers oder Frauenlist und Männerlist: Ein galantes Puppenspiel in zwei Akten frei nach einer Geschichte des Kardinals Bandello (The Scorned Lover's Revenge)*. Berlin: Paul Cassirer, 1925.

_____. *Das Schwalbenbuch (The Swallow-Book)*. Potsdam: Gustav Kiepenheuer Verlag, 1924.

_____. *Seven Plays*: Comprising *The Machine-Wreckers, Transfiguration, Masses and Man, Hinkemann, Hoppla! Such is Life!, The Blind Goddess, Draw the Fires!*, together with *Mary Baker Eddy* (with Hermann Kesten). With an introduction by the Author. London: John Lane The Bodley Head, 1935.

_____. *Der Tag des Proletariats: Requiem den gemordeten Brüdern: Zwei Chorwerke (The Day of the Proletariat: Requiem for the Murdered Brothers: Two Choral Works)*. Potsdam: Gustav Kiepenheuer Verlag, 1925.

_____. *Verbrüderung: Ausgewählte Dichtungen (Brotherhood: Selected Poems)*. Berling: Arbeiter-Jugend, 1930.

_____. *Vormorgen (Before Dawn)*. Potsdam: Gustav Kiepenheuer Verlag, 1924.

_____. *Die Wandlung: Das Ringen eines Menschen (Transfiguration)*. Potsdam: Gustav Kiepenheuer Verlag, 1920.

_____. *Der Weg nach Indien (The Way to India)*. Film manuscript. Toller Collection, Yale Univ. Approximate date: 1937.

_____. and Kesten, Hermann. *Wunder in Amerika: Schauspiel in 5 Akten (Miracle in America*; trans. as *Mary Baker Eddy* in *Seven Plays)*. Berlin: Gustav Kiepenheuer Bühnenvertrieb, 1931.

Secondary Literature

Abusch, Alexander, "Einige Bemerkungen zu Piscator und Toller." *Die rote Fahne*, No. 210 (Sept. 7, 1927), Beilage.

Adler, Georg. "Anarchismus." In *Handwörterbuch der Staatswissenschaften*. Vol. I. 2nd ed. edited by J. Conrad et al. Jena: G. Fischer, 1902, pp. 296-327.

Albrecht, Friedrich. *Deutsche Schriftsteller in der Entscheidung: Wege zur Arbeiterklasse 1918-1933*. Berlin: Aufbau, 1970.

Altenhofer, Rosemarie. "Ernst Tollers politische Dramatik." Diss. Washington Univ. 1976.

Anders, Achim. "Ernst Tollers grosser Theaterskandal. Zum 75. Geburtstag des Dichters." *Der Literat*, 10 (1968), 208.

Angress, Werner *Stillborn Revolution: The Communist Bid for Power in Germany 1921-1923*. Princeton: Princeton University Press, 1963.

Arnold, Matthew. *The Poems of Matthew Arnold*. Ed. Kenneth Allott. New York: Norton, 1965.

Aschieri, Annheide. "Ernst Toller: Analisi di una sconfitta." *Belfagor*, 28 (1973), 474-481.

Astel, Arnfried. In *Aussichten: Junge Lyriker des deutschen Sprachraumes*. Edited by Peter Hamm. Munich: Biederstein Verlag, 1966.

Bab, Julius. *Chronik des deutschen Dramas: Teil V: Deutschlands dramatische Produktion: 1919-1926*. Berlin, 1926. Reprinted Darmstadt: Wissenschaftliche Buchgesellschaft, 1972.

Bakunin, Michael. "Bakunin and Nechaev: An Unpublished Letter." Trans. by Lydia Bott. *Encounter*, 39, No. 1 (July, 1972), 81-91.

Barbusse, Henri. *Under Fire*. Trans. F. Wray. London: Everyman-Dent, 1917.

Barnouw, Dagmar. "Literary Politics in World War I: *Die Aktion* and the Problem of the Intellectual Revolutionary." *German Quarterly*, 52, No. 2 (March 1979), 227-247.

Beckley, Richard. "Ernst Toller." In *German Men of Letters*. Vol. III. London: Wolff, 1968, pp. 85-107.

Bergson, Henri. *Les deux sources de la morale et de la religion*. 20th ed. Paris: Alcan, 1937.

Berlau, A Joseph. *The German Social Democratic Party*. New York: Columbia Univ. Press, 1949.

Bernstein, Eduard. *Die Voraussetzungen des Sozialismus und die Aufgaben der Sozialdemokratie*. Edited by Günter Hillmann. Reinbek bei Hamburg: Rowohlt, 1969.

Beyer, Hans. *Von der Novemberrevolution zur Räterrepublik in Bayern*. Berlin: Rütten und Loening, 1957.

Bock, Hans Manfred. "Bibliographischer Versuch zur Geschichte des Anarchismus und Anarcho-Syndikalismus in Deutschland." In *Arbeiterbewegung. Theorie und Geschichte. Jahrbuch I: Über Karl Korsch*. Edited by Claudio Pozzoli. Frankfurt/M.: Fischer, 1973, pp. 295-336.

_____. Syndikalismus und Linkskommunismus von 1912-1923. Marburger Abhandlungen zur politischen Wissenschaft, No. 13. Meisenheim/Glan: Hain, 1969.

Borries, Achim von and Ingeborg Brandies, eds. *Anarchismus: Theorie. Kritik. Utopie.* Frankfurt/M.: Joseph Melzer, 1970.

Bracher, Karl Dietrich. *Die Auflösung der Weimarer Republik: Eine Studie zum Problem des Machtzerfalls in der Demokratie*. 2nd ed. Stuttgart: Ring, 1957.

Brauneck, Manfred, ed. *Die rote Fahne: Kritik, Theorie, Feuilleton 1918-1933.* Munich: Fink Verlag, 1973.

Brecht, Bertolt. "An die Nachgeborenen." In *Gesammelte Werke in 8 Bänden*. Edited by Suhrkamp Verlag in collaboration with Elisabeth Hauptmann. Frankfurt/M.: Suhrkamp, 1967. Vol. IV, p. 722.

_____. *Die Massnahme*. In *Gesammelte Werke in 8 Bänden*. Edited by Suhrkamp Verlag in collaboration with Elisabeth Hauptmann. Frankfurt/M.: Suhrkamp, 1967. Vol. I, pp. 631-664.

Bruggen, Max F.E. van. *Im Schatten des Nihilismus. Die expressionistische Lyrik im Rahmen und als Ausdruck der geistigen Situation Deutschlands*. Amsterdam: Uitgeverij J. H. Paris, 1946.

Buber, Martin. *Hinweise*. Zurich: Manesse Verlag, 1953.

_____. *Ich und Du*. Leipzig: Insel, 1923.

_____. *Pfade in Utopia*. Heidelberg: Lambert Schneider, 1950.

_____. *Paths in Utopia*. Trans. R.F.C. Hull. Introduction by Ephraim Fischoff. Boston: Beacon Press, 1971.

_____. *Pointing the Way*. Trans. and ed. by Maurice Friedman. New York: Harper and Brothers, 1957.

Büchner, Georg. *Dichtungen und Übersetzungen mit Dokumentation zur Stoffgeschichte*. Vol. I of *Sämtliche Werke und Briefe*. Ed. by Werner R. Lehmann. Hamburg: Wegner, 1967.

Büchner, Ludwig. *Kraft und Stoff*. 21st ed. Leipzig: Th. Thomas, 1904.

177

Bullivant, Keith, ed. *Culture and Society in the Weimar Republic.* Manchester: Manchester University Press, 1978.

Bütow, Thomas. *Der Konflikt zwischen Revolution und Pazifismus im Werke Ernst Tollers. Mit einem dokumentarischen Anhang.* Hamburg: Hartmut Lüdke, 1975.

Cafferty, Helen. "Georg Büchner's influence on Ernst Toller: Irony and Pathos in Revolutionary Drama." Diss. Univ. of Michigan 1976.

Camus, Albert. *The Rebel.* Trans. by Anthony Bower, with a preface by Sir Herbert Read. New York: Kopf, 1954.

Carr, E.H. *Michael Bakunin.* London: Macmillan, 1937.

Carsten, F.L. *Revolution in Central Europe: 1918-1919.* Berkeley: Univ. of California Press, 1972.

Carter, April. *The Political Theory of Anarchism.* London: Routledge and Kegan Paul, 1971.

Cattepoel, Jan. *Anarchismus. Rechts- und staatsphilosophische Prinzipien.* Marburg: Wilhelm Goldmann, 1973.

Codigno, Luciano. "Toller rivistato." *Studi Urbinati di Storia, Filosofia e Letteratura,* 45 (1971), 660-669.

Cole, G.D.H. *Marxism and Anarchism.* Vol. II *A History of Socialist Thought.* London: Macmillan, 1957.

Conrad, Michael Georg. *Die clerikale Schilderhebung: Aus italienisch-deutschen Gesichtspunkten betrachtet.* Breslau: Schottländer, 1878.

Craig, Gordon. *Germany: 1866-1945.* New York: Oxford University Press, 1978.

Darwin, Charles. *The Descent of Man.* London: J. Murray, 1888.

Deak, Istvan. *Weimar Germany's Left Wing Intellectuals. A Political History of the Weltbühne and Its Circle.* Berkeley and Los Angeles: Univ. of California Press, 1968.

Denkler, Horst. "Ernst Toller: *Die Wandlung.*" In *Das deutsche Drama vom Expressionismus bis zur Gegenwart: Interpretationen.* Ed. Manfred Brauneck. 2nd expanded ed. Bamberg: C.C. Buchners Verlag, 1972, pp. 52-63.

Diehl, Karl. *Die Diktatur des Proletariats und das Rätesystem.* 2nd ed. Jena: G. Fischer, 1924.

_____. *Über Sozialismus, Kommunismus und Anarchismus: 25 Vorlesungen.* 4th expanded ed. Jena: Gustav Fischer, 1922.

Domke, Helmut. "Tollers Münchener Tage. Eine Dokumentation." In *Dichter in ihrer Landschaft. Oder das Unheil des Daseins.* Munich: Prestel, 1969, pp. 189-206.

Dorst, Tankred. "Materialien und Aufzeichnungen zu 'Toller.'" *Emuna,* 4 (1969), 119-124.

_____. *Toller.* edition suhrkamp 294. Frankfurt/M.: Suhrkamp, 1968.

_____. Hartmut Gehrke, and Peter Zadek. *Rotmord oder I was a German.* Munich: Deutscher Taschenbuch Verlag, 1969.

Dostoevsky, Feodor. *The Possessed.* Trans. by Constance Garnett. New York: Macmillan, n.d.

Dukore, Bernard F. and Daniel C. Gerould. "Explosions and Implosions: Avant-Garde Drama Between the Wars." *Educational Theater Journal.* 21 (1969), 1-16.

Bibliography

Eichenlaub, René. "Les Intellectuels et la révolution manquée de 1918-1919 en Bavière." *Bulletin de la Faculté des Lettres de Mulhouse*, 3 (1970), 40-47.

Eisner, Kurt. *Die halbe Macht den Räten*. Ausgewählte Aufsätze und Reden eingeleitet und herausgegeben von Renate und Gerhard Schmolze. Cologne: Jakob Hegner, 1969.

_____. *Die neue Zeit*. Munich: Georg Müller, 1919.

Eliot, Thomas Stearns. *The Complete Poems and Plays, 1909-1950*. New York: Harcourt Brace, 1952.

_____. *Selected Essays*. New Edition. New York: Harcourt Brace & World, 1964.

Elsasser, Robert B. "Ernst Toller and German Society: The Role of the Intellectual as Critic, 1914-1939." Diss. Rutgers Univ. 1973.

Eltzbacher, Paul. *Anarchism: Exponents of the Anarchist Philosophy*. Trans. Steven T. Byington. Ed. James J. Martin, New York: Libertarian Book Club, 1960.

Engels, Friedrich. *Anti-Dühring*. In Vol. XX of Marx-Engels, *Werke*. Ed. Institut für Marxismus-Leninismus beim ZK der SED. Berlin: Dietz, 1973.

Esper, Thomas. "The Anarchism of Gustav Landauer." Unpub. Master Thesis. Univ. of Chicago, Dept. of History, 1961.

Espinoza, Enrique. "Ernst Toller y sus 'Cartas de la prisión.'" *Humboldt*, 35, 78-79.

Fähnders, Walter and Martin Rector. *Linksradikalismus in der Literatur. Untersuchungen zur Geschichte der sozialistischen Literatur in der Weimarer Republik*. 2 vols. Reinbek bei Hamburg: Rowholt, 1974.

_____. *Literatur im Klassenkampf. Zur proletarisch-revolutionären Literaturtheorie 1919-1933*. Munich: Hanser, 1971.

_____. "Proletarisches Theater 1919-1921." *Alternative*, 14 (1971), No. 76, 25-32.

Fechenbach, Felix. *Der Revolutionär Kurt Eisner*. Berlin: J.H.W. Dietz, 1929.

Fishman, Sterling. "Prophets, Poets and Priests: A study of the Men and Ideas that made the Munich Revolution of 1918/1919." Diss. Univ. of Wisconsin 1960.

Der Freihaften, III. Hamburg: Verlag der Hamburger Kammerspiele (1920), 5-7.

Freyhan, Max. "Tollers 'Hinkemann.' Residenz-Theater." *Deutsche Allgemeine Zeitung*. No. 336/337. Reichsausgabe, July 20, 1924.

Friedman, Maurice S. *Martin Buber: The Life of Dialogue*. Chicago: Univ. of Chicago Press, 1955.

Fritzsche, Walter. "Die Intellektuellen der Bayrischen Revolution." *Kürbiskern*. Nos. 2 and 4 (1969), pp. 356-371 and 690-703.

Frölich, Paul. "Pravda ob Ernste Tollere." *Pravda*. 64 (March 20, 1926), 3-4.

Frühwald, Wolfgang. "Exil als Ausbruchsversuch. Ernst Tollers Autobiographie." In *Die deutsche Exilliteratur 1933-1945*. Edited by Manfred Durzak. Stuttgart: Reclam, 1973, pp. 489-498.

_____. "Kunst als Tat und Leben. Über den Anteil deutscher Schriftsteller an der Revolution in München 1918-1919." *Sprache und Bekenntnis: Hermann Kunisch zum 60. Geburtstag*. Berlin: Duncker und Humblot, 1971, pp. 361-389.

Furness, N.A. "Toller and the Luddites: Fact and Symbol in 'Die Maschinenstürmer.'" *Modern Language Review*. No. 4 (October, 1978), pp. 847-858.

Gábor, Andor. "Drei Berichtigungen, die berichtigt werden." *Die Linkskurve*, Feb., 1930.

Gallas, Helga. *Marxistische Literaturtheorie: Kontroversen im BPRS.* Neuwied and Berlin: Luchterhand, 1971.

Gay, Peter. *The Dilemma of Democratic Socialism: Eduard Bernstein's Challenge to Marx.* New York: Collier Books, 1970.

———. *Weimar Culture: The Outsider as Insider.* New York: Harper & Row, 1968.

Geifrig, Werner. "Ernst Toller-Dichter und Politiker 'Zwichen den Stühlen.'" In *Vergleichen und Verändern. Festschrift für Helmut Motekat.* Edited by Albrecht Goetze and Günther Pflaum. Munich: Hueber, 1970, pp. 216-223.

Gerstl, Max. *Die Münchener Räterepublik.* Munich: Verlag der politischen Zeitfragen, 1919.

Gilles, Werner. "Eine expressionistische Moritat. Zu Hansgünther Heymes Heidelberger Ausgrabung der Tragödie 'Hinkemann' von Ernst Toller." *Mannheimer Morgen,* Feb. 17, 1959.

Godwin, William. *An Enquiry Concerning the Principles of Political Justice and its Influence on General Virtue and Happiness.* Facsimile of the 3rd ed. with notes and introduction by F.E.L. Priestley. 3 vols. Toronto: Univ. of Toronto Press, 1946.

Goethe, Johann Worfgang von. *Faust: Eine Tragödie.* Edited and annotated by Erich Trunz. Vol. III of *Werke.* Hamburg: Christian Wegner, 1962.

Goldman, Emma. *My Disillusionment in Russia.* Garden City, New York: Doubleday, 1923.

Gorodetskii, Sergei. "T. Komediia 'Eugen Neschastnyi.'" *Iskusstvo truiaschahimsia.* No. 2 (Moscow, 1925), 10.

Götze, Dieter. "Clara Zetkin über Ernst Toller. Ein Artikel aus dem Jahre 1926." *Weimarer Beiträge,* 22, No. 3 (1976), 163-164.

Graf, Oskar Maria. "Gedenkrede auf Ernst Toller." *Sinn und Form,* 21 (1969), 897-900.

———. *Wir sind Gefangene: Ein Bekenntnis aus diesem Jahrzehnt.* Berlin: Aufbau, 1948.

Guérin, Daniel. *Anarchism.* Translated by Mary Klopper with introduction by Noam Chomsky. New York: Monthly Review Press, 1970.

Guillaume, J. *L'Internationale: Documents Souvenirs 1864-1878.* 4 vols. Vol. I. Paris: P-V. Stock, 1905-1910.

Gumbel, E.J. *Vier Jahre politischer Mord. Statistik und Darstellung der politischen Morde in Deutschland von 1919 bis 1922.* Berlin: Verlag der neuen Gesellschaft, 1922.

Gumplowicz, Ludwig. *Der Rassenkampf.* Vol. III of *Ausgewählte Werke.* Edited by G. Salomon. Innsbruck: Universitätsverlag Wagner, 1928.

Guthke, Karl S. *Geschichte und Poetik der deutschen Tragikömodie.* Göttingen: Vandenhoeck und Ruprecht, 1961.

———. *Die Mythologie der entgötterten Welt.* Göttingen: Vandenhoeck und Ruprecht, 1971.

Haar, Carel ter. *Ernst Toller: Appell oder Resignation?* Munich: tuduv

Verlagsgesellschaft, 1977.

Hampel, Fritz. "Eröffnung der Piscator-Bühne: Mit Ernst Tollers 'Hoppla, wir leben!.'" *Die rote Fahne*. No. 209 (September 6, 1927, Beilage.

Hannover, Heinrich and Elisabeth Hannover-Drück. *Politische Justiz 1918-1933*. With an introduction by Karl Dietrich Bracher. Frankfurt/M.: Fischer, 1966.

Harich, Wolfgang. "Zur Kritik der revolutionären Ungeduld." *Kursbuch* 19 (1969), 71-111.

Hegel, Georg Wilhelm Friedrich. *The Philosophy of Right*. Translated with notes by T.M. Knox. Oxford: Clarendon Press, 1942.

Heller, Peter. "The Liberal Radical as a Suicide." *Modernist Studies*, 2, No. 1 (1976), 3-13.

_____. "The Writer's Image of the Writer. A Study in the Ideologies of Six German Authors, 1918-1933." Diss. Columbia 1951.

Hermand, Jost. *Unbequeme Literatur: Eine Beispielreihe*. Literatur und Geschichte, No. 3. Heidelberg: Lothar Stiehm Verlag, 1971, pp. 128-149.

Hern, Nicholas. "The Theatre of Ernst Toller." *Theatre Quarterly*, 2 (Jan.-Mar. 1972), No. 72-92.

Hillmann, Günter, ed. *Die Rätebewegung I*. Texte des Sozialismus und Anarchismus. Reinbek bei Hamburg: Rowohlt, 1971.

Hirsch, Werner. "Piscator-Bühne und die Arbeiterschaft." *Die rote Fahne*, No. 211 (Sept. 8, 1927), Beilage, 1.

Hofstadter, Richard. *Social Darwinism in American Thought*. Revised ed. New York: Braziller, 1955.

Horowitz, Irving L. *The Anarchists*. New York: Dell, 1964.

Hug, Heinz. *Erich Mühsam: Untersuchungen zu Leben und Werk*. Glashütten im Taunus: Detlev Auvermann, 1974.

Hulse, James W. *Revolutionists in London: A Study of Five Unorthodox Socialists*. Oxford: Clarendon Press, 1950.

Hunt, Richard N. *German Social Democracy*. New Haven: Yale Univ. Press, 1964.

Hurlbert, William H. "State Christianity and the French Revolution." *The Nineteenth Century*, XVIII.

Hussong, Friedrich. "Der deutsche Hinkemann." *Berliner Lokal-Anzeiger*. No. 181 (April 15, 1924).

Isherwood, Christopher. "The Head of a Leader." In *Exhumations*. New York: Simon and Schuster, 1966.

Iwabuchi, Tatsuji. "Tankred Dorsts Toller. Schauspieler seiner Selbst." *Doitsu Bungaku*, No. 50 (1973), pp. 41-52.

Jackson, J. Hampden. *Marx, Proudhon and European Socialism*. New York: Collier Books, 1962.

Jászi, Oscar. "Anarchism," *The Encyclopedia of the Social Sciences*. Vol. II. New York: Macmillan, 1930, 46-53.

Joll, James. *The Anarchists*. New York: Grosset & Dunlap, 1964.

_____. *Europe Since 1870: An International History*. London: Weidenfeld & Nicolson, 1973.

_____. *The Second International: 1889-1914.* New York: Harper and Row, 1966.

Kadečková, Helena. "Zwei nicht verwirklichte Islandreisen: Eine Bemerkung zur Biographie Ernst Tollers und Egon Erwin Kischs im [Jahr] 1936." *Philologica Pragensia*, 13 (1970), 51-53.

Kaiser, Georg. *Die Koralle.* Potsdam: Gustav Kiepenheuer, 1928.

Kalz, Wolf. *Gustav Landauer: Kultursozialist und Anarchist.* Meisenheim / Glan: Hain, 1967.

Kändler, Klaus. "'Soll es ein andrer Mensch sein? Oder eine andre Welt?' Zur Vorgeschichte des sozialistischen Dramas der zwanziger Jahre." *Weimarer Beiträge*, 14 (1968), Nos. 1-2, 25-72.

_____. *Drama und Klassenkampf: Beziehungen zwischen Epochenproblematik und dramatischem Konflikt in der sozialistischen Dramatik der Weimarer Republik.* Beiträge zur Geschichte der sozialistischen Literatur, No. 4. Berlin: Aufbau, 1970.

Katzenstein, Simon. *Der Anarchismus und die Arbeiterbewegung.* Berlin: Vorwärts, 1908.

Kaufmann, Eva. "Zwei Dramatiker im Epochenumbruch." *Wissenschaftliche Zeitschrift der Friedrich Schiller Universität Jena*, 17 (1968), 475-482.

Keene, Donald. *Modern Japanese Literature.* New York: Grove Press, 1956.

Kerr, Alfred. "Toller und Brecht in Leipzig." *Berliner Tageblatt.* No. 571. Abend-Ausgabe (December 11, 1923), 2.

Kessler, Harry. *In the Twenties: The Diaries of Harry Kessler.* New York: Holt, Rinehart & Winston, 1971.

Kesten, Hermann (ed.). *Deutsche Literatur im Exil: Briefe europäischer Autoren, 1933-1945.* Vienna, Munich, Basel: Kurt Desch, 1964.

_____. *Meine Freunde die Poeten.* Munich: Donau Verlag, 1959.

Klarmann, Adolf. "Der expressionistische Dichter und die politische Sendung." In *Der Dichter und seine Zeit. Politik im Spiegel der Literatur.* Edited by Wolfgang Paulsen. Heidelberg: Lothar Stiehm, 1970.

Klein, Alfred. "Zwei Dramatiker in der Entscheidung: Ernst Toller, Friedrich Wolf und die Novemberrevolution." *Die Dichter des sozialistischen Humanismus. Porträts.* Edited by Helmut Kaiser. Wissen der Gegenwart, No. 7. Munich: Dobbeck Verlag, 1960, pp. 15-37.

Klein, Dorothea. "Der Wandel der dramatischen Darstellungsform im Werk Ernst Tollers (1919-1930)." Diss. Bochum 1968.

Klein, H.M. "'Sangrado'—Byron before Scott." *Notes and Queries*, 17 (1970), 174.

Knobloch, Hans-Jörg. *Das Ende des Expressionismus: Von der Tragödie zur Komödie.* Regensburger Beiträge zur deutschen Sprach- und Literaturwissenschaft, No. 1. Bern: Lang, 1974.

Kolb, Eberhard. "Geschichte und Vorgeschichte der Revolution von 1918/1919 in Bayern." *Neue Politische Literatur*, 16 (July-Sept. 1971), No. 3, 383-394.

_____. *Die Arbeiterräte in der deutschen Innenpolitik 1918-1919.* Düsseldorf: Droste, 1962

Kolinsky, Eva. *Engagierter Expressionismus. Politik und Literatur zwischen Weltkrieg und Weimarer Republik*. Stuttgart: Metzler, 1976.

Kreuzer, Helmut. *Die Boheme: Beiträge zu ihrer Beschreibung*. Stuttgart: Metzler, 1968.

Krimerman, Leonard L. and Lewis Perry, eds. *Patterns of Anarchy: A Collection of Writings on the Anarchist Tradition*. Garden City, New York: Anchor Books, 1966.

Kropotkin, Peter. *The Conquest of Bread*. London: Chapman and Hall, 1913.

_____. "Anarchism." *Encyclopaedia Britannica*. 11th ed. (1910- 1911), pp. 914-919.

_____. *Ethics: Origin and Development*. New York: McVeagh, 1924.

_____. *Fields, Factories and Workshops Tomorrow*. Introduced and edited by Colin Ward. New York: Harper and Row, 1974.

_____. *The Great French Revolution*. Trans. N.F. Dryhurst. London: Heinemann, 1909.

_____. *In Russian and French Prisons*. New introduction by Paul Avrich. New York: Schocken, 1971.

_____. "Law and Authority, an Anarchist Essay." London: William Reeves, n.d.

_____. *Mutual Aid: A Factor in Evolution*. Edited by Paul Avrich. New York: New York Univ. Press, 1972.

_____. *Mutual Aid: A Factor in Evolution*. Boston: Expanding Horizons Books, 1955.

_____. *The Place of Anarchism in Socialistic Evolution: An Address delivered in Paris*. Trans. Henry Glasse. London: William Reeves, n.d.

_____. "On the Present Condition of Russia." *The Outlook, LVIII (January 8, 1898)*.

_____. *Les Temps nouveaux*, V (Jan.-Feb., 1900).

_____. *The Terror in Russia: An Appeal to the British Nation*. London: Methuen, 1909.

Lamb, Stephen. "Ernst Toller and the Weimar Republic." In *Culture and Society in the Weimar Republic*, ed. Keith Bullivant. Manchester: Manchester U.P., 1977.

Landauer, Carl. "Anarchismus and Sozialismus." *Hamburger Jahrbuch für Wirtschafts- und Gesellschaftspolitik*, 18 (1973), 11-24.

Landauer, Gustav. *Aufruf zum Sozialismus*. 2nd ed. Cologne: F.J. Marcan Verlag, 1909.

_____. *Beginnen: Aufsätze über Sozialismus*. Edited by Martin Buber. Cologne: F.J. Marcan Verlag, 1924.

_____. *Ein Weg deutschen Geistes*. Munich: Forum Verlag, 1916.

_____. *Shakespeare: dargestellt in Vorträgen*. Edited by Martin Buber. 2 vols. Frankfurt/M.: Rütten und Loening, 1920.

_____. *Skepsis und Mystik: Versuche im Anschluss an Mauthners Sprachkritik*. 2nd ed. Cologne: Marcan, 1923.

_____. *Die Siedlung* (1910). In *Beginnen*.

_____. *Was ist zunächst zu tun?* (1909). In *Beginnen*.

_____. *Was will der sozialistische Bund?* Oct., 1908. In *Beginnen*.

_____. *Der werdende Mensch: Aufsätze über Leben und Schrifttum*. Edited by Martin Buber. Potsdam: Kiepenheuer, 1921.

Laqueur, Walter. *Weimar: A Cultural History*. New York: Putnam, 1974.

Lasker-Schüler, Else. "Ernst Toller." *Emuna*, 4 (1969), 259-260.

Lenin, V.I. *Ausgewählte Werke*. Berlin: Dietz, 1959. Vol. II.

_____. *Sonderheft zum XXXV. Jahrestag der Großen Sozialistischen Oktoberrevolution*. *Neue Deutsche Literatur*. 5th ed. Berlin: Volk und Welt, 1952.

_____. *State and Revolution*. New York: International Publishers, 1974.

Leroy, Maxime. *De Montesquieu à Robespierre*. Vol. I of *Histoire des idées sociales en France*. Paris: Gallimard, 1946.

Lichtheim, George. *Marxism: An Historical and Critical Study*. 2nd edition revised. New York: Praeger, 1965.

Linse, Ulrich. "Der deutsche Anarchismus 1870-1918: Eine politische Bewegung zwischen Utopie und Wirklichkeit." *Geschichte in Wissenschaft und Unterricht*. 20, No. 9 (1969), 513-519.

_____. *Gustav Landauer und die Revolutionszeit 1918/19: Die politischen Reden, Schriften, Erlasse und Briefe Landauers aus der November-Revolution 1918/1919*. Ed. Ulrich Linse. Berlin: Karin Kramer, 1974.

_____. *Organisierter Anarchismus im deutschen Kaiserreich von 1871*. Berlin: Duncker und Humblot, 1969.

_____. "Die Transformation der Gesellschaft durch die anarchistische Weltanschauung. Zur Ideologie und Organization anarchistischer Gruppen in der Weimarer Republik." *Archiv für Sozialgeschichte, 11 (1971)*, 289-372.

Lipinski, Richard. *Die Sozialdemokratie von ihren Anfängen bis zur Gegenwart*. 2 vols. Berlin: J.H.W. Dietz Nachf., 1927-1928.

Lösche, Peter. *Anarchismus*. Erträge der Forschung, Bd. 66. Darmstadt: Wissenschaftliche Buchgesellschaft, 1977.

_____. "Rätesystem im historischen Vergleich." *Politische Vierteljahrsschrift*, Sonderheft (1970).

Lukács, George. *Essays über Realismus*. Berlin: Aufbau, 1948.

_____. *Die Zerstörung der Vernunft*. Vol. IX of *Werke*. Neuwied: Luchterhand, 1962.

Lunn, Eugene. *The Prophet of Community. The Romantic Socialism of Gustav Landauer*. Berkeley and Los Angeles: The Univ. of California Press, 1973.

Luxemburg, Rosa. "The Russian Revolution" and "Leninism or Marxism." Ann Arbor: Univ. of Michigan Press, 1961.

Maloof, Katharina. "Mensch und Masse: Gedanken zur Problematik des Humanen in Ernst Tollers Werk." Diss. Univ. of Washington 1965.

Malzacher, Werner. "Ernst Toller—ein Beitrag zur Dramaturgie der zwanziger Jahre." Diss. Vienna 1959.

Marcuse, Herbert. *Versuch über die Befreiung*. Frankfurt/M.: Suhrkamp, 1969.

Markov, P. "Eugen Neschastnyi." *Pravda*, 21 (Jan. 27, 1925), 7:5-6.

Marks, Harry J. "Movements of Reform and Revolution in Germany from 1890 to 1933 with an Epilogue: 1903-1914." Diss. Harvard Univ. 1937.

Marnette, Hans. "Untersuchungen zum Inhalt-Form-Problem in Ernst Tollers Dramen." Diss. Päagogische Hochschule Potsdam 1963.

Marx, Karl et al. *Marx, Engels, Lenin. Anarchism and Anarchosyndicalism*. New York: International Publishers, 1972.

Maste, Ernst. "Der Anarchismus in den Lehren seiner Klassiker." *Politik und*

Zeitgeschichte, 14 (1971), 27-40.

Maurer, Charles. *The Call to Revolution: The Mystical Anarchism of Gustav Landauer.* Detroit: Wayne State Univ. Press, 1971.

Mauthner, Fritz. *Beiträge zu einer Kritik der Sprache.* 3 vols. First ed. Stuttgart: J. Cotta Nachf., 1901-1902.

Mehring, Franz. *Geschichte der deutschen Sozialdemokratie.* 4 vols. 12th ed. Stuttgart: J.H.W. Dietz Nachf., 1922.

Mehring, Walter. "Ernst Toller." *Das neue Tagebuch,* 7 (May 27, 1939), 523-524.

Mennemeier, Franz N. "Das idealistische Proletarierdrama: Ernst Tollers Weg vom Aktionsstück zur Tragödie." *Der Deutschunterricht,* 24, No. 2 (1972), 100-116.

Michel, Karl Markus. "Herrschaftsfreie Institutionen? Sieben Thesen über die Unmöglichkeit des Möglichen." *Kursbuch* 19 (1969), 163-195.

Mitchell, Allan. *Revolution in Bavaria 1918-1919.* Princeton: Princeton Univ. Press, 1965.

Mitzman, Arthur. "Anarchism, Expressionism and Psychoanalysis." *New German Critique,* 10 (Winter, 1977), 77-104.

Morgan, David. *The Socialist Left and the German Revolution: A History of the German Independent Socialist Party 1917-1922.* Ithaca: Cornell Univ. Press, 1975.

Mühsam, Erich. *Die Befreiung der Gesellschaft vom Staat. Was ist Kommunistischer Anarchismus?* Fanal Sonderheft. Berlin: Fanal Verlag, 1933.

_____. "Lenin und die Scheinräterepublik." *Die Weltbühne,* 28 (May 3, 1932), 681ff.

Munteanu, Romul. "Toller si sensul militantismului in teatrul expresionist." *Secolul, XX 15 i (1972),* 63-67.

Nettlau, Max. *Der Anarchismus von Proudhon zu Kropotkin. Seine historische Entwicklung in den Jahren 1859-1880.* Berlin: Verlag Der Syndikalist, 1927.

_____. *Anarchisten und Sozialrevolutionäre. Die historische Entwicklung des Anarchismus in den Jahren 1880-1886.* Berlin: Asyl Verlag, 1931.

_____. *Der Vorfrühling der Anarchie. Ihre historische Entwicklung von den Anfängen bis zum Jahre 1864.* Berlin: Verlag Der Syndikalist, 1925.

Neubauer, Helmut. *München und Moskau 1918/19. Zur Geschichte der Rätebewegung in Bayern.* Munich: Isar Verlag, 1958.

Niekisch, Ernst. *Gewagtes Leben: Begegnungen und Begebnisse.* Cologne: Kiepenheuer und Witsch, 1958.

Nozick, Robert. *Anarchy, State, and Utopia.* New York: Basic Books, 1974.

Oberländer, Erwin, ed. *Der Anarchismus.* Dokumente der Weltrevolution, Vol. IV. Olten: Walter Verlag, 1962.

Orwell, George. "Politics vs. Literature." In *Shooting an Elephant.* New York: Harcourt Brace and Company, 1945.

Pachter, Henry. "Was Weimar Necessary? The Räte Movement 1918-1921 and the Theory of Revolution." *Dissent,* No. 1 (Winter, 1977), pp. 78-88.

Papic, Mitar. "Ernst Toller auf dem PEN-Kongress in Jugoslawien 1933." *Weimarer Beiträge,* 14 (1968), Sonderheft 2, 73-77.

Park, William M. "Ernst Toller: The European Exile Years 1933-36." Diss. Univ. of Colorado 1976.

Paterson, R.W.K. *The Nihilistic Egoist Max Stirner.* London: Oxford Univ. Press, 1971.

Pennock, J. Roland and John W. Chapman, eds. *Anarchism.* Nomos 19. New York: New York Univ. Press, 1978.

Peter, Lothar. *Literarische Intelligenz und Klassenkampf. "Die Aktion" 1911-1932.* Cologne: Pahl-Rugenstein, 1972.

Peterson, Carol. "Ernst Toller." In *Expressionismus als Literatur: Gesammelte Studien.* Bern: Francke, 1969, pp. 572-584.

Piscator, Erwin. *Das politische Theater.* Reinbek bei Hamburg: Rowohlt, 1963.

Pittcock, Malcolm. "*Masse-Mensch* and the Tragedy of Revolution." *Forum for Modern Language Studies,* 8 (1972), 162-183.

_____. "Die Maschinenstürmer." *Durham University Journal,* 35 (1974), 294-305.

Plechanoff, George. *Anarchism and Socialism.* Chicago: Charles Kerr, 1912.

Poor, Harold. *Kurt Tucholsky and the Ordeal of Germany.* New York: Scribners, 1968.

Pörtner, Paul. "The Writers' Revolution: Munich 1918-19." *Journal of Contemporary History,* 3 (1968), 137-151.

Pross, Harry. "Die Literaten und die Münchner Räterepublik," *Vorgänge. Zeitschrift für Gesellschaftspolitik,* 16, No. 26 (1977), 79-89.

Proudhon, Pierre-Joseph. *Carnets de P.-J. Proudhon.* Vol. I. Paris: Marcel Rivière, 1960.

_____. *L'Idée générale de la Révolution au 19ᵉ siècle.* Paris: Marcel Rivière, 1929.

_____. *Oeuvres Complètes: Programme Révolutionnaire.* Paris: Marcel Rivière, 1938.

_____. *La Révolution sociale démontrée par le coup d'état du deux décembre.* Paris: Marcel Rivière, 1938.

_____. *Système des contradictions économiques.* Vol. II. Paris: Marcel Rivière, 1923.

Puech, J.L. *Le Proudhonisme dans l'Association des Travailleurs.* Paris: F. Alcan, 1907.

Quinet, Edgar. *Die Schöpfung.* Leipzig: Weber, 1871.

Rammstedt, Otthein. *Anarchismus. Grundtexte zur Theorie und Praxis der Gewalt.* Cologne: Westdeutscher Verlag, 1969.

Read, Herbert. *Anarchy and Order. Essays in Politics.* With an introduction by Howard Zinn. Boston: Beacon Press, 1971.

_____. *Poetry and Anarchism: The Philosophy of Anarchism.* London: The Freedom Press, 1940.

_____. "Pragmatic Anarchism." *Encounter,* 30 (January-June 1968), 54-61.

Reimer, Robert C. "The Tragedy of the Revolutionary: A Study of the Drama of Revolution of Ernst Toller, Friedrich Wolf, and Bertolt Brecht: 1918-1933." Diss. Univ. of Kansas 1971.

Reso, Martin. "Gefängniserlebnis und dichterische Widerspiegelung in der Lyrik Ernst Tollers." *Weimarer Beiträge,* 7, No. 3 (1961), 520-556.

_____. "Der gesellschaftlich-ethische Protest im dichterischen Werk Ernst Tollers." Diss. Jena 1957.

_____. "Die Novemberrevolution und Ernst Toller." *Weimarer Beiträge,* 5, No. 3 (1959), 387-409.

Reszler, André. "L'Esthétique de l'anarchisme." *Revue d'Esthétique,* 24, No. 2 (1971), 167-184.

Bibliography

Rey, William H. "Der Dichter und die Revolution. Zu Tankred Dorsts Toller." *Basis*, 5 (1974), 166-194.

Riedel, Walter. *Der neue Mensch: Mythos und Wirklichkeit.* Studien zur Germanistik, Anglistik und Komparatistik, No. 6. Bonn: Bouvier, 1970.

Ritter, Alan. "Anarchism and Liberal Theory in the Nineteenth Century." *Bucknell Review*, 19, No. 2 (Fall, 1971), 37-66.

———. *The Political Thought of Pierre-Joseph Proudhon.* Princeton: Princeton Univ. Press, 1969.

Ritter, Gerhard and Susanne Miller, eds. *Die deutsche Revolution 1918-1919: Dokumente.* Frankfurt/M.: Fischer, 1968.

Rodgers, Jacqueline Helen. "Ernst Toller's Prose Writings." Diss. Yale University 1972.

Rolland, Romain. *Jean-Christophe in Paris: The Market-Place. Antoinette. The House.* Trans. Gilbert Cannan. New York: Henry Holt, 1915.

Rothe, Wolfgang. *Der Expressionismus: Theologische, soziologische und anthropologische Aspekte einer Literatur.* Frankfurt/M.: Klostermann, 1977.

———, ed. *Expressionismus als Literatur: Gesammelte Studien.* Bern: Francke, 1969.

Rotteck, Carl von. "Anarchie." In *Staats-Lexikon oder Encycklopädie der Staatswissenschaften.* Ed. Carl von Rotteck and Carl Welcker. Vol. I. Altona: Hammerich, 1834, pp. 546-550.

Rubiner, Frida. "Zur Toller-Aufführung bei Piscator: Großes Können am untauglichen Objekt." *Die rote Fahne*, No. 210 (Sept. 7, 1927), Beilage.

Runkle, Gerald. *Anarchism: Old and New.* New York: Delta, 1972.

Rurup, Reinhard. "Problems of the German Revolution 1918-1919." *Journal of Contemporary History*, 3 (October, 1968).

Russell, Bertrand. *Proposed Roads to Freedom: Socialism, Anarchism and Sydicalism.* New York: Henry Holt, 1919.

———. *Theory and Practice of Bolshevism.* New York: Simon and Schuster, 1964.

Ryder, A.J. *The German Revolution of 1918.* Cambridge: Cambridge Univ. Press, 1967.

Schatz, Marshall, ed. *The Essential Works of Anarchism.* New York: Bantam, 1971.

Schmolze, Gerhard, ed. *Revolution und Räterepublik in München 1918/1919 in Augenzeugenberichten*, Düsseldorf: Rauch Verlag, 1969.

Schorske, Carl. *German Social Democracy 1905-1917.* Cambridge, Mass.: Harvard Univ. Press, 1955.

Schürer, Ernst. "Literarisches Engagement und politische Praxis: Das Vorbild Ernst Toller." In *Rezeption der deutshchen Gegenwartsliteratur im Ausland.* Ed. by Dietrich Papenfuss und Jürgen Söring. Stuttgart: Kohlhammer, 1976, pp. 353-366.

Serke, Jürgen. *Die verbrannten Dichter: Berichte, Texte, Bilder einer Zeit.* 2nd ed. Weinheim and Basel: Beltz Verlag, 1977.

Shelley, Percy Bysshe. *Selected Poems, Essays, and Letters.* Selected and edited by Ellsworth Barnard. New York: The Odyssey Press, 1944.

———. *Shelley's Poetry and Prose.* Selected and edited by Donald H. Reiman and

Sharon B. Powers. A Norton Critical Edition. New York: Norton, 1977.

Soergel, Albert. *Dichtung und Dichter der Zeit. Eine Schilderung der deutschen Literatur der letzten Jahrzehnte. Neue Folge: Im Banne des Expressionismus.* Leipzig: R. Voigtländer, 1925.

Sokel, Walter. "Ernst Toller." In *Gestalten.* Vol. II of *Deutsche Literatur im 20. Jahrhundert: Strukturen und Gestalten.* Edited by Otto Mann and Wolfgang Rothe. 5th ed. Bern: Francke, 1967.

Soudek, Ingrid Helene Waithe. "Man and the Machine. A Contrastive Study of Ernst Toller's *Die Maschinenstürmer* and Elmer Rice's *The Adding Machine.*" Diss. Univ. of Michigan 1974.

Spalek, John M. "Der Nachlass Ernst Tollers: Ein Bericht." *Literaturwissenschaftliches Jahrbuch der Görres-Gesellschaft,* 6 (1965), 251-266.

_____. "Ernst Toller: The Need for a New Estimate." *German Quarterly,* 39, No. 4 (November, 1966), 581-598.

_____. *Ernst Toller and His Critics: A Bibliography.* Charlottesville: Univ. of Virginia Press, 1968.

_____. "Ernst Tollers Vortragstätigkeit und seine Hilfsaktionen im Exil." In *Exil und Innere Emigration. II. Internationale Tagung in St. Louis.* Edited by Peter U. Hohendahl and Egon Schwarz. Frankfurt: Athenäum, 1973, pp. 85-100.

_____ and Wolfgag Frühwald. "Ernst Tollers amerikanische Vortragsreise 1936/37. Mit bisher univeröffentlichten Texten und einem Anhang." *Literaturwissenschaftliches Jahrbuch der Görres-Gesellschaft,* 6 (1965), 267-312.

Spencer, Herbert. *Principles of Sociology.* Vol. II. New York: D. Appleton, 1897.

_____. *The Study of Sociology.* New York: Appleton, 1882.

Der Spiegel (March 26, 1973), p. 160.

Stalin, Isoif Vissarionovic. "Anarchismus oder Sozialismus?" *Kursbuch,* 19 (1969), 58-69.

Stekel, Ernst. "Zur Diskussion über die Piscator-Bühne." *Die rote Fahne,* No. 202 (Sept. 9, 1927), Beilage.

Sterne, Laurence. *A Sentimental Journey.* Introduction by Virginia Woolf. London: Oxford Univ. Press, 1963.

Stirner, Max. *The Ego and His Own.* Trans. Steven Byington. New York: Libertarian Book Club, 1963.

Taëni, Rainer, "Die Rolle des 'Dichters' in der revolutionären Politik. Über *Toller* von Tankred Dorst." *Akzente,* 15 (1968), 493-510.

Taine, Hippolyte. *De l'Intelligence.* Introduction to the 4th ed. Paris: Hachette, 1906.

Tönnies, Ferdinand. *Gemeinschaft und Gesellschaft.* 2nd ed. Berlin: K. Curtius, 1912.

_____. *Soziologische Studien und Kritiken.* Vol. I. Jena: G. Fischer, 1925.

Tourmin, Walter. *Zwischen Rätediktatur und sozialer Demokratie.* Düsseldorf: Droste Verlag, 1954.

Trommler, Frank. *Sozialistische Literatur in Deutschland: Ein historischer Überblick.* Stuttgart: Kröner, 1976.

Trotsky, Leon. *What Next? Vital Questions for the German Proletariat.* Trans. Joseph Vanzler. New York: Pioneer, 1932.

Bibliography

Tucholsky, Kurt. *Gesammelte Werke*. Eds. Mary Gerold-Tucholsky and Fritz Raddatz. 3 vols. Hamburg: Rowohlt, 1960-1961.

Turnowski-Pinner, Margarete. "A Student's Friendship with Ernst Toller." In *Leo Baeck Institute Yearbook*, 15 (1970), 211-222.

Unger, Wilhelm. "Für die Revolution ohne Terror und Blut. Ernst Toller war schon immer von Tragik umwittert." *Emuna* 4 (1969), 186-187.

Vries, Monica Fidélia de. "Das historische Drama in Deutschland 1918-1933: Stoffe, Formen, Tendenzen." Diss. Univ. of Capetown 1969.

Vorwärts. Morgen-Ausgabe, No. 11 (Jan. 8, 1926).

Weber, Marianne. *Max Weber: Ein Lebensbild*. Tübingen: J.C.B. Mohr, 1926.

Weber, Max. *Gesammelte politische Schriften*. Ed. Johannes von Winkelmann, 3rd expanded edition. Tübingen: Mohr, 1971.

Wedekind, Frank. *Die Büchse der Pandora*. Munich: Langen-Müller, 1970.

Werfel, Franz. *Schlusswort von der christlichen Sendung*. In *Tätiger Geist*. Vol. II of *Ziel-Jahrbücher*. Ed. by Kurt Hiller. Munich & Berlin: Georg Müller, 1917-1918.

Wilde, Oscar. *De Profundis*. London: Methuen, 1950.

Willett, John. *Arts and Politics in the Weimar Period: The New Sobriety: 1917-1933*. New York: Pantheon, 1978.

Willibrand, William Anthony. *Ernst Toller and His Ideology*. Iowa Humanistic Series. Vol. VII. Iowa City: Univ. of Iowa Press, 1945.

Wolff, Kurt. *Briefwechsel eines Verlegers*. Ed. by Bernhard Zeller. Frankfurt/M.: Heinrich Scheffler, 1966.

Woltmann, Ludwig. *Politische Anthropologie*. Eisenach: Thüringische Verlagsanstalt, 1903.

Woodcock, George. *Anarchism: A History of Libertarian Ideas and Movements*. New York: World, 1962.

Woodcock, George and Ivan Avakumović. *The Anarchist Prince: A Biographical Study of Peter Kropotkin*. London: T.V. Boardman, 1950.

Wurgaft, Lewis D. "The Activist Movement. Cultural Politics on the German Left 1914-1933." Diss. Harvard 1970.

Wyler, Paul E. "'Der neue Mensch'im Drama des deutschen Expressionismus." Diss. Stanford Univ. 1943.

Zanasi, Giusi. "Note sul 'Teatro' di E. Toller." *Studi Germanici*, 10 (1972), 619-647.

Zetkin, Clara. "Dem deutschen Dichter Ernst Toller bester Willkommensgruss." *Weimarer Beiträge*, 22 (1976), No. 3, 161-162.

Index

Index

Index

194